Twenty ~~years~~
to say
Goodbye

Twenty Miles to say Goodbye

a family memoir

ANDI DAUNT

Copyright © 2015 Andi Daunt.

Photographic Credits to Hugh Anderson
Cover Designed by Amanda Ragg

All rights reserved. No part of this book may be reproduced, stored, or transmitted by any means—whether auditory, graphic, mechanical, or electronic—without written permission of both publisher and author, except in the case of brief excerpts used in critical articles and reviews. Unauthorized reproduction of any part of this work is illegal and is punishable by law.

ISBN: 978-1-4834-3721-7 (sc)
ISBN: 978-1-4834-3720-0 (e)

Because of the dynamic nature of the Internet, any web addresses or links contained in this book may have changed since publication and may no longer be valid. The views expressed in this work are solely those of the author and do not necessarily reflect the views of the publisher, and the publisher hereby disclaims any responsibility for them.

Any people depicted in stock imagery provided by Thinkstock are models, and such images are being used for illustrative purposes only.
Certain stock imagery © Thinkstock.

Lulu Publishing Services rev. date: 09/10/2015

Dedicated
to

Savana and Sirri
blessed to share the journey with you, and yours.

'many lanterns one light'

Grateful thanks;
to Hugh, for your help, photographic expertise, and for being who you are and going that extra mile.
to Lee, for all the love, adventure, encouragement, and support along the way.

Introduction

A touching family narrative, veiled beneath shifting cultures, and changing times.

Returning home to Kenya in the 1970s, we experience a unique self-sufficient safari in the vast Masaai Mara. Exploring the country further, we meet the local people and discover their stories, as well as my mother's fascinating journals, which reveal a hidden depth to the magic of Kenya.

Twenty Miles to say Goodbye, fills a literary niche in an interesting period of Kenya's transition, between its Colonial era and Africanisation. Long before the current turbulence, it captures a time, and a place, when black and white tentatively reached out and began to accept one another's ways.

Initially there were troubled times. The Mau Mau rebellion was an horrific period when members of the family were drawn in, and became actively involved in quelling the uprising. The natural difficulties and hardships that had to be overcome while farming in remote parts of the country, all tell of my parent's courage, tenacity, and humour. Their love of the land and its people were passed on to us, gifting a carefree and adventurous childhood that could only have been found in this Africa.

Twenty Miles to say Goodbye is fast paced, interesting and enjoyable. It delivers a colourful kaleidoscope of intriguing stories and insights that take place in East Africa, and beyond, as our travels lead us to work in the Middle East, Australia, and New Zealand.

Journals and letters have been kept in their original form, and are in italics.

Prologue

A child of the land has returned.

In my absence I had hitchhiked through Europe, travelled to New Zealand, married, and had a baby. It was good to be back home in Kenya at last. Mum and Dad had driven the two hundred miles up to Nairobi to meet us, taking us back to Maraba, their home in the Songhor Valley. There had been many special moments as they opened their hearts to their little granddaughter and got to know my husband, Lee. Now they had lent us their car so we could explore the country, and visit friends and family.

1. A Safari - a journey

A moment of solitude slipped into eternity. Far below, the Great Rift Valley stretched beyond the blue horizon: vast, exquisite, and tantalizing. Sleepy volcanic mountain ranges embraced the rift on either side, until they too, were absorbed into the hazy distance. Mount Longonot rose above the rolling golden savannah, and a tiny straight dirt road marched for miles across the plains. This was the road we would be taking to Mau Narok.

Only an hour before, we had been negotiating the bustling streets of Nairobi. Pausing for a coffee at the Thorn Tree, outside the New Stanley Hotel, we watched our baby, Sirri, stand alone for the first time. Unremarkable to most, but more significant to us, as this was the same hotel in which her grandmother, my mother, had spent her first night in Kenya a couple of lifetimes ago.

Tearing ourselves from the beautiful scenery, we drove on down the steep, winding escarpment, eventually passing a tiny chapel nestled in a rocky corner. Built by Italian prisoners of war, St Mary of the Angels stood silently beside a sharp hairpin bend, where a friend had died, driving home too late.

Soon after reaching the floor of the Rift Valley, we turned off the main Nairobi Nakuru highway, onto a long dusty road disappearing into the distance towards the western ranges of the Rift. We were looking forward to our stay in Mau Narok with my cousin and her husband, who had offered to take us on safari to the Maasai Mara Game Reserve.

We pulled to a sudden halt. We had run into a huge pack of baboons – hundreds of them, each side of the road, in front of us, and behind. Quickly we wound up the windows, hurriedly hiding any food that might excite the primates. Several baboons jumped up on the bonnet, peering through the windscreen at us. They clambered all over the car, great big hairy creatures with ugly bald bottoms, long snouts, bared yellow teeth and small round eyes. Meanwhile dozens and dozens more loped across the road on all fours. Baboon mothers with babies on their backs or clinging to their underbellies, were flanked by single adults and scampering youngsters. The odd burly male sauntered by, eyeing us menacingly. Evidently the tribe was on a mission. Nine or ten baboons explored the car, leering through the glass as they hung from the roof ogling our little baby through the back window. She was equally fascinated. Quietly, we sat and waited until the baboons were ready to take leave of us. Eventually, they scurried off to join the rear guard, and we were able to continue our journey. Dust billowed out behind us, while the highlands ahead invited us closer. Climbing into the Mau Ranges, the air became cooler, as we tunneled through forests, emerging into rolling wheat land, pastures and farms. We were now in Mau Narok, where Liz and Bruce lived on a farm that had been worked by Bruce's father long before his sons were born.

Later, relaxing by a smoldering fire in a huge stone hearth, we excitedly discussed details of our safari to the Mara. We were heading into the real wild Mara. This was before tourist hotels, airstrips, hot air balloons, zebra busses, or cell phones and petrol stations. We would be out there on our own, and our survival depended on our self-sufficiency plans. The Maasai Mara, a beautiful, ageless land where wild life roamed free, as it had since time began, was a vast game reserve of 1,500 square kilometres, flowing south into the Serengeti in Tanzania.

Liz and Bruce's two girls were away at boarding school. We left our little daughter in the kind hands of friends, where she was enthralled by their tame, house-trained owl. Until this point Sirri had been everywhere with us, and we had seldom left her with a baby sitter, but now we were off on safari in the Maasai Mara Game Reserve, not the place for a baby. It wrenched me to leave her behind but I knew she'd be safe, and happy, with Vanda. We were joined by Jenny, an English girl, coming on safari with us, and the five of us loaded up the Toyota four-wheel drive and trailer with tents, food supplies, first aid kit, milk churns of drinking water, and drums of petrol and oil.

Leaving the farm behind us, we travelled through forests, sighting black and white colobus monkeys swinging through ancient bearded trees. Then, descending onto the plains, we passed Narok, a sleepy settlement of dusty dukas, where skinny cattle and goats wandered aimlessly over the road. The afternoon wore on and we eventually pulled up beside a group of Maasai, sheltering beneath an isolated thorn tree. It was hot and still, and the air thick with flies. A languid lazy stupor hung around like a slow Sunday afternoon. No one was going anywhere. There was nowhere to go. Tumbling out of the truck, we greeted the Maasai and curiously observed one another. The men, with earthy ochre hairdo's, were attired in simple faded red blankets draped over one shoulder, revealing their dark skin, and supple bodies, leaving little to the imagination. Chattering, bare-breasted young women stared at us, before touching our arms and hair and dissolving into fits of giggles. Bruce talked to the group in Maa, translating back to us. He was told that the necklaces, bracelets and earrings each person wore signified the wearer's particular status. The women wove the hundreds of little coloured beads onto leather thongs in patterns of their own, to express whether they were single, married, with child, a mother, grandmother, or widowed. They were partial to red beads, which were the Maasai colour. Green beads signified grass, and blue was God's colour. A young girl took off a necklace she was wearing and offered it to me. Perhaps she was soon to change her status? The necklace was beautiful and I am still its proud owner. The morani warriors had gathered round Lee and Bruce, proudly displaying their spears. Lee asked Bruce to offer a warrior a good price for his spear. Quicker than an arrow the answer came back; "A spear is necessary. What use would money be out here?" Lee's face acknowledged his understanding and respect for this Maasai warrior in his own vast, remote world, and we bid farewell. As we clambered back into the Toyota, the Maasai strode off into the long grass in single file. They were the last people we'd see for several days.

Standing in the back of the truck, we observed the wilderness unfold through two open roof hatches. Hundreds of gazelle, wildebeest, and zebra grazed all around but initially Liz and Bruce were the ones to spot more obscure animals in the undergrowth. Our eyes ached from searching the tawny grassland dotted with stunted acacia trees. Even nearby elephant in the shadows were surprisingly hard to see. Sometimes it was only a slight movement that attracted our attention, and before too long we'd adjusted our peripheral vision and cried out in excitement as we spotted creatures camouflaged beneath the trees. Bruce, who had been coming here since childhood, kept us informed with interesting snippets about the wild animals and our surroundings.

Liz and Bruce took us to a favourite campsite at a bend in the Mara River, and we pitched our tents in the shade, on the banks above the river overlooking a small beach. Bruce tagged little cloth strips to tree trunks leading to and from our toilet, in the bush. From here you looked down the steep bank to the river below where hippo wallowed and sighed. This had to be the prettiest loo in the world. It could also be the scariest. If, while you sat and gazed about you, you were surprised by a snort or a rustle in the bushes, you quickly hot tailed it back to camp, thanking God, or Bruce, for the coloured strips along the way!

Lulled by earthy sweet scents, we lounged beside the fire embers, gazing at the bright starry sky. Our ears tuned into the noises of the night. Millions of insects droned, frogs croaked, night-birds screeched, zebra barked, jackals cackled, hyenas laughed, and a lion coughed – somewhere out there. It felt good to be alive, to be here, alone and far away, wrapped in the soft velvety African night. Someone shone a torch around, and from the darkness, a thousand golden eyes reflected in the beams. It was amazing, as though the sky had fallen, filling the earth with scattered stars. All around eyes twinkled in the light. There were hundreds and hundreds of grazing eyes, watching eyes, hunting eyes. We certainly were not alone, we were totally surrounded by a multitude of creatures. Wildlife was everywhere, revealed only in a beam of light, invisible in the darkness of night. The night really does have a thousand eyes.

We lay in our tents, listening to strange snuffles and grunts. My imagination kept sleep at bay, as I mentally gauged the strength of the tent's fabric against a hungry lion's claws! At last, in the steel grey of a new day, Liz woke us with cups of hot tea. We piled into the truck to search for game at first light, the active hour.

Later, as the day grew hotter, animals would retire to rest or hide in the cool shade of the undergrowth and would be difficult to see. Now creatures were busy hunting or heading home. Herds of antelope, wildebeest, and zebra grazed contentedly in close vicinity to a pride of lion grouped on a rock. Bruce explained that the herbivores grazing were aware of the hunters, but somehow they instinctively knew they would not be troubled by their natural enemy, as the lion had eaten recently and there was no danger. We trundled across the plain, and Lee called out as he spotted a cheetah moving catlike through the long grass, leaving a trail in the dew. We bumped our way closer, and watched him in awe. His fur bristled in the first fiery rays of the morning sun, as he rhythmically padded onwards, paying scant regard to us.

Hours later we returned to camp and a welcome breakfast of bacon, eggs, and coffee. While we washed the dishes and put the camp to rights, Bruce and Lee repaired the daily half a dozen punctures, pulling thick six inch thorns from the rubber. The day grew hot, and leaving our clothes on the little beach, Lee and I bathed and washed our hair. We swam and splashed in the river as happily as anybody would in Eden. Late afternoon we climbed into the Toyota again, and Bruce drove the truck off-road in our insatiable search for wildlife. We saw a massive herd of buffalo, several hundred metres away. The herd, a sprawling patch of dark grey, mirrored a stormy sky above. We stopped. The silence was heavy, the heat intense, a storm was brewing. Was it a far off growl of thunder or the sudden snap of twig? Suddenly the enormous herd of buffalo stampeded. The huge powerful creatures moved in our direction en masse. Bruce started the truck up and we crawled carefully away over the rough terrain. The stampeding herd charged towards us, gathering speed. The earth thundered with a thousand pounding hooves. Hell bent, the beasts drew level with us. Hundreds of hefty, powerful buffalo surged on in a sea of tossing, grunting, grey. With massive heads armoured with huge thick horns, the enormous muscled bodies powered past in swirling dust. A couple collided with the back of our truck, lurching us forward. Others buffeted and shunted us as they hurtled onwards. The main herd split each side of our crawling truck, joining up in front like water, and rushed headlong onwards. Wow!

On safari, the only certainty is the unexpected. The natural high of observing another species in its own habitat is incredible. There is a special thrill that goes with sharing a moment in time with the wilderness. To see a tiger at the zoo, is to see an animal adjusting to your environment. To see an animal, or sea creature, living wild and free, as it has since time began, is exhilarating and special, and you feel a sense of utmost respect for that creature in its own domain. Often the sheer size, power, or speed, amazes you, and a sense of wonder and intensity absorbs you totally in the moment.

Driving along the river, Bruce was telling Lee that crocodile basking in the sun, can feel the vibrations of an approaching vehicle and quickly disappear into the water. Nearing a particular spot, he told Lee to get ready to jump out and run up the dune in the hope of seeing a croc before it disappeared. Lee did this, with the rest of us hurriedly scrambling after. At the top, Lee stood in awe, pointing to a vague ripple. Visibly moved, he told us that an enormous crocodile. 'Massive! As wide as a car', had slipped into the murky water, vanishing with hardly a trace, only moments before. He had no idea a crocodile could be that big, never mind move so quickly.

Night had fallen by the time we pulled into camp. Bruce shone the Toyota spotlight around, and there, in the river, beside our little beach, were several pairs of red eyes lurking in the dark water. Crocodile! Crocodile in the exact spot we had been bathing that morning. We stayed dirty for the rest of the safari.

We took turns as driver for the day, and whoever was driving was free to choose where they wanted to take us. As a boy, Lee had watched movies of jeeps dramatically tearing across the African savannah in pursuit of wild animals, and had dreamt that he'd be able to do that too. So now, here he was, at the wheel, off-road, on safari in Africa, when two hefty rhino appeared ahead. We lumbered closer to the large beasts. Rhino have limited vision, but their sense of smell is strong. Sensing our presence, they quickly became agitated. They blundered around, pawing the ground, sniffing and snuffling. They turned, and turned again, trying to hone in on our scent. Finding it, then losing it again, they became panicky and confused. They went through the sequence several times, before snorting and trotting off. Keeping our distance, in respect of the rhino, as well as our own safety, we followed behind, jerking and jolting over the rough terrain. The rhinos stopped to stamp and snort and face us, before running on again. It was tremendously exciting, but then the pair ran into a belt of dense dried bushes. They turned back to challenge us. We were no longer in open grassland and were now in an environment that favoured them. We stopped and watched for a while, before they finally grunted and crashed off into the undergrowth. Lee was ecstatic that his childhood dream had been realized and that it was so much more thrilling in reality.

It was time to pack up camp. After five magical days our supplies were getting low, and we loaded our gear into the truck. Leaving our lovely campsite as we found it, we drove off across the plains towards Narok. During our time in the Mara we hadn't seen another soul. Now, on our last day, we sighted a car in the distance, and everyone waved like long lost friends! Our wonderful Mara safari over, I couldn't wait to be back with our little baby Sirri. As a mother, I felt I had been away far too long and the endless miles were achingly slow for me. I wanted only to hold my wee lass in my arms again. How sweet the moment was.

***

"Quick, quick, there's a man out there. He's cut up horribly. He's bleeding badly."

"Yeah, O.K. What would you like to drink?"

"I don't think you understand. He's in a real bad way. He needs help."

"Yeah, yeah, in a minute. What are you drinking?"

"Listen man, it's serious. He's been in a fight - slashed all over, blood everywhere. He needs to get to hospital, else he'll bleed to death. He's out the back ..."

With an impatient sigh the thickset man handed someone a beer, muttering, "OK, OK, I'll go and have a look - munts, more trouble than they're bloody worth."

Liz had taken us to play tennis on a nearby ranch, and afterwards we'd been invited up to the house for drinks. Nipping out to the car to get a jumper for the baby, Lee heard angry shouts and a woman's screams. Following the frightening noises behind a shed, he saw a couple of Africans fighting. One was unarmed, the other hacked at him with a *panga* - a heavy duty machete. Catching sight of Lee, the assailant ran off, leaving his viciously slashed victim slumped on the ground.

Lee had been shocked at the brutality he'd just witnessed, and stunned by the rancher's attitude and lack of compassion. New to Africa, he was becoming aware of the often harsh realities of daily life in this beautiful sad, country.

Everything had changed, but nothing had changed. It was 1972, nine years since Kenya's independence, and life went on much the same. Still there were whites who regarded the black people as a lesser species. Still an element of blacks hated the whites. Others were hell bent on exploiting their own people, and bribery and corruption were rife. But at least peace prevailed. Next door, in Uganda, under Idi Amin's regime, the brutal butchering of Ugandans in their thousands was a regular occurrence. Asian families fled for their lives, and horror stories filtered out, of border beatings, rapes, and fingers severed for rings.

The day after the machete fight we drove back across the Rift Valley floor, heading homewards. Sirri slept in her cradle on the back seat, and I sat with her, while Lee was in the Nakuru Post Office. He was taking an age and I waited and waited. Eventually he emerged, shrugged, and smiled knowingly saying, "Now the boot's on the other foot." He told me there were three windows open in the Post Office and he had queued patiently, but when he reached the front, he was continually overlooked by each of the three tellers as 'locals' were served instead.

"It just is, and I guess there'll always be a 'them and us' no matter where in the world you are. You can be on the right side at the wrong time, or the wrong side trying to make it right, or anywhere in between!"

"Yeah" said Lee, "Right from childhood, people identify themselves by taking sides – whether its boy or girl, black or white, this or that religion, rich or poor. It's the old 'divide and rule' system at play. Come to think of it, the entire British Empire was built on such a system, but like any system, it eventually rules itself out and it's time for change."

"Yeah, I try not to take sides – if I can. But that's only easy when you are not emotionally involved. Things change dramatically the second you feel strongly about something." I added.

Leaving the scruffy township of Nakuru in our wake, we pass beneath an avenue of purple flowering jacaranda trees. The straight road opens up ahead. Heat haze mirages lure us towards illusory lakes that flow across the road and evaporate into thin air as we approach. Banana busses and *matata* taxies, loaded to the hilt, hurtle past at break neck speeds, and I am reminded of a similar experience to Lee's, in the same town.

A few years before, I had booked a seat on a *matata*, a Peugeot station wagon taxi, that, for a reasonable fee, crammed it's passengers in for long haul journeys. I needed to get from Nakuru to Kericho, where Mum and Dad were meeting me. I arrived at the depot before opening time, hoping to be on the first matata, but the African manager loaded the car up with others. Patiently I waited for an hour when the next vehicle was scheduled to leave. The same thing happened, and I approached this surly man to explain that I had booked, and my parents would be waiting, and probably worrying, in Kericho. It made no difference. He continued to squeeze new arrivals of his own colour into each taxi throughout the day, until, just before closing time, he reluctantly squashed me into the back of a loaded matata.

"There's no accounting for it" Lee responded. "I suppose these things just happen, and it might be because you are the wrong colour or class, or it might simply be that someone is having a bad day and is taking it out on you."

"You can't really generalize can you. Another time, I could quite easily have been put in my place, insulted, belittled, or simply kicked out. Ironically it was in Nakuru again, but late at night. Everything had closed, and driving around, looking for a bit of action, we'd spotted an African night club. The five of us, three guys and two girls, all young and white, and probably a bit drunk, approached the noisy, somewhat sleazy backstreet night club. The place was rocking with loud jazzy African music reverberating down the dark dingy stairwell. On entering the dim, noisy room, we were immediately made to feel welcome. We soon realized it was also a brothel, but the ladies of the night and customers alike were friendly and genuinely happy to chat and dance with us, accepting us 'outsiders' into their world without any bother or ill will."

Now, I was finding it interesting, seeing a different take on Kenya through my husband's eyes. To me it was home, the place where I was born and grew up, but for Lee it was all new. Although he was well travelled, this was his first visit to Africa. His senses were startled by the ever-changing kaleidoscope of spectacles and curiosities. He told me he felt Kenya was a country you wore, like a mantle. Its energies and ancient mysteries settled round you, and you became of it, and were absorbed into its every nuance. However his cloak didn't always fit comfortably, and he found it hard to handle the blatant poverty, the flies, and being waited on by a houseboy.

We drove on, through the green tea growing highlands of Kericho, and down into the hot Kavirondo Basin near Lake Victoria. By early evening we were in the Mtete Valley and eventually arrived at Maraba's little wooden house amongst the trees, where Mum and Dad worked on a small, remote, cattle and coffee farm. '*Maraba*' means 'the meeting place' in Swahili. It certainly was an ideal meeting place, and it was great to be welcomed home again.

That night, we lay in our little hut listening to the throb of drums, shrill whistles, shrieks and wails. There was an *ngoma,* a dance, in a village further down the valley. Dad had warned us earlier, that it was likely to go on all night, and that it was a circumcision ceremony. While the rest of the village performed its traditional dances, girls of eleven or twelve, spent the night sitting in the river singing. They were numbing themselves in the cold water in preparation for their clitoridectomy the next morning. It was considered a special occasion, and the young girls were proud and happy to be welcomed to womanhood in this way. To us, the idea is horrific, unhygienic, and barbaric, but to the women of the tribe it was an accepted and anticipated part of their life.

In the morning sunshine, we joined Dad at the makeshift factory, where coffee beans were spread out on trays to dry in the sun. Work stopped as we approached, and we were greeted profusely by the old headman, Kipsang, a wiry wizened eccentric with a will of steel, who exuded character from his stretched earlobes to his gnarled splayed feet. The coffee pickers, all women and children, gathered round to say 'jambo' and stroke the baby, while the men who had been bagging up the dried beans, paused for a smoke and chat.

Home again, with the people I loved, I was as content as our baby, crawling amongst the butterflies and lilac jacaranda flowers. Mum and I unravelled the years we'd been apart while her fingers busily spun stitches into little garments. Lee wandered off to help the mechanic, Daniel, in the workshop. With no common language between them, they'd quickly developed an understanding that revolved around tractor parts and cigarettes.

2. All in the fullness of time

Just before the light faded, having started the generator, which provided our electricity, Dad came in to relax with a 'sundowner' beer. Lee was reading through some notes Mum had written on her arrival in Kenya. My parents, Peggy and Jim Anderson, met when they were both stationed in Egypt during the war. They married in 1945, and from the Suez Canal, sailed south to their life together in Kenya.

I peered over Lee's shoulder to read Mum's records;

After a speedy voyage round the Horn of Africa, our ship the S.S. Arundel Castle ploughed down the East African coast. A strange unknown smell wafted across the water. Before it was light, the East African troops were lining the ship's rails, excited to be returning home after two or three years in the Middle East. European Officers and N.C.Os were shouting the word "kwenda". There was no mistaking its meaning "Go! You're free!" The sun had risen by the time the ship entered Mombasa Harbour, and red roofed houses with verandas appeared amongst the lush vegetation. I was as excited as the troops. Disembarkation took hours as the returning soldiers stopped at the bottom of the gangway to put on their boots – they were not going to step onto their homeland with bare feet now that they were the proud soldiers of 'Kingi Georgie's Army'.

Mombasa Station was ablaze with flowering shrubs, which, I was later to learn were bougainvillea, frangipani, and hibiscus amongst others. The daily 4.30pm train for Nairobi was a social event. We had afternoon tea in the Buffet Car with some of my husband's Officers. There was spotless napery, gleaming silver, and attentive Goan Stewards. Carnations, lovely colours and of enormous size in a silver vase caught my attention. I could not believe such beautiful flowers could be completely scentless. One of the grinning Lieutenants said, "I was waiting for that reaction". He explained that in the tropics I should often find the loveliest bright flowers would have little or no perfume.

I said goodbye to Jim and his Officers, who were travelling later with their men in a troop train. With a series of jerks, we were off! We passed through lush countryside with coconuts and other palms, crossing rivers whose waters were a thick orange brown. I'd not then heard of Kenya's problem of fertile topsoil eroding and being washed down to the ocean. Night came suddenly. Whilst at dinner, attendants converted the seats into bunks, making them up with starched but off-white linen. Waking early in the dawn, I noticed the tropical coastal belt had given way to dry, almost tree-less plains with occasional hills lazy in the distance. Then there was more excitement at my first sighting of plains game, zebra, buck, and giraffe. Before long the train was running into Nairobi, with more colour and noise.

I managed to get a room in The New Stanley Hotel, and set off to explore the city. There was not a great deal to see in those days, just a minaret and domed mosque or two, a variety of peoples, gaily coloured dresses, saris and rags. The white men all wore uniform, and so many had crowns on their shoulders. No wonder Kenya was known as 'the Crown Colony' at that time.

"It's hard to imagine Nairobi in those days." I said.

"It's certainly progressed since then, but the two main colonial hotels are still there – the Norfolk and the New Stanley, although that wasn't a modern skyscraper then."

"The New Stanley!" added Lee, "Wasn't that where Sirri stood up, only it was a street café underneath a sprawling thorn tree? And you told me that, no matter where in the world you came from, if you sat outside the Thorn Tree for long enough you would see someone you knew go by."

"That's what they say!" I replied teasingly.

"So how come I didn't see anyone I knew?"

"Maybe you didn't sit there for long enough!"

Biffing me lightly, Lee picked up the next page and continued reading.

Two days later, Jim, having settled his battalion into the Depot out at a place called Ruiru, joined me, bringing his Colonel, Sandy Arrish to meet me. Sandy told me I could leave off my stockings and gloves, but I was to buy a shady felt hat. Pointing to a passing vehicle, a sort of motorcar with four poles supporting a roof, he said, "If that was what your husband were to purchase, don't protest, just appreciate how lucky you are to have a motorcar." Cars, trucks, and in fact all consumer goods were difficult to come by as during the seven years of war, ships sailing into Mombasa were not carrying luxury items. I was stunned as Jim had told me not to bring anything out for our home as we'd get everything we needed in Kenya. Fortunately I had bought some bed linen and huge towels from the Naval Stores whilst in the WRNS. All these 'whites' were soon to be dyed dark green or blue as the brown waters of Nandi stained everything. Army wives aboard the trooper had told me I was very silly not to have brought everything including furniture out for the home. There was an Army allowance of four and a half hundredweight of baggage per family! Many months later, Whiteaways, Kenya's one department store, received a consignment of goods. I was able to buy half a dinner service, a vegetable dish, and gravy boat, using our wedding present money. The only china made at that period in East Africa was a dull pale earth colour, very utilitarian.

February 1947 our employers, East African Coffee Plantations, wanted us to move down country to a sister estate, Kiamara in Kiambu for six months. Jim refused, "No, we couldn't go until later, our baby was due the second week in March, the doctor and hospital were booked ready." Our little baby son, Hugh, arrived prematurely on 24th February, weighing only five pounds at birth. I didn't get to see my baby until the next day and spent the entire night worrying that something was terribly wrong with our little premature baby, and that was why they wouldn't let me see him, but it was simply a misunderstanding between staff changing shifts.

We still had to proceed with the move only two weeks after our return from Eldoret Hospital. It was a nightmare journey with the tiny baby. From the farm in Nandi Hills at 7,200 feet above sea level, down the escarpment to Muhoroni, 4,000 feet. We boarded the train in the afternoon and chugged up to Lumbwa, at over 7,000 feet. Dinner was in the Dak Bungalow and then back on the train and down gradient to Nakuru, another long slow climb to Uplands, 8,500 feet, and finally down into Nairobi. Hugh, by then was as yellow as a china-man. The last section was by truck to Kiambu, only fourteen miles out of Nairobi, but the road was always appalling, and either a foot deep in dust in the dry season or sticky mud in the rains. It took our wee son a long time to recover from jaundice.

Lee paused and looked up at Mum, "This makes interesting reading Peggy. Have you always kept a diary or a journal?"

"No, Lee, there are no journals. I liked to write down some of my impressions and experiences during the war years and my early years in Kenya, but sadly it was pretty spasmodic and there are many things I wish I'd recorded but never did. I just kept the notes together in a box, which came with us whenever we moved."

"Actually it's quite remarkable you have kept these. You have captured a time that has already gone, a time when things were completely different to the way it is now. Funnily enough the way it is now is all so different for me – even now!"

Laughing we returned our attention to Mum's narratives;

A month or two later, Irene, an ex WRNS friend came out to stay. When we met her in the early morning, after she'd travelled over night from Mombasa, Jim asked her if she would like to see lion that evening. Irene, told me later she said a mental, "O yeah! They produce lion just like that do they?" Jim and I had been going to Nairobi Game Park every weekend since arriving down country. Game Wardens tipped us off, telling us where to find the king of beasts, but we never had a glimpse. That evening with Irene, we sat in the dusk watching a pride of six or seven lion crossing the track right in front of us. Irene was not the only one to be astonished and thrilled. In those days the Nairobi Game Park was only new and there were no entrance fees.

Jim taught Irene to play chess. One wet evening they were concentrating on their game sitting in front of a smoking log fire. I donned raincoat, and taking a dutch lamp, set off down the path into a little wood, where the loo was hidden away. Just seated, I felt something move underneath me. Letting out a terrible shriek, I grabbed my lamp and ran, still screaming. Jim and Irene, startled by the yells, jumped up, sending the table and chessmen flying, rushed out in time to see me emerge from the woods and trip over my knickers! Jim was so cross with me spoiling their game, just because a bat had caressed me!

Our six months drew to an end. I loved being close to Nairobi and hated the idea of returning to Nandi Hills, but I had the arrival of my family to look forward to. My parents, Sue and Arthur, and youngest brother, Teddy, had been on a waiting list for two years, and finally had berths on a ship to Cape Town in October. They had sold the guest house and in late 1947 arrived in Cape Town, where they bought a car and motored up to Durban. They had intended keeping the car and driving north, but discovered it was illegal to take cars out the country, so the car was sold and the Chapmans sailed up the coast to Kenya. From Mombasa, they travelled inland by train to Nairobi, spending a couple of days in the city, before taking the overnight train down across the Rift Valley to Muhoroni, near Lake Victoria.

Jim and I left our new baby, with friends, Peggy and Syd Outram, and drove down the Nandi Escarpment to meet the Chapmans at a tiny isolated station at 3 o'clock in the morning. The journey back up the steep rugged escarpment wasn't without adventure, as everyone had to get out at the Twin Bridges and all the many S bends, to push the loaded car. It was dark, lonely, steep, rugged country, and the new arrivals were terrified of snakes and leopards. This was young Teddy's introduction to Kenya, where he was later to play his part admirably. Up in the Nandi Hills, we stopped for an early breakfast with the Outrams, and my parents were able to meet their grandson. The Chapmans stayed with us on the farm at Savani where Jim was working.

My mother, Sue, was a great success in the district and was the life and soul of Christmas and New Year parties. However, it was my father, Arthur who took the dancing honours. Driving home one night, he stopped the car on the grass track to adjust the headlights. Suddenly he was yelling and jumping about, arms waving wildly. Then he ripped off his shirt, trousers and underpants. Sue was horrified, what on earth was he playing at? Arthur was undergoing his African initiation, compliments of siafu - soldier ants that travel in massive armies devouring everything in their path. Anyone unfortunate enough to be standing in their way, soon feels the nasty nips as the ants swarm up your legs and into your clothing at lightning speed. However, to an observer it is usually an amusing sight!

In the New Year, Leonard Foster, a neighbour and pre-war friend of Jim's, who'd returned to his farm as soon as he was de-mobbed from the R.A.F., decided he needed a holiday. He asked Arthur and Sue to mind his farm, Kaparak, for three weeks while he was away. He brushed aside their protests of 'no knowledge or experience' telling them all they'd have to do was look after the animals and supervise the labour. Sue and Arthur duly took responsibility of Kaparak, and the weeks passed, but Leonard Foster did not return to his farm. Animals died, a leopard got into the kitchen creating havoc, and Arthur had to rush himself to Kapsabet Hospital to have dog bites cauterized. Sue was getting very worried. After six weeks a postcard arrived from Leonard. It had been posted in Kingston, Jamaica, and read, "Having a lovely time. See you soon." It was several more weeks before Leonard reappeared. He nonchalantly remarked, "Why did you worry Sue? Those animals would have died if I'd been here anyway!"

During this time, my elder brother Jim arrived unexpectedly, discharged from the Royal Engineers, and en route to Tanganyika (now Tanzania) to join the infamous Ground Nut Scheme. Driving through the night, he collided with an ant bear. Stunned by its size and strange shape, he thought he was seeing things! A few days later, it was getting dark, and Sue was anxious because her boys hadn't returned home. Then she heard shouting in the distance. Arthur, with great presence of mind, quickly jumped into the car, and with headlights full on, and horn blaring, he rounded the corner. Jim and Teddy had been sent scurrying up a tree by a leopard and were unable to get down until the leopard had been frightened away! It was an exciting start to life in Africa for the boys.

The ground nut scheme was situated in a notoriously unhealthy area, and Jim quickly realized it was doomed before it got going. He took on another position in Uganda, working as an engineer at Buchanans, near Jinja, where they grew coffee, vanilla beans and rubber. The family travelled up to Kampala for Jim's wedding to Pam Cashmore. However, it wasn't long before tribal unrest forced the young couple to leave Uganda and join us in Kenya. They settled in Nakuru, where Jim worked with the Kenya Farmers Association until the Mau.

Arthur, Sue and Teddy moved to Eldoret, known locally as 'Sleepy Hollow' or '64'. Sue bought a café, 'Barty's Tea Room', and Arthur managed a bookshop & stationers. They lived in a corrugated iron house near the old Hill School, which Teddy attended. In those days the Hill School comprised of old army huts from World War 1. A couple of years passed before Norrie Duncan opened his own café above his bakery in Eldoret. Knowing this would take away her trade, Sue sold quickly, and the family moved to Nakuru. Arthur became the radiographer in the native hospital and Sue went to Nairobi as governess to the American Consul's children. She returned home when she could, but on completion of her governess job, was asked to manage Ankole Hotel in Usambara for three months while the owner was on overseas leave. Later Sue became a nanny to a Greek family who took her by ship to France with them, motored through to Rome, and flew to Athens. Part of the agreement was that the family would pay Sue's return airfare to Kenya, but they also paid for her to go home to the UK for a holiday first. While Sue was away working, Arthur and Teddy spent their weekends with us.

"Wow!" I exclaimed. "Granny Sue certainly had an interesting life, especially in those days when women weren't supposed to be so independent. What a character – always lots of fun, a real free spirit."

Mum replied that, yes, her mother believed anything was possible as long as you took the chances when they came along.

"Didn't Granddad mind her always disappearing for new adventures?"

"No." said Mum, "He was clever enough to know nothing would hold her back, and life was certainly more peaceful when he let Sue do whatever she wanted!"

"Hey Lee, you'd better be warned that I have Granny Sue's genes in me!"

"I'd better adopt some of Granddad's wisdom then!" he retorted.

Laughing I replied, "Yes, but I have his genes too!"

***

With all the recent travelling, different times zones, climate changes, and new people and places, our baby had lost all sense of any sleep patterns she may have had, so we tried to establish a bit of routine. Like most new mothers, I had been besieged with endless well-intentioned but conflicting advice and old wives tales. Is it better to feed your baby regularly every four hours or 'on demand'? Should the baby be picked up whenever it cries, or trained to be less dependent? We had never used a pram, preferring to carry our baby around in our arms or in a sling, and having grown up alongside the Africans, I favoured the ways they brought up their children. They never seemed to pander to their *toto's* - little ones, who seldom grizzled or demanded undue attention. African mothers took their babies with them wherever they went, wrapped in a sort of cloth hammock on their backs. This way, the mothers continued with their daily chores, working in the fields, collecting firewood and water, or going to market. On the other hand, our European ways demanded more schedule in our days, as we ate and slept at specific times, and I was struggling with what I'd like to do, and what would be best, considering we would be staying with several different people over the next few months. Eventually we decided that Sirri, now ten months old, needed her sleep, and that we would encourage her to have a nap in her cot every afternoon and to settle down for the night at a certain time. The first afternoon was difficult to say the least, as she screamed from the moment I put her in her cot. I forced myself to ignore her protests, although I hated every minute, becoming really tense and uptight. The next afternoon, the same thing. But this time, as I passed through the kitchen, Mango, our old loyal house boy, surprised me, saying, "How can you do this? You are the mother, how can you let your baby cry like that?"

He was right! I couldn't. After that, either Lee or I would lie on our bed reading by the baby's cot, and happy that we were in the vicinity, Sirri would eventually lie down for an afternoon snooze. The evening wasn't so simple, as we slept in a little guest hut separate from the main house, so we tended to let Sirri stay up until she was practically asleep before tucking her up for the night.

A day or two before Christmas, I noticed Mango rummaging through the rubbish bin. He explained that he'd thought I might have thrown a baby's teat away. Mango was from the Luo tribe, who live along the shores of Lake Victoria in Western Kenya. He was a staunch catholic, kind, serious, and a good father to his three teenagers. He'd always been determined his son, Michael, should have a good education, and most of his wages went towards this.

Unsure why Mango needed a baby's teat, I asked. He explained that one of the farm labourers, Otunda, had recently lost his wife. She had died in childbirth. The baby had survived and now Otunda was up all night with the crying baby. He also had two other children to look after, as well as a job to hold down. Mango thought that if we had an old teat, it would help Otunda feed the baby from a bottle, instead of dipping cloth into milk for the baby to suck on. I told Mango I'd get him a bottle and some teats, and moved by Otunda's story, immediately repeated it to Lee and Mum.

We dug out blankets, towels, and baby clothes. Then Lee and I drove the eleven miles to the *duka* – local shop. To our delight, there amongst the bags of salt and maize, hurricane lamps, and batteries, were two plastic baby's feeding bottles with screw on teats. We also stocked up on sugar, tea, powdered milk, rice, sweets and cigarettes for Otunda and his children. Back at Maraba, we asked Mango to pass these on. Early the next morning Otunda was at the door thanking us profusely with watery eyes. He was so grateful. It was probably the best Christmas present we would ever give – and it had been so easy.

After that Otunda waved and called out to us whenever our paths crossed on the farm, and with his beautiful smile, he'd ask after Sirri and tell us how his children were. He taught me much, even then. In spite of his grief, he radiated a genuine warmth and appreciation of life. He carried on alone, looking after his tiny baby Margaret, his older children, and doing a day's work at the coffee factory, yet he was always so considerate and friendly.

Above the monotonous throb of the generator and drone of insects, night birds screeched in the darkness. I joined the others in the lounge, where Dad was relaxing with his pipe, listening to the news through the static on the radio, while Mum concentrated on her needlework. Lee was reading more of Mum's notes, and as he completed each handwritten page, he passed it over to me.

In May 1948 we moved to Lugari Sisal Estate, 19,000 acres, 12,000 under sisal, 500 maize. The bungalow was newly built in a clearing in the sisal. Water was brought from the river each day in three forty gallon drums on a sledge pulled by a team of oxen. Catering was easy as the estate bordered the railway line and three times a week the Uganda bound train stopped at Lugari Station where we collected three baskets, from the butcher, the baker, and the greengrocers, as well as our mail. We had a good social life here too. The Turbo and Kipkarren districts had opened up 'Soldier Settlement Scheme' farms for young ex-servicemen and their wives. I made many friends, and we visited each other, played tennis, and danced at Turbo Club.

In the bungalow the outlet for the bath and basin was a square hole about 6" high and wide at floor level. I was terrified as I could not get Kipling's Riki Tiki Tavi out of my mind. I used to peer around the door, then kneel to look beneath the bath, keeping one eye on the outlet all the time I was in the bathroom. The inevitable happened after about six weeks. "Noika, noika" – snake, snake. I grabbed my baby, slamming the nursery door behind us, only to realise if the snake came under the door, we would be trapped, as the windows were meshed with wire gauze to keep out the mosquitoes. The snake was killed with a great deal of shouting and banging with sticks. It was quite small and black, and the boys pronounced it a baby mamba. Jim told me I was a fool not mentioning my fears before, and quickly made a gauze frame to cover the outlet.

Another hazard at Lugari was the bees. In the bungalow they loved the sitting room chimney. We overcame them by using special Amtil Bee Candles. The bees took revenge by keeping us out of the master bedroom from about 10 in the morning, swarming inside my wardrobe, getting through the tiniest crack. The swarm was about the size of a soccer ball, and every afternoon, when the heat had died down, we threw handfuls of raw pyrethrum powder over them, later sweeping up the dead bodies so we could have our room back for the night. The bees were a constant hazard in the sisal too, being the indirect cause of terrible fires. Careless Kitoshi tribesmen used to smoke the bees out of their hives to collect the honey, often failing to put the fires out after them. A European always had to be on duty as "firewatcher" at weekends. On a neighbouring estate our friend Wallace Linscott was out in the fields when he received a message that his wife and little son had been stung by bees and had died. He rushed back to the house to find his wife unconscious and little Guy terribly stung all over. Fortunately he was able to administer help immediately. The bees had been disturbed by the engine of the D8 tractor. Later discussions with other farmers confirmed that these noisy engines always upset bees.

Two year old Hugh was now joined by his new baby sister, Heather Jane. Because of the abundance of snakes, and the fact that Hugh was now running about everywhere, Jim felt that Hugh needed someone with him all the time and that the children should have an ayah, a nanny, to look after them. I was adamant that we didn't need an ayah, and was not going to have anyone to look after my children, and a long row ensued! However, the snakes were a real danger and finally an ayah was employed. Cheppichi was a young widow from the Nandi tribe and became an integral part of our family. Still not entirely convinced an ayah was necessary, I admit to being a bit stand-offish towards her on her first day, but that soon changed when I was sitting on the steps sewing. Cheppichi came and sat down beside me, saying "Now sewing is something I **can** do". We quickly became friends and I taught Cheppichi how to cut clothes out from patterns and to use the sewing machine. She created beautiful crochet work and whenever I was visiting friends and noticed an interesting piece of crocheting in someone's house, I would call Cheppichi in to look at it. She had a photographic memory and was able to just look at the crochet piece, remember the patterns, and later would reproduce a similar work of art from memory. She was a happy, friendly soul, who liked to play games and sing Nandi songs to the children. She was much loved by all the family, but sadly, when the children were a little older, a change in circumstances meant that we had to let her go. She found work quickly with another white family, and kept in touch with me for years. At one stage I told her we'd love to have her back if she ever wanted. Cheppichi answered that she would love to come back to her little family, but the people she was with were decent folk, and she could not leave them unless they did something bad to her, or no longer needed her. What wonderful loyalty and integrity. I still have some of her pale green crochet mats, laced with her warmth and hints of hidden memories of happy early days.

In 1950 Jim applied for a Settlement Scheme farm in Kipkarren, but was turned down due to insufficient capital. The required starting amount had just been increased from the formerly required £1,000 to £1,500. Immediately after this disappointment an opportunity arose to go into partnership working a sawmill and clearing 500 acres of forest cedar and native podo. Because we were already employed, we had to keep these negotiations secret. On the final settlement day, Jim had gone into Nakuru to sign the contracts, and while he was away, Billy arrived. Billy had been one of Jim's young Lieutenants in Egypt, and was now a good friend and neighbour. I was being evasive about Jim's whereabouts and when he was due back. After a cup of tea and chat, Billy, who was able to see into the unknown, offered to read my palm. He told me that I would be moving into a little wooden house in the woods. He then became terribly upset and said he didn't feel like going on. He appeared to be in shock so I quickly got up to get him a brandy. Just then Jim arrived home, and beaming happily, announced that he was now a saw-miller. Billy was full of genuine relief. He explained that looking into the future he had seen the woods, and the saw-mill, but had also seen me running from the house, into the arms of a man coming from the forest. Poor Billy had thought that I was to leave Jim for another man! After that Billy stopped telling fortunes.

Soon after settling in to the little wooden house in the forest, I saw a beautiful rainbow, ending at the foot of the waterfall. I remember thinking that our 'pot of gold' was there in the forest and was convinced that we would make our fortune here. All these years later, I realise that we did indeed find our 'pot of gold' – it was our lives.

There were rumblings of fear and discontent as the Mau Mau Rebellion grew. Sightings of Mau Mau were often reported in the area, and the local headquarters were not far up the road. We acquired a gun for protection, which was kept locked in the safe when we were home. However, on car trips, as a precaution, should we be ambushed or have to slow to negotiate any impromptu road blocks, I sat with a revolver on my lap, hidden beneath a jumper, hoping like hell I'd never have to use it.

We were only saw-millers for two years. Prior to buying the property, the Subukia woods had been surveyed by The Forestry Department, and were reported to have five years cutting in them. Alas, after less than two years, it transpired that the cedar trees were diseased. We came out, breaking even after selling the house and land to cattle breeders. Only months after leaving the Waterfall Estate, the Mau Mau raided the house. The new owners hired Kipsigis herdsmen to look after their cattle, and the ten Kipsigis men, with their bows and arrows bravely fought off the Mau Mau gang. This is why I referred to our 'pot of gold' being our lives. Jim said that we had been truly blessed by the timber running out when it did.

There was a small event that gives the general Mau Mau savagery a little human touch. Before we left the woods, Jim was at work at the mill, the baby asleep, and I was ironing, thinking Hugh was with the ayah. In turn, Cheppichi had thought Hugh was with me. Realising that my little boy was nowhere to be seen in the house or garden, I went running up the drive. Coming down the road towards me, were two African men pushing Hugh home on his little tricycle. Young Hugh had decided he was going to ride his bike to Nakuru to see his Grandad! En route he passed a hut where several African men were holding a meeting. It turns out that this particular hut was the local Mau Mau headquarters, and yet those hard and dangerous men kindly returned this little white boy unharmed to his mother.

Handing the notes back to Mum, Lee said, "Wow! What amazing experiences you have had. It's hard to imagine what you went through in the early years here – incredible really. But what about the Mau Mau? That must have been a very difficult time for everyone. What was it all about?"

Turning off the wireless, Dad gave Lee an overview of the Mau Mau; "Basically, the Mau Mau was a rebellious uprising by the Kikuyu tribe against white colonialist oppression. Jomo Kenyatta, Dedan Kimathi and others, lead the freedom fighters in an attempt to drive the white farmers from their land, and ultimately from their country. Farmers and their wives and children were brutally attacked in their homes at night. Several settler's families, as well as their African workers, were found hacked to death, and livestock mutilated or stolen. Huts were burnt with the occupants inside. Gangs appeared, people disappeared, strangers crisscrossed the farms, and sinister secret meetings were held in huts at night. Long serving and loyal staff were discovered to have let Mau Mau gangs into their owner's houses, many more lost their lives defending their employers. White settlers carried guns wherever they went, and everywhere there was an atmosphere of fear and mistrust. Thousands of Kikuyu lived in constant dread of being meted out and forced to take 'the oath'. Huge numbers of Kikuyu men and women, who resisted these demands, were murdered.

The oathing ceremonies involved disgusting initiation rituals, which were inhumane and terrifying in themselves. The hold over the people and power of these rituals was magnified by deep seated local superstition, spells and curses. The Kikuyu were understandably terrified of insulting or upsetting the spirits of their ancestors by refusing to join their people's fight, or by betraying them. Those taking the oath were cursed with evils far worse than death, should they violate or betray their brothers in any way. Once they had taken the oath, kikuyu men were expected to act with unfailing loyalty, and initiates would commit atrocious crimes during raids to obtain ammunition and supplies, and they maimed, mutilated, and murdered on command.

The Mau Mau were a formidable force to deal with. Their barbaric acts of degradation and depravity put fear and dread into the hearts of Africans and Whites alike. It was difficult to police the vast areas affected by the Mau Mau. The rebels operated a huge net spread out across the plains and isolated farms, hiding out in the dense forests of the Abedare Mountains. The great distances caused serious time delays to the Police, and information was hard to come by and often unreliable as no one knew who to trust.

To help combat the Mau Mau, the Kenya Police and Reserves, joined forces with the K.A.R, Kenya Regiment, and a Home Guard, which was formed by Kikuyu who had refused to take the oath. Also several units of the British Army were sent out to Kenya to quell the uprising."

Mum interrupted, adding that both her brothers were involved with the police and army during the Mau Mau. "Jim was seconded to the Rift Valley Police HQ when the state of emergency was declared, and was with the police throughout the Mau Mau years, working in the Operations Department, where he was often called out on raids. Because of the distance between farms, and poor communication, as well as cut phone lines, Jim invented a warning rocket, a flare device that farmers could fire up their chimneys if they were attacked.

My younger brother, Teddy, also began working with the Special Police Force, translating Kikuyu to English. On his seventeenth birthday, he voluntarily signed up with the army, The Kenya Regiment, altering the date on his birth certificate so it looked like he was 18. He served as an interpreter to the Gloucesters, Buffs, and Royal Inskillans, up in the Aberdare Mountains."

Putting her needlework aside, Mum paused a moment before continuing her story, "I remember that Christmas so well. It was usual for local European families to invite visiting soldiers into their homes for Christmas. These troops, far from home, enjoyed the chance to share a family Christmas, and soldiers were given 48 hour leave and dispersed far and wide to enjoy the Christmas festivities and a bit of R&R. Teddy came home to Arthur and Sue's in Nakuru, bringing a friend from the Black Watch with him for Christmas, and our little family came in to town and stayed with my brother Jim and Pam. Jim had been on police duty on Christmas night, and returned at breakfast time, with the alarming news that there had been a battle, near Thika, and that Major Wavell, a popular Black Watch C.O, had been killed. This news had to be suppressed until all the men from the Black Watch, and other regiments, were back from their 48 hour Christmas Leave. Wavell was so revered by his troops that it was feared that the unsettled men, perhaps with the aid of alcohol, might over-react causing incidents to flare up with local natives all over the country. So having been given the disturbing news by Jim, the Chapman households had to spend Boxing Day pretending that nothing untoward had happened until Teddy and the other lad had left to join the troops. Once all the soldiers were safely back in their barracks they would be briefed with the news.

Mau Mau terrorists had their hide outs and headquarters up in the dense wet forests of the massive Abedare ranges, where Teddy was stationed, and the situation was always tense. As well as his normal duties as an interpreter to the Black Watch Battalion, Teddy liked to help cook the daily meal of rice or curry for the boys in the evenings. Like his mother, Teddy was psychic and intuitively knew where people were hiding. He had an uncanny sense of danger and would warn others of any impending menace, often helping to save lives, including his own. Once, tracking down on the plains, his group paused for a cigarette. The other two lit up and offered him a light. Suddenly he remembered 'the third light story' from his father's days in the trenches. He declined saying he'd light his own. Seconds later, as he lowered his head to strike his own match, a bullet whistled over his head, actually parting his hair. Alas, sadly his sixth sense was to fail him not long after. In August 1955, Teddy had been seconded as Assistant District Officer of the Kikuyu Reserve, and was now stationed near Nyeri. He had taken a couple of days leave to come down to Nairobi to see us off on our overseas leave to England. I will never forget the last sight of my 19 year old brother, looking up, smiling, and waving to us from the foot of the gangway. A week later Teddy was dead."

Tears filled Mum's eyes as she talked about her young brother. Dad consoled her, putting his arm gently around her shoulders, he continued with her story, "Back in Nyeri, Teddy had joined Wynne Cashmore, Jim's mother in-law, for supper at the White Rhino Hotel. He met up with two other soldiers for the journey home in the rain. The driver had had too much to drink, so a young Scot volunteered to drive. This young lad had only been in the country a few weeks and wasn't familiar with the Kenya bridges that often had no sides and were constructed of wood, which became very slippery when wet. The Land-Rover skidded on the bridge and careered over the edge into the raging waters. The young Scot was pinned behind the driver's wheel and Teddy was thrown onto rocks and drowned. Both Teddy and the young Scot were killed instantly, while the third passenger was unhurt.

Teddy was buried the following day with Full Military Honours at St Peters Church in Nyeri, where Lord Baden Powell, founder of the scouts, is also buried.

At the time, Teddy's parents, Arthur and Sue, were travelling through the Red Sea and were unaware of his death, and we did not know the sad news until a telegram reached Peggy in Scotland. Wynne Cashmore kindly stood in for the family and arranged all the necessary details for his funeral. 'At the going down of the sun, and in the morning, we will remember him'."

With her voice catching, Mum said, "He was too young to die. Always so full of life, so adventurous, and you know, he showed great kindness and warmth to everyone. He spent hours playing with young Hugh, making catapults and model boats, or looking for chameleons and tortoises. Teddy also had a special bond with you, Heather. When he first left school at 16, he asked if he could borrow you. You were little more than a toddler, and he took you to meet all his friends, their parents, his old teachers, in fact everyone he knew! Several hours passed and Dad and I were getting anxious that something had happened, but Teddy finally returned with his little niece, having run out of people to show her off to!"

Mum smiled at the memory, and I reached for her hand. I had never heard the full story before. All I knew was that, as kids, we missed our Uncle Teddy, who we adored. His young face smiled at us from a photo Mum kept on her dressing table, and Hugh and I used to talk about a joyous time when Uncle Teddy had turned up unexpectedly in his first car, a rusty chassis of a pick-up truck, open to the elements. He took us for rides along the bumpy farm roads, and we all sang at the top of our voices as we bounced about on the wooden boards of his old jalopy.

3. Punda Milia and Uhuru

Hugh, my elder brother, was living in the Cayman Islands with his young wife, Linda. He was running the office while he surveyed and mapped the Cayman Island coastline. To do this he was sub-aqua diving to take measurements and photographs, compiling his findings with land and aerial photographs and readings.

Our younger brother, Robin was working on a coffee farm in Kiambu, near Nairobi, and in the New Year we went to stay with him. We enjoyed our time with the young bachelor Robin, squeezing into his tiny flat, which was completely taken over by an entire motor bike stripped down into hundreds of greasy pieces - very difficult to keep our crawling baby out of! The shower outlet was blocked and so showers were remarkably quick as you balanced on tiptoe, trying to avoid standing in the scummy foam. We were served meals by 'The Spook', the serious, silent, creeping houseboy, who had an incomprehensible ability to make green omelettes, which he served often. The conditions in the flat encouraged us to spend as much time as possible outside, and we'd eagerly jump in the Land-Rover with Robin as he went about his rounds. As our visit drew to an end, we decided to have a good night out in Nairobi, but on that particular day the heavens opened. Late afternoon found Robin and Lee knee deep in mud, trying to get two tractors out of a ditch. Needless to say, this took hours, and although I was dressed and ready to hit the high spots, the boys returned exhausted and caked in mud, wanting only a hot bath, a meal and a drink. A scungy shower, green omelette and a beer sufficed!

Robin and I had lived out this way in the early sixties, and much of our chatter revolved around those times and people we knew then. We had lived further out in an area known as Makuyu, where Dad managed Punda Milia Sisal Estate. This estate was named after the vast herds of zebra that once roamed the land freely. In 1906 two Irish settlers, Swift and Rutherford, planted the country's first commercial sisal here. Apparently they had one bicycle between them. When they both wanted to go to Nairobi, 50 miles away, one would set off on the bike, while the other walked or trotted. After bicycling so far, the rider would leave the bike beside the road, and continue on foot. Later, the walker would reach the bike, and ride on, past his friend, until he too had cycled the agreed distance. And so in turn, walking and riding, they would both arrive in Nairobi!

From the house, we had lovely views of distant Mt Kenya in the early mornings, and clear evenings. There was a story, about some courageous Italians and Mt Kenya. During the war, for security reasons, as Italy was a German ally, all the Italian men in East Africa were rounded up and kept in Prisoner of War camps for the duration. While they were POWs, the Italians did an incredible job building roads, bridges, hospitals, houses, and farm buildings throughout Kenya. To their on-going credit they constructed the difficult, steep, rocky road twisting down the Great Rift Valley Escarpment, and half way down, the little chapel, St Mary of the Angels.

Three Italian prisoners in Nanyuki made a bid for freedom one night. The idea was not so much to escape, but more to escape the endless boring hours of imprisonment. The challenge that loomed invitingly over them day and night, was the snowcapped peak of Mt Kenya. The three broke out and climbed for three days, with meagre rations, and dressed only in prisoners' clothes. They had no maps or knowledge of climbing routes, came up against a herd of elephant, survived a mountain blizzard, and against all odds, scaled Lenana Peak and planted the Italian flag there! Early the following morning, local officials awoke to see the Italian flag flying from the top of Mt Kenya! The three Italians stumbled back to their POW camp, and quite rightly, the British Officials took a lenient view of this heroic escapade.

After the war, many Italians stayed on in Kenya. They were married by proxy, to Italian girls they had never met. Back in Italy, the young women were desperate to escape the bleak and hopeless existence in bombed and ruined cities, and bravely travelled out to a new land faraway to wed men they knew nothing about.

When we moved to Punda Milia, we inherited two springer spaniels. Tiger was the older wiser dog and Tess was little more than a puppy, but she had a way with snakes. Snakes were abundant in the area, and it was not uncommon to find a puff adder on the doorstep in the mornings. The snakes slithered up the steps to coil up on the warm concrete in the cool of the night. Whenever Tess discovered a snake in the garden, she would bark continuously, swaying from side to side, mirroring the movement of the snake. It is unclear whether it was the snake that became mesmerized by the dog, or vice versa, but both were incapable of escape, remaining where they were until someone responded to Tess' monotonous 'snake bark' and ran to deal with the snake. The dogs also warned us of impending earth tremors, cowering under the table or desk several minutes before a shake was felt. Both dogs loved riding in the Land-Rover, heads stuck out the sides, and ears flying in the breeze! However, being long haired dogs, they picked up a multitude of burrs, black jacks, and grass seeds, which knotted up their fur, creating thick matted havens for fleas. It took hours to trim and brush their coats and ears back to an acceptable state, and you'd generally find they'd been bush again the following morning!

Tiger had been a gun dog for his previous master and was an experienced and instinctive retriever. His instincts took over when we took an old rowboat out on the dam. Splotches of delicate pale blue water lilies decorated the pond, which was surrounded by reeds and peppered with water fowl. Tiger couldn't bear to be left on the shore, and in spite of his advanced age, he hurled himself through the reeds and swam out to join us in the middle of the dam. He doggy paddled to the boat but was exhausted and panting on arrival. There was no option but to try and get him on board, at the risk of capsizing us all into the water. But that was part of the adventure for us kids. Eventually, after a struggle we were able to haul the slippery heavy dog into the wildly rocking boat and row back to shore. Alas, one afternoon, Tiger padded into my room and, as usual, put his nose on my bed for a pat. I was engrossed in a book and didn't pay him enough attention. He lay down by the bed and died quietly in his sleep. I was heartbroken, and don't think I ever forgave myself for not making more effort to be with him in his last moments.

Hugh was at secondary school in Nairobi, and Robin and I went to Nyeri Primary, closer still to Mt Kenya, which loomed above the school in fascinating, majestic, splendour. We were boarders, and travelled by train at the beginning and end of terms. It was a happy school and we excelled at sports, and enjoyed games of tennis with the teachers. A dilapidated school bus took us, all singing our lungs out, to and from weekly swimming lessons at the Outspan Hotel, and at weekends the older kids gathered under the pepper trees, where we played '45s' on a portable gramophone, enjoying the likes of Elvis, Buddy Holly, and the Everly Brothers. Late Sunday afternoons we'd usually find ourselves involved in a wild game of British Bulldogs or Buck-buck with the boys.

Our house was surrounded by sisal plantations. The large sharp pointed plants grow a dramatic central rigid pole three metres high to support their creamy flowers. Harvesting the succulent leaves was carried out in an on-going basis. Leaving the upper pointed leaves, the long lower leaves would be neatly sliced off at the base and the sisal plants would resemble huge pineapples growing in rows. The harvested leaves were fed into a decorticator and the leaves were stripped into metre-long white fibres, which were spread out on wires in the sun to dry. The fermenting waste smelt disgusting, but was used to fertilize the adjacent coffee plantation. Once dry, the long white, coarse fibres were baled and freighted, to be twisted and woven into rope, string, or sisal mats. The emergence of nylon rope was soon to seriously affect the sisal industry.

The weather was usually hot, and during the school holidays Hugh, Robin and I spent our days down at the concrete water tanks swimming with Mum. We loved collecting frogs, and back home we'd run cold water into the bath and hold frog races and Olympic frog jumping events! We also spent hours climbing in a huge sprawling fig tree, or playing energetic games of soccer, tennis, and hockey in the garden. We particularly enjoyed the free for all hockey games at Christmas, or whenever we had lots of visitors. Everyone joined in, no matter their age or ability. There were a few hockey sticks, but the rest had to play with whatever kind of stick they could find, from golf clubs, walking sticks, cricket bat, stumps, tennis racquets, to bits of four-by-two. A wonderful spontaneous game followed, with few rules, lots of cheating by the adults, and much laughter.

Dad gave us occasional target practice using a rifle or revolver, so that we'd all be able to handle a gun, should the need arise. Thankfully it never did, but we all liked shooting at bulls eyes on boxes placed at the bottom of the garden. I have to admit the boys were much better shots than me, and they sometimes went off hunting mouse birds and rabbits together. I'd hear them whistling as they returned home. Both were able to whistle a good tune and it was nice hearing them around the place. They especially liked whistling while we were out in the boat, where, I am told, the resonance was good. However, you knew what was coming if they tried to whistle the 23rd psalm together. Somehow they'd always end up giggling. For reasons best known to them-selves, it was impossible to get through this particular tune without one or other of them smiling, and any whistler knows you can't smile and whistle, and they would end up laughing instead! I don't think they ever managed to complete that tune. Maybe that was just the finale to their repertoire.

Easter was synonymous with the East African Safari Rally, and although we always each had our Fry's Cream Easter egg, our hearts were with the rally drivers as they rocketed through 3,000 miles of typical rough African terrain over the long weekend. There were the big guns from overseas, international rally drivers, like Stirling Moss, Erik Carlsson and Gunnar Palm, who came every year to compete in the world's toughest rally, but there were also the local entrants, and we followed every detail as the exhausted drivers battled their way through thick mud or dust at death defying speeds to reach check points before they were time barred. We listened with eager ears to every Safari Bulletin on the radio and filled out our Safari Score Sheets, noting the latest positions in the field, times, penalties, and mechanical problems. Mum groaned every year when the Safari 'reared its ugly head again' but she was a good sport and would pack a picnic if the rally route came through our part of Kenya. We'd pile in the car and travel miles to watch the safari cars race past. With Dad at the wheel, we'd drive on and on, until we were satisfied that we had the best, most spectacular spot to watch the rally cars. Our excitement never palled as we watched rally cars hurtle through tricky sections. The cars screamed into sharp bends, drifting out sideways, with clouds of thick red dust billowing out behind. In the wet season, with engines throbbing the drivers changed down to negotiate deep sticky muddy ravines. Hugh and Robin chattered endlessly about each car and what they'd do when they were Safari drivers. The boys dream was simply to grow up and be Safari drivers. The only goal being to finish the Safari. The actuality of winning the Safari was out of reach of locals due to competition from experienced overseas drivers and works teams, but young Kenyans were more than determined to do up their own cars and get them round the grueling route to 'finish the Safari'.

On previous farms we'd always been a good distance from the nearest sign of civilization, which was usually just a *duka,* a local shop with an assortment of necessities, from salt, sugar and paraffin, to bolts of cotton, sweets, cigarettes, bicycle tubes, plastic combs and pens. Living at Punda Milia we were fortunate to actually have a *duka* almost within shouting distance of the house. Hugh, Robin, and I happily wandered down past the Police Station to the *duka* on errands, because we liked to have a bit of cheeky fun with Babu, the shopkeeper. We'd ask him for left handed screwdrivers, bladeless knives with no handle, or topless bikinis with bottoms to match. The ever helpful Indian would mutter, "Oh yes, yes, I can find for you, just one minute please" returning a few minutes later to politely tell us "Velly velly solly, but we have not this thing at this moment." No wonder the family's annual Christmas present from the *duka* diminished each year! Our first year at Punda Milia we were given a lovely set of six cut glasses, and by the last year we were lucky to receive a small box of dated faded chocolates.

Although the Mau Mau uprising drew to a close in 1956 it wasn't officially declared over until 1960. A year later, Jomo Kenyatta, a Kikuyu freedom fighter, was released, after 7 years in prison. While confined, he had studied law, politics, agriculture, and reflected on human nature. He was known as 'Mzee' and was 70 when he emerged from imprisonment. He had good oratory skills, and a wisdom that was to prove essential in harnessing the gaping diversity of Kenya's people in the 'spirit of *harambee*' - all pulling together in the spirit of unity. Kenya's *Uhuru* - independence was due to take place in December 1963, and after 68 years of British Colonial Rule, the popular Jomo Kenyatta, ex Mau Mau terrorist, was certain to become the first President.

However, as *Uhuru,* approached, the entire country became shrouded in an atmosphere of uncertainty. People of all colours and tribes were concerned about their future. What would happen with the change of government? Would 'Africanisation' work? Could things possibly continue as before? Would there be tribal infighting depending on who was in government? Would Indian business men and Europeans be pushed out in order to provide jobs and land for Africans? Would there be anarchy? Would there be riots? Nobody had any idea what the future held, and anxiety was rife. The area we lived in was populated by the Kikuyu, the majority tribe who were responsible for the Mau Mau rebellion. Political 'hot heads' and young trouble makers, who, with their arrogant attitudes, and derogatory remarks and threats, exacerbated the situation, causing arguments, fights, and confusion. Fists held high in black power salutes became a common sight, but sometimes the faces said so much more.

Prior to Uhuru, there was a national amnesty. All Mau Mau rebels, oath administrators, activists, and the like, were to be released from detention camps,

Twenty Miles to say Goodbye

to be rehabilitated and integrated back into society. Rebels, still hiding out in the Abedare mountain ranges, were rounded up and pardoned.

One hot afternoon, wandering back from the duka, we happened upon an unforgettable and chilling sight. Only yards from us, in front of the Makuyu Police Station, three Mau Mau rebels clambered out of a police van. These men had been eking out a living in the thickets of the Abedare forests since the Mau Mau days, and were now being taken to Nairobi. The disheveled men looked terrifying, dressed in skins and covered in mud and animal grease, with long hair matted in original dreadlocks. They looked wild and mean as they glared at us, possibly the first white people they'd seen since the Mau Mau uprising ten years earlier. Perhaps this incident helped fuel my nightmares?

Although Hugh slept on his own in his little detached cottage out the back, I spent my nights indoors, in fear. With a ridiculously vivid imagination at 13, I was terrified that some gang would break in to our house during the night. I would wait until everyone had gone to bed, then creep round the house checking all the windows and doors had been closed and locked properly. If I heard noises in the night, I'd lie trembling, thinking that 'they' would be coming to get the gun. A rifle was kept locked in a safe in the floor, under my bed. I was convinced that anyone who wanted a gun would know we had one, and exactly where it was kept!

On 12th December 1963, Kenya became an Independent nation. We gathered round the radio listening, and on the stroke of midnight, Jomo Kenyatta, waving his fly whisk, was sworn in as President. The Union Gap was lowered and the Kenya flag raised. The country celebrated its freedom, '*Uhuru!*' The following day, Punda Milia Estate put on a huge all day party for the workers and their families. I accompanied Dad when he went down to the festivities to ensure that everything was going well. The brand new red, green and black flag fluttered gaily from trees and goal posts. Celebrations were in full swing and everyone was in good humour. We were the only white faces amongst the cheerful black crowds. People were shouting and applauding relay races and a fierce tug of war. A whole beef sizzled over a large fire. *Pombe*, the home brewed beer, was provided, along with bottles of Fanta orange, and boiled sweets for the children.

Across the field there were dancers, drums, horns, and whistles. Dad and I strolled over and joined the circle watching some spirited African dancing. The men looked wonderful, dancing wildly in their flowing feathered headdresses and colobus monkey skins. Bracelets, necklaces, and anklets of beads, shells, and bells, rattled and shook to the rhythm. Spears flashed in the sunlight. Everyone was caught up in the urgency of the dance. The drumming grew louder, the beat faster and faster. The dancing became wilder. Stomping, whirling, whooping and leaping, the dancers responded to the ever increasing tempo of the drums, pounding quicker and quicker into a frenzied crescendo. Suddenly it stopped. Silence. Nothing moved. As one, the music and dancers had halted. With spears raised and bodies taut, the dancers confronted us. The hushed crowd stood stock still. The dancers crouched in front of us, spears poised and pointed at us. Tension filled the air. We held our breath. For an endless terrifying moment we looked at one another. Then spontaneously everyone laughed! The drums took up again, dancing continued and Dad and I waved goodbye. As we walked away, Dad squeezed my hand and said to me "I'm very proud that you didn't flinch when they did that." I remember squeaking, "Daddy, I was too scared to do anything".

4. That's the spirit

Back at Maraba, enjoying the warm morning sun with a cup of coffee, Mum showed her concern asking how I'd found Robin.

"Did you think Robin was alright? Was he well and full of energy, or a bit wan?"

To me, he'd seemed his normal carefree, lively self, and we'd had a lovely time staying with him. But Mum explained that his bilharzia had never really left him. She filled me in on his illness, and I was shocked how little I knew and how unconcerned I had seemed as a kid. There had been a fishing picnic with some friends by a dam. Everyone knew not to paddle or swim in still water dams or slow rivers because of the danger of contracting bilharzia. It is a parasitic disease caused by infected worms that enter the blood system through cuts and scratches on the skin. Accidents happen, and I remember Robin slipping in and his gum boots filling with water.

Mum got up and brought through the notes she had written at the time.

In 1963 I went to South Africa for the first time, to see my parents, and my brother Jim and his wife Pam. They had returned from New Zealand about 1960. I had not seen them since they left Kenya towards the end of 1954. There was a special excursion on an Italian Liner. I didn't travel First Class, even Second. The special was Steerage Class. No white starched linen, crystal or silver in the dining room. We had trestle tables and benches, but free red wine was served with meals! Just as well, as I couldn't afford to buy a beer, or anything in fact. I just had enough to buy Jim and the children a small gift in South Africa. Six days fast steaming, eight days in Natal, and six back to Mombasa.

I missed school Half Term. Jim came down to meet the ship. He'd been up to Nyeri for Sports Day and the Half Term weekend, and showed me photos of Robin on the rostrum etc. I asked what was wrong. Robin looked ill with sunken eyes and his face had fallen in. Nothing, he hadn't been ill. When the children came home from school, we went to the coast for two weeks holiday. In a hotel, near Likoni Ferry, looking at the menu, Robin asked, "Can we order anything we like?" "Oh good, my favourite, and can I have that for pudding?" He tucked in, really enjoying his meal, but half way through, he turned to me with an antagonized face, "I can't eat any more". He was so disappointed, and this was the pattern for every meal. Once home, he'd be slamming the ball against his tennis wall on the front veranda, then silence. I started creeping round and peering in his window. He'd be flat out – exhausted. There were no symptoms at all. I took him down to a Mission Hospital on the Tana River, about twenty five miles from Punda Milia. There were several doctors and a pathologist, all nuns, and all tropical disease specialists. We took samples down. A few days later, Mother Superior phoned and confirmed my suspicions. Robin had bilharzia. She recommended a doctor in Nairobi. Robin went into Gertrude's Garden Children's Hospital for a week, then we were told we could take him home. When I was the paying the bill, the accountant, an older lady asked why this child had been here as there were no charges for treatment or medication. After I explained he had bilharzias, she said, "It's not my business, but if he was my child, I'd be getting a second opinion." We went to Nairobi and found the doctor, who astonished us, "Yes, your son has bilharzias. I couldn't do it. I have a son the same age and I couldn't do it to him." In those days the treatment required a horrendous daily injection into the stomach for fifty six days. I phoned Mother Superior and explained what had happened. Robin was due back at Nyeri Primary on the Sunday and Mother Superior offered to get in touch with the school doctor. So on Sunday I reported to the San Matron at school and filled her in. Twenty four hours later the Matron phoned, "I have Robin in the San for meals and to sleep, but he's attending regular classes". The doctor had taken more samples and arranged for Robin to see another doctor and be hospitalized for treatment at Princess Elizabeth Hospital in Nairobi. On meeting the new doctor, he said, "Good news. We've just received the new Ciba Treatment for bilharzias in pill form. No more terrible tummy inoculations necessary." After his treatment Robin came home for six weeks recuperation. He did lessons in the morning, and after his rest we played scrabble every afternoon. He had to go for check-ups every three months, which he did for nearly four years. At sixteen, the night before returning to school, he insisted, "Don't book an appointment for me to see Dr Marshall, because I won't go. You will be wasting Dad's money. I'm better." A year later he was back in hospital having a repeat treatment.

"Now you are a mother, you will understand the ongoing concerns for your child. It doesn't matter how old your children are, you are always uneasy when things go wrong, if there is an accident or illness. How awful I've always felt about Hugh's nasty accident as a little boy. Even now, when I see the scar on his face, I feel a chill, and blame myself for not doing more to prevent it."

"You mean when he fell down the well? I don't remember that at all. I was probably too young."

"Yes you were quite small then. Dad had taken us down to the coast for a holiday and we were staying at Kikambala, in a thatched cottage nestled under coconut palms. Labourers were digging a well, which was covered and lit up by a couple of hurricane lamps at night. Dad had gone fishing before dawn, and I was strolling along the path to breakfast with you two children. The lanterns were no longer alight, and Hugh ran ahead, stepping onto the boarding that covered the hole. I watched in horror as it instantly gave way and Hugh fell twenty feet down into the well. Seeing this, a staff member from the Jeluo tribe, rushed into a cottage, tore sheets off a bed and tied them together. Other staff members hurried over to help lower him down into the well to rescue Hugh. With everyone hauling on the sheets, he brought Hugh up out of the well in his arms. Young Hugh was badly bleeding from coral cuts and there were deep cuts on his face from the asbestos covering. Amazingly there was a doctor staying at the hotel, who attended to Hugh and drove him to Mombasa Hospital. Hugh was kept in hospital for the rest of the holiday as there were concerns that he would get septicemia from the coral cuts, but thankfully he healed well. How often the quick actions and kindness of others, usually strangers, make all the difference to our lives."

Mum topped up her coffee, shook a cigarette from its orange 'Crown Bird' package, tapped it, lit it, and leant back to inhale before continuing.

"After that holiday we moved back to the Nandi Hills, where Dad managed Kibabet Estate, growing maize, cattle, and planting tea at an altitude of 6,000 feet above sea level. We lived in a shed with our belongings stored under a tarpaulin sheet while the house was built. It was wonderful moving into our brand new stone house, and much appreciated after the months of spartan living in the shed with a family. The shed had a dirt floor, and when it was dry and dusty we had awful problems with fleas, and when it rained, puddles formed in our lounge, and it was a constant battle keeping everything dry. However, Hugh thoroughly enjoyed the chance to play with his boats without having to go outside!

Our third baby was expected soon, but the rains came earlier. It rained incessantly for weeks. Loud grumbling thunder rumbled and echoed through the limestone hills, and often two inches fell in a night. The roads were now quagmires and I fretted that I wouldn't be able to get off the farm and into Eldoret Hospital to have the baby, so Dad arranged for a tractor and driver to be on standby should we need assistance getting over the seven miles of farm track to the main *murram* road. There were no phones on the farm, nor on neighbouring estates, and the journey to Eldoret took over an hour. Finally a week before the baby's due date, Doctor Ashton ordered me into hospital.

Dad and Hugh came in to visit me at the end of the week, battling their way through the mud, across the Uasin Gishu Plateau to Eldoret, but there was still no baby. They returned to the farm for a few more anxious days, before setting off again on the afternoon of 2nd July. Halfway through the journey, Dad noticed a gang of Post & Telegraph African workers, and one of the men was working up the top of a telegraph pole. Getting out of the car, Dad explained that his wife was expecting their baby and asked the workers if there was any chance they could to get through to Eldoret Hospital to see if there was any news. The man up the pole was able to tap in to the Chief P&T Engineer in Eldoret, who in turn phoned the hospital. Minutes later a broadly grinning face looked down, calling out the message. "Fine son, born five minutes ago!" Smiles and much back patting and joyous shouts of *"dumi* - a boy!" Having handed out *baksheesh* - tips all round, Dad and Hugh roared on into Eldoret to welcome Robin John into the world.

While I was in hospital, you Heather, had been staying with friends. Lively and petite, with a head of beautiful soft blonde curls, you returned home to hear the good news. Dad again made the long trip in to Eldoret, this time bringing both you children to see me and the new baby. In those days children were not allowed inside the hospital buildings, so you waited outside the ward window until Dad went round to lift you up. When Hugh's little ginger head appeared at the window, he was grinning from ear to ear as I held the baby up for him to see. Then I gasped in horror as a scraggly urchin child's tufted head appeared. What on earth had happened to my pretty little daughter?

Apparently Hugh was so thrilled with his new brother, that he decided to make his little sister into a brother – by cutting off her hair!"

Suddenly animated, I exclaimed, "I remember that Mum! I think it's my earliest memory. I was sitting on a pouffé by a window, playing hair dressers with Hugh. I didn't know he wanted to turn me into a boy though!"

***

In the cool of the evening, we walked beside the coffee bushes, accompanied by Macora, who scampered about in zigzags. We returned home at sunset to bath Sirri and enjoy sundowners. As we sipped our drinks, Dad played with his little granddaughter on his lap, and we talked about Mum and Dad's war time experiences, and how they came to be in Kenya. Once again, now that I was an adult, I loved all the details that had not concerned me as a child.

Dad had grown up in the Scottish town of Kilmarnock, where he was born in 1906. His father, John William Anderson worked as an engineer at Young's Paraffin Works in Kilmarnock, where they extracted paraffin from shale. However, after many years of service, John either walked out suddenly, or was fired, over a dispute that erupted when he tried to introduce a by-product. Apparently Young's Paraffin Works did finally introduce this particular by-product some 40 years later! Meanwhile John Anderson went to work for an elder brother at his family mill in Stewarton. The business was struggling with the brother refusing to move with the times, and they eventually went bust.

None of us kids ever met this Grandfather. He was reputed to be rather domineering with a Calvinistic attitude, keeping his family under strict control. He and his wife, Margaret had four children. Three girls, Anne, Wynne, and Pix, and the youngest, a boy, was James Matthew, Dad. Margaret (nee Muir), was well liked, and remembered as a kind loving soul by her children. She was musical, and played the violin in The Walker Family Orchestra. The Walkers, of Johnny Walker

Whisky fame, were good friends of the Muirs, and apparently when Margaret was in her late teens, a nasty abscess appeared on her nose. Panicking, she sent a note to Mr Walker telling him that she would be unable to attend the concert the following evening. Mr Walker responded by sending her a phial of 100% proof whisky with a note telling her she'd cure her infection by dabbing it often with the whisky, and that she'd be playing at the concert the next day. She was! All four children had to learn to play a musical instrument and in time Anne became a proficient pianist. However Dad told us he hated the tedious enforced practices so much that he vowed he would never impose music lessons on any children he might have. He kept this promise, but, nevertheless, expected us to put total effort into whatever we did, and always do our best.

Dad's mother, Margaret, died in 1925, after a long and horrible struggle with cancer. Prior to the family's move to Stewarton, Dad had attended Stuarts College in Edinburgh until he was thirteen. This prestigious school would not let him sit the Matric Examination as his marks weren't good enough, so he sat them privately and was rewarded with a 1st Class Pass. He briefly attended Kilmarnock Academy, but with his father's business demise, the family fell on hard times and he was sent to the local public school. With the exception of Dad's father, all the Anderson males had been doctors, and it was Dad's dream to follow in their footsteps. However, unable to pursue a medical career due to lack of funds, he went to Agricultural College in Glasgow where he studied for two years for a National Diploma, receiving three honours certificates in Agriculture, Survey, and Hydraulic Engineering. While he was completing the course, his father arranged for him to be sent out to East Africa to work as a pupil on an associate's farm. Dad had no say in the matter.

Dad took up his story, "After the Great War, a Soldier Settlement Scheme had been developed in the colony of Kenya. A thousand acres of virgin land, next to Lord Kitchener's, was allotted to George Martin. George had been injured while fighting for the Royal Artillery in France during the 1st World War, and was unable to continue his military career. His new estate, 'Kwisos', was on the Kavirondo Plains, close to the equator and Lake Victoria. At this time, land owners were paid large amounts of money, between £300 and £400 a year, for 'tuition' of a student. Fathers in the UK paid these vast sums so their sons could gain agricultural experience in the colonies. My father, John Anderson, had arranged for me become one of George's students. George had also agreed to take on two other pupils, a cousin of mine, Tom, and another lad, Ian Barbour, who's parents had answered an advertisement in the paper. George was also engaged to marry my sister, Pix, and had obviously got off to a good start with his eminent father in-law. In those days long engagements were the norm, and Pix and George were to be engaged for five years before George returned to Scotland for the wedding, and to take his bride back to his farm in Kenya.

I remember the cold, drizzly, February morning when we gathered at the Glasgow dockyards. It was 1927, and I was excited about going to Africa, as were Tom and Ian. We thoroughly enjoyed our voyage and the days of freedom, unaware of the difficult years ahead.

From the port of Mombasa, we crossed Kenya by rail, arriving at 'Kwisos Estate' in the Songhor Valley in the early hours of the morning. The farm was situated in a hot, dry, rocky area, and there was an abundance of snakes, mosquitoes, and leopards. Kwisos produced a small amount of coffee, maize, sugar and milk. We students worked long hours through the heat of the day, six days a week, and were constantly hungry. We lived in a grass hut out the back of the main house, and had to wait to be called in for the evening meal. Often this was not until 10 o'clock at night. Completely exhausted, all we wanted to do was to have a bite to eat and get some sleep".

Mum interrupted, "Dad seldom mentions this period of his life, but Ian Barbour, who became a close family friend, told me bits and pieces over the years. Ian still hated bananas, because they had eaten so many as students. They bought bunches of bananas to stave off their hunger and keep them going through the day until their evening meal was served. Poor Tom was sent home in disgrace after six months, because of rumours connecting him to a native girl. Ian maintained that they were too tired to do anything, and Tom probably only winked at her anyway. At any rate, neither of the lads knew anything about this, but Tom was expelled never the less, and George never mentioned his name again."

Dad cleared his throat and continued, "On completion of my two years, I was offered a position managing a nearby maize farm in Chemelil, which I accepted without hesitation!"

"Wasn't that about the time you scraped the fare together to go back to Scotland to ask Isobel to marry you?" asked Mum.

"Well yes. She was a friend from teenage years. But it was not to be. I arrived in Scotland too late, to find that Isobel had just become engaged to my old pal, Norman."

"Oh Dad, that's so sad! What did you do then?"

Mum chipped in, "Dejected and penniless, Dad managed to get to Paris, where his sister Anne was living with her accountant husband Wilf Turner. Anne was very chic, lively, and a talented and sought after pianist. She was horrified to see her little brother on her doorstep looking like a scarecrow in farming clothes! Anne was furious with her sister Pix and George for not looking after their brother better and resolved to make sure he enjoyed the rest of his leave. Dressing Dad in Wilf's clothes, they took him off to Parisian night clubs, cafés and restaurants."

"I even played rugby for an English team in Paris! So you see, it wasn't so bad. I had a good holiday in *La belle France*. I returned to my new job in Kenya, and joined up with the Kenya Defence Corp, the Territorial Army, and for two weeks every year I went off on camp with them. These annual training camps were very enjoyable and were the closest I got to a real holiday for several years.

Late in 1929, my father, John Anderson sold his house and furniture in Scotland and joined me in the Songhor Valley, not far from Pix and George. Father and I bought our own farm, 'Balcorrough', growing maize and planting sugar. In retrospect, this was not the best time to venture out into a new business, let alone invest in land. 1930 was of course the start of the 'Great World Depression', which caused drastic falls in commodity prices and led to poverty and distress as it impacted on the industrialised western world and those dependent on it. Maize prices slumped, and in 1931 locust swarms destroyed the crops en masse. The swarms returned to wipe-out everything again the following year. The locust swarms were so huge that they completely blocked out the sun, and could be seen in the distance like massive rain clouds forming. As they neared, the temperature would drop as if it was about to rain. Only this was more devastating than any storm, for if locusts descended on your farm, they would alight in their thousands on the lush green crops and proceed to munch noisily until they had devoured every inch of foliage. An hour or two later a healthy crop had become a field of shredded, khaki desolation. Another time, I had a run in on my motor bike with hoppers, the precursors to locusts. They were piled up on each other crawling in their thousands across the road. Riding down the dirt track, I had noted the different colours on the road, suggesting a change in soil type. Suddenly the bike hit the hoppers, throwing me one way and the bike the other. It was like hitting a foot high log across the road.

Soon after that, a leopard crept up to our verandah and attacked my dog. The struggles on the farm continued. Banji, who owned the local Indian duka store, allowed us to live on credit until he bought the farm from us himself - at a very low price in 1938. Debts were paid off and any balance went to my father, who then moved in with George and Pix at Kwisos, where he stayed until 1944. Father utilized his time working with wood, becoming a skillful carpenter, creating attractive carved cabinets and coffee tables.

It was not until the 1960s that sugar became a thriving industry in this area, and the huge sugar mill now stands only 2 miles from our old house at Balcorrough where we had unsuccessfully planted sugar so many years before.

No doubt you have read many accounts about the construction of the railway, 'The Iron Snake'. Beginning in Mombasa, at sea level, the lines stretched 500 miles across the plains and through the highlands of Kenya, into Uganda. In the early days, you could flag a train down, in the middle of nowhere, between stations. Farmers would board the train at one end of their farm, returning by another train that evening or the next day, promising to pay their fares later. I believe the money was usually forthcoming as such was the system of trust that operated in those days. A little give and take goes a long way, as the young Nandi warriors discovered, and much of the Nandi tribes' jewelry to this day was created from lead from the railway tracks and copper taken from the early telephone wires.

I had been a keen rugby player in my school days and played for the Kilmarnock Academics First XV. We had a Scottish International playing with us then! However, as young men farming in western Kenya, rugby was our only sport and social activity.

If we combined all the available players in the Songhor Valley through to Kericho and Kisumu, we could almost rustle up a complete rugby team. Games were played on a Saturday afternoon up in Nandi Hills. The odd vehicles, of the Model T Ford type, would set off around the farms in the area on Saturday morning in an attempt to round up as many players as possible. Lads were hijacked from their work. Sometimes everyone would lend a hand to get a job finished first, before heading for the next estate. Finally, with the cars jammed with players, we would head off up the Nandi Escarpment. There was much camaraderie and high spirited enjoyment and this scene was replayed in reverse on Saturday night or Sunday morning getting everyone back to work, often after a few too many drinks! There was a period when the owner of one of the Model Ts had problems with the rack and pinion steering. Hastily repairing the steering on Friday night, he had put it together incorrectly. The result being that to turn right, the driver had to turn the steering wheel left! You can imagine how difficult it would be to handle this monstrous vehicle on normal roads, but we had to drive up the Nandi Escarpment, a rise of over 3,000 feet. The stony dirt roads had sheer vertical drops, and numerous snaky twists and turns, hairpin bends and the infamous Twin Bridges at right angles to each other. So much fun was had with this vehicle over that first weekend that the steering was left as it was for several more weeks!

Playing rugby at an altitude of 7,000 feet presented a few oxygen problems, and when the home team were in need of a breather, we would kick a long ball into touch, and with a bit of skill, the ball would land in the adjoining stream or swamp. Of course the time you had to get your breath back would largely depend on who was retrieving the ball!

Occasionally there was a rugby tournament over in Eldoret, which necessitated an over-night stay. One particularly amusing Saturday night it was just like the Wild West – more like El Dorado than Eldoret! The three hotels down the one street were lively and bursting at the seams with rowdy men in town for the Saturday night. A herd of cows had escaped from their stockade, and stampeded down the main street, drawing dozens of drunken revelers out onto the road to show off their cattle droving skills. The result was mayhem. Whistles, 'yee-ha's', and incoherent commands from legless 'cowboys' up and down the street only served to confuse the stricken animals further. Cows ran amok in every direction, while hopelessly drunken men staggered about trying to round them up. Raucous laughter ricocheted about as the rest of us, jeered and shouted, from windows and porches, calling out wise-cracks or silly suggestions!"

As we all laughed, Mum got up, put her knitting away, and smiling at the baby, said "I'll just go check supper is OK. You carry on. Tell them what you did in the war."

Dad continued, "Well, my next job was in the Nandi Hills working as Assistant Manager to East African Coffee Plantations. Letters reached me there addressed simply to 'Jim, Nandi'! But things were hotting up in Europe and Britain declared war on Germany. I left my job the day war broke out, joining the Kenya Defence Corp. Initially I drove supplies up through the Northern Frontier District to Abyssinia to the forces fighting the Italians in the Ethiopia – Somali Land Campaign. I was commissioned into the Royal Army Service Corp and in 1941 was promoted to Captain. Because I spoke a few native languages and generally got on with the Africans, I volunteered to train African troops for the Pioneer Corp. In 1942 I was assigned to take the African Labour Battalion to the Middle East. We had to get supplies through to the troops in the 8th Army fighting at El Alamein. Much later we were prevented from continuing on into Italy because black troops from East Africa were restricted from leaving African soil."

Giving me a grin, because he knew we'd loved this story as kids, Dad added, "There was a humorous incident when I was travelling by train with my troops through Egypt. Some dignitary or other was also on board in the first class carriage. As the train pulled into a station, the troops noticed a red carpet had been laid out, and a welcoming committee of soldiers stood to attention on either side of the carpet. However, the train failed to stop at the correct place to enable the dignitary to step from his carriage onto the red carpet. The welcoming committee hurriedly gathered up the long red carpet, and rushed to place it outside where the VIP's carriage had pulled up, quickly lining up and standing to attention alongside. Alas the engine driver shunted the train back again, necessitating the poor soldiers pick up the carpet, and scramble to a new position. My troops were leaning out the train windows and doors, enthusiastically commentating on this fiasco. Now they doubled over with laughter as the train shunted backwards and forwards, perpetuating the farce and humiliating the confused soldiers. The VIP finally stepped out of his carriage onto the carpet, taking it all very seriously and never even smiled – pompous ass!

Towards the end of 1944, I was in Beirut on leave from Alexandra. Neutral Beirut was a carefree lively hub where troops from all over the Middle East converged to enjoy a bit of well-earned R&R away from the fighting. There were cafes, restaurants, hotels with swimming and tennis, and night clubs with bands and dancing."

With a wink, Dad looked up at Mum, who had just returned. "Tell them what happened next Peg".

"Ah" Mum said, "I had come down with sandfly fever and pneumonia, and was sent up to the mountains of Lebanon to recuperate. A WREN friend invited me to join some others sailing, and it was here I met your Dad. He was my friend's date! Shortly after this, I was transferred to Alexandra. Dad got in touch with me, and took me out whenever we could both get away. Then on the 24th February 1945, my last day in Egypt, Dad proposed to me. In July, he took special leave to return to England to marry me. In order to take this time off from the army, he had had to agree to work an extra year after discharge date, once the war was over, as well as forfeiting the pip to his crown, which would have been his next promotion to Lieutenant Colonel. The wedding was at St Peters, Lowestoft, in Suffolk, and my parents Arthur and Sue, my brother Teddy, and Dad's sister Anne, were present. Our little wedding party had lunch at a hotel in Lowestoff, before returning to Arthur and Sue's guest house on the sea front. We newlyweds rushed off to catch the only train back to London, and our connections to Edinburgh. We spent a few lovely weeks together in Scotland before Dad had to report back for duty in Egypt. But while we were enjoying the serenity of the Scottish lochs and glens, we heard the chilling news that the Americans had dropped atomic bombs on two Japanese cities. We heard nothing else as we travelled through the remote highlands, until we drove into a small town with an extraordinarily happy atmosphere. Everyone was out in the street celebrating, and we were quickly enlightened – "The war's o'er! Awa an hav a wee dram!"

Dad was then stationed in Kantara on the Suez Canal, about 30 miles from Port Said. In May 1946, I was summoned to an interview in London with army personnel. Officers in London were trying to find employment for the troops returning home. When they realised that my husband was due to return to his job in East Africa, I was given a priority passage to Kenya. I was told that I would probably be leaving in a month. It was three weeks! Luckily, my brother Jim arrived home unexpectedly, on leave from his duties in Germany and Holland, and we spent a few days together before I left for Africa. A couple of Wren friends came to see me off as my father and I, boarded the London train south. As the train drew into Southampton Station, I hung out the window waving to my good friends Pat and Reg, and to my surprise, waiting with them was a handsome naval friend of mine from early '41 days. We all had a wonderful evening at Pat and Reg's home. The next morning was an emotional one as I said goodbye to my father, and he bravely fought back tears as he hugged me and stood waving as my ship, The Arundel Castle, slipped out to sea. Thankfully Pat and Reg looked after Dad and took him back to the station for his lonely return journey to Suffolk.

Meanwhile, in Suez, troopers were being scheduled to sail down the East African coast. Dad was to take his battalion of 600 men and officers home to East Africa at the end of the month. I had wired him that I would be passing through the Suez on my way south to Kenya, on the HMS Arundel Castle. Dad managed to swap duties with another Major, who didn't want to leave Egypt quite so soon, and he was able to board the Arundel Castle just before the Red Sea and join me on the voyage to Kenya."

5. London to Kenya, via Egypt

While we were talking, our little baby had fallen asleep on Grandpa's lap. I took her off to our guest hut, changed her and tucked her in, staying with her a while she settled into a deep sleep. Returning to the house, and preparing the trolley for supper, I overheard snatches of conversation as Mum and Lee discussed the Jews, Israel, and Palestine.

Lee's voice was a little agitated, "I just don't get it. How can a nation of people who have gone through the horrors of genocide, who have been subjected to so much, turn around and subject another nation to similar cruelties. Look at the way Israel treats the Palestinians, you'd think they'd have more compassion. I just can't understand it …"

Moths, attracted by the light, fluttered against the wire netting. I turned my attention to our evening meal. We usually ate a light supper in the evenings, having had our main meal at lunch as everything revolved around the workings of the farm. Mango started work about eight in the morning, finishing in the afternoon, and he would now be with his family, in their hut up the hill.

Becoming more aware of the conversation in the lounge, I quickly took our meal out of the oven and warmed the plates. Voices were raised now, and things were getting pretty heated. I suppose I had expected this. It was inevitable that Mum and Lee would clash from time to time as they were both strong minded individuals with their own deep set opinions. My heart beat faster. I felt nervous and I was anxious that the argument wouldn't escalate into something bigger. I knew what Lee was like. I knew what Mum was like.

Hurrying towards the lounge, I heard Dad intervene calmly, "It is never easy being a free thinker Lee, and you have some very valid points. However, every generation wants to be, and mercifully is, different to the previous one, and diverse life experiences lead to a vast range of ideas." He paused then added, "I have told you how I came to be in Kenya, now let Peg tell you her story."

"Oh Lee doesn't want to hear about all that!"

"Yes I do" replied Lee. "I know you're from London, and I'd really like to hear what you did during the war. But where's Andi? She's been a while."

I appeared on cue, pushing in the supper trolley. The talk became general as we helped ourselves to macaroni cheese and settled down to eat. Then Dad encouraged Mum to tell us about her war years. How strange I knew so little about her. She had always been there, always good to us kids, and although she was very strict about manners and standards, she allowed us a lot of freedom, prudently guiding us from a distance. But sad to say, as a teenager, I was more concerned with myself, showing little curiosity in the person who was my mother. Upon reflection, both Mum and Dad were special parents, allowing us to explore and make our own decisions, expecting little in return; only the knowledge that we did what we did with integrity and behaved like decent human beings. As we grew older, we seldom felt obligated, and whether we wrote, visited, or helped our parents in any small way, we did it simply because we wanted to, rather than feeling we ought to. In fact as children, Mum had always praised us highly if we did things before anyone had to ask or tell us. She'd say, "Well done! You did that off your own bat - you didn't wait to be told." In retrospect it was a clever way to bring us up, and encouraged us to think for ourselves, be responsible, and use our own initiative. I'd do well to remember that when we're bringing up our own children.

Initially hesitant, but soon warming to her story, Mum began, "Life in London as a girl had been good. I was fortunate to have had a happy childhood with loving, interesting parents. When I was young, my father, Arthur Chapman, fitted a little seat onto his bicycle and took me for long rides through the woods and country lanes. Later he bought a Dunnolt motor bike with a side-car, and with my mother and brother Jim in the side-car, and me up behind Dad, we'd roared off for the day. We often met up with Uncle Harry, Aunty Ethel and Dorothy. Years later Arthur and Sue bought a motor car and we ventured further afield at weekends. One unforgettable day we had breakfast in Stonehenge. With the world to ourselves, we fried sausages over a campfire in the silent circle of the great ancient stones. Another special memory was early in October 1930, when Arthur hired a rowing boat to take us children out on the upper reaches of the Thames. The massive 777 foot zeppelin R101 floated above us, thrilling us to the core. It was the largest airship in the world and a truly awesome sight. Only two or three days later the nation was stunned when R101 crashed in France on its maiden overseas voyage.

After leaving school, I worked in the Research Laboratories of General Electric Company, initially as the office junior, and later as a librarian. General Electric supplied books and equipment to the BBC. While working there, I was able to watch the original television in 1936. Along with five other companies, GEC was short-listed to produce the first television. Presentations were shown in the oak shelved library, and each day a procession of technicians and dignitaries from the BBC and associated companies came to view the television. Many photographs were taken of people gathered round to watch the first television, but for advertising purposes, everyone was cut out and only one pretty girl at the front was left! Unfortunately GEC missed out and Baird won the contract. Later, in 1941, after I had left the company, another young librarian wrote telling me about the same room being crowded with men watching the GEC's first showing of colour TV. She had been called in for this momentous event, and afterwards the boss exclaimed, "Well we've cracked it! We've produced colour TV. Now we put it on the shelf until the war is over". World War II necessitated General Electric putting their TV research on hold and concentrating on electrical requirements for war. Television was being worked on simultaneously in America where they were able to continue their developments unimpeded, and eventually television became a household item.

During the winter, Arthur took me with him to visit an out of town hospital. I was staggered by the vast amount of patients in beds crammed together out on the verandas. Arthur explained that these patients had tuberculosis, which was then very common due to the dense fog in the atmosphere, caused by the vast amounts of coal being burned in factories and homes everywhere. It was thought the best cure for tuberculosis was for people to have plenty of fresh air, hence the masses sleeping outside in the cold."

I interrupted, "Weren't we given tuberculosis injections at Nyeri Primary?"

"Yes you are right. The children at your school were amongst the first 'guinea pigs' for the new anti-TB inoculation. At the time, I thought it was quite ironic that 25 years after seeing all those tuberculosis patients out on the veranda in England, my own children in Africa had a part in helping to research a better cure."

"I only remembered they were tuberculosis injections because I had such a bad reaction and needed daily dressings on my arm for weeks after. Anyway carry on Mum. How old were you when the war began?"

"I was 19 when World War Two was declared on 3rd September 1939. It was a Sunday and Arthur called us all inside just before 11am to listen to the radio broadcast by the Prime Minister, informing the nation that we were at war. Less than an hour after the broadcast, the first air raid sirens wailed out ominously over London, filling the hearts of the people with fear and dread. Back at work on Monday, I was sent to the Patent Office, the Science Museum Library, and Her Majesty's Publications, because the young messengers who normally did these delivery jobs had already gone to war – they were all territorials. That same day the children of London were evacuated and sent to stay in villages and farms in the country. When I got back to Marylebone Station, thousands of children were on the platforms and in waiting trains. They clutched their wee bundles in brown paper bags or tiny cardboard cases. Gas masks were slung across their shoulders with string. The forlorn wee boys were trying to look so brave, in their long shorts and tackity boots. A heart breaking sight, never forgotten, even by the good time girl I was back then.

Arthur, Sue and the two boys lived in a little summer bungalow called 'Destiny' in Shepperton on the banks of the River Thames. The house was on stilts and the floor was about 20 feet above water level. That winter, just after Christmas, a section of the River Thames froze over, and I remember actually walking across the River Thames to Weybridge with Sue to go shopping. It transpired that the general public had no knowledge of the river freezing over because the Government had put a 'D Notice' on it. They had kept this hushed up to prevent the Nazi's learning the river was frozen, because if bombs were dropped on London, Greater London would have had no water to fight the fires. As it was, the Luftwaffe tended to drop their bombs on London when the river was at low tide for this very reason. The icebreaker was working up and down the river leaving the surface lumpy and uneven, extinguishing any thoughts of skating. Thaw and torrential rains followed in January and the water rose to within six inches of Destiny's floorboards. I was renting a bedsit closer to work and only went home at weekends. Arthur and Jim used to punt over the neighbours flooded gardens, happily adding to their personal tally of decapitated submerged garden gnomes! They stocked up on supplies, met me at the end of the lane and ferried me back to Destiny. We'd enter the house by climbing through the bathroom window from the punt! After a couple of days of freezing cold and listening to the eerie sound of water lapping just below the floor, I was glad to be ferried out again. However Sue wasn't so lucky. She was scared of climbing out the window into a dubious rocking punt and was consequently marooned in her house for another three weeks.

Most of the other bungalows were empty. In normal times they were summer holiday homes along the banks of the Thames. However, by the end of 1940 all these bungalows were occupied as the German blitz took its toll on London buildings.

In the spring of 1940 the Chapman family moved to up to Bend Cottage on Riverside Road. This was still in Shepperton and also faced the Thames. Arthur was working at Middlesex Hospital and Sue ran a Bed & Breakfast at Bend Cottage. One Sunday, sitting in the garden enjoying a cup of tea with my cousin and Aunt, we noticed a group of people strolling past. Then we heard them say, "That looks a nice place" and they all turned back for afternoon teas. Soon my cousin and I were waitresses! The table in the garden was taken, as well as those inside! Bend Cottage Bed & Breakfast now became Bend Cottage Tea Rooms. After that, whenever business was slow, to entice patrons, all available bods sat outside to give the impression the café was busy. A little later, as the bombing of London became more devastating, the bedrooms were all taken by men working in London, who had sent their wives and children to the country for safety.

In May 1940 I was rushed to hospital for an appendicitis operation. After an appendectomy, patients were expected to convalesce for six weeks. However, my stitches were removed and I was sent home within three days. Expecting bombs to be dropped on London at any time, hospitals were at the ready. Prepared for a mass influx, they were keeping every available bed-space free. Meanwhile I was restless and rang my employers to ask if I could go back to work. They wouldn't hear of it and kindly insisted on paying me in full for the entire six weeks. At this point I realised it was probably a good time for a change and rang General Electric back to explain and hand in my notice.

I moved to Bath to live with my friends Pat and Reg, and was out looking for a job. I was actually in an interview and being offered the job, when I found myself thanking the interviewer and telling him I wouldn't take the position. Back at the labour exchange, while waiting in the queue, I noticed a poster for the W.R.N.S. (Women's Royal Naval Service), and on reaching the counter I again surprised myself by telling the clerk I would like to join the W.R.N.S. He directed me to the Headquarters in Bristol, and told me that if I hurried I would catch the correct bus up at the corner in 5 minutes! Within a couple of hours, I had been interviewed by the Chief CO, and undergone a medical examination. Two days later I received a telegram from the Navy, "REPORT HMS CABOT, BRISTOL...."

The following morning I received a second telegram, this time from my father, "STOP NONSENSE. UNDER AGE. REPORT HOME IMMEDIATELY. REPEAT UNDER AGE."

Fate was to ensure that all Arthur and Sue's children went to the forces at the earliest possible age, just as Arthur himself had done in the Great War. In view of his own horrific experiences, it is little wonder he tried to steer his children away from the forces. However, I was now too caught up in the promise of new opportunities to listen to my father. I became a 'Wren', and settled happily into naval life, duly receiving my stripes on completion of my first year. I started in the Navy in Bristol on the same day as Felicity and we became firm friends, spending a lot of time together until Felicity was commissioned and posted to Gibraltar. Bristol was subjected to enemy invasions and bombing. When the air raid warning sounded over the city, everyone had to rush underground and sleep in huge cold cavernous tunnels, which smelt musty, and were always dirty and crowded. All the Wrens were rostered on fire watch duty, and most hated these all night shifts, sitting on duty, alone and cold through the long dark hours, but Felicity and I often swapped with the others, preferring this shift to enforced nights in 'the tunnel'. After air raids, I would listen anxiously to the morning radio bulletins to reassure myself that my family and friends were safe, and that the areas they lived in hadn't been bombed. I was transferred to Brightening Sea for the next two years, and received my Anchor Stripe as Leading WRNS, denoting my 3 years' service.

Before the war, I used to ride pillion on a boyfriend's motor bike, which was fairly unusual in those times. However my next boyfriend, Frank, actually had a plane! Frank and Gerald's father had been a pilot in the 1st World War, and he and his sons had saved hard to buy their own plane, a canvas, two-seater German Clem. The body of the plane was housed in a long dog kennel like hangar, and both wings were removed and stored alongside. It always took a minimum of three people to get the plane out or put it away. After hauling the body from the hangar, I would help carry the wings out with one of the boys. We'd hold each wing steady against the body, while the third person dropped a bolt in to secure the wings to the plane. The pilot could never bank too severely for fear the bolt would slip out. I often used to go up with Frank, flying 'on a wing and a prayer' in this fragile plane.

One afternoon in 1939, Frank received a telegram from his father, requesting him to meet urgently at Stanstead Station. We set out quickly, arriving late that night at the deserted station. A dim blue light revealed a lone man in military uniform, rhythmically slapping his leather gloves against his thighs. It was Frank's father. Now 56, and aware the Air Force age limit was 47, he had pretended he was 46 and signed up to fly planes. Probably wise to this, the Air Force had accepted him as they were desperate for experienced pilots, and assigned him to train young military pilots in Canada. He was leaving first thing next morning and wanted to see his son before he left.

Before this, Frank's brother, Gerald, had gone to Italy where he had a job installing auto-pilot mechanisms into fighter planes. As the pressure for war increased, and Italy allied itself with Germany, Frank's family became embarrassed about his job, as it appeared he was working for the enemy.

Much later, possibly four years after Frank and I had gone our separate ways, we bumped into each other in the street. Frank explained that Gerald had been missing for three years. The family had searched everywhere, contacting camps and Red Cross units all over Europe to check 'missing in action' and 'wounded' lists, but there was no trace of him. Eventually the family heard from Gerald. He and a friend quit their jobs when the war commenced and escaped to the Alps, where they were aided by partisans. The young men hid out in the mountains carrying messages, assisting in escapes, and helping in the partisans fight. Finally an opportunity presented itself to them and they managed to leave Italy on a ship bound for India. They eventually turned up in Australia, and immediately joined the Australian Air Force as pilots.

My brother Jim was conscripted at 18. His best friends, two brothers, came from Yorkshire. This Yorkshire family had moved down to London specifically because they didn't want their boys to have to spend their lives down the coal mines, as had all previous generations. Fate, or Bevan, had other plans. Bevan, a politician, insisted that two thirds of all the young men conscripted were to go and work in the mines as fuel was needed for the war effort. Jim and the two brothers were called up at the same time and after health checks and interviews, were lined up at random. A military personnel simply went along the line, pointing at each man in turn, handing out his fate; "mine, mine, regiment, mine, mine, regiment, mine, mine ...." In a few seconds flat the unfortunate young Yorkshire men, who had stood on either side of Jim, were consigned to the mines as 'Bevan's Boys'. After all the effort their parents had made so their sons wouldn't have to work in the mines, the boys were now being sent off 'down pit'. Jim was incredibly lucky and was allocated to the Royal Engineers, immediately put through rigorous training, and commenced his war service in Holland. Here, and in Belgium, and

Germany, the Royal Engineers repaired the war ravaged railway systems and got trains running again for the movement of troops and supplies. Jim, to his delight, saw his boyhood dream come true and was occasionally able to drive the steam engines! Lee chuckled suddenly, "Steam engines, driving racing cars, being a fireman, a pilot, or a soldier – even chasing rhinos! It's funny really how all the boyhood dreams are much the same all over the world, no matter what generation."

"Then when they grow up they find themselves doing something completely different ...." mused Dad. "But then the war changed a lot of things for everyone."

Mum agreed, "Yes, such was the urgency of war. I was transferred to the Middle East in December 1943. Those of us in the W.R.N.S. were commonly known as *'Wrens',* and there were sixty of us on the ship. I was the only 'striped' Wren as most of the others had not even completed a year's service before being sent off to serve overseas. A large contingent of army and navy personnel were dispatched to build up the forces in The Middle East. I was amongst this re-enforcement and was consigned to the Stratheden Castle, as were six thousand men from a Cameronian Battalion, and a New Zealand Regiment. There were also seventy army doctors, seventy nurses, and eleven army girls on board. The Stratheden Castle was part of a large fleet, of seven or eight destroyers and ten ocean going liners, sailing from the Clyde Dockyard. The fleet was held up in the Clyde by fog for three days before it was able to slip out into the Irish Sea. In order to avoid detection by enemy U-Boats, all ships were forbidden to travel at more than 26 knots, and the fleet followed a roundabout course. It sailed north of Ireland, well out into the Atlantic Ocean, round the Azores, and finally through the Straits of Gibraltar into the Mediterranean Sea three weeks later. For security reasons those on board never knew the ship's position at any time, and only once, on Christmas Day, did the captain give any clue as to our whereabouts. He announced that the Holy Land, although far off, was straight ahead, and Malta was 1,000 miles to the left.

This being a military assignment, strict rules were adhered to at all times. Each military group kept to its allocated deck, and if an alarm sounded the starboard side was to be cleared immediately for the ship's crew. Compulsory exercising for everyone was held daily on 'A Deck'. The Cameronian Battalion's full pipe band played lively tunes while all the men and women enjoyed Scottish dancing! Our women's uniform consisted of men's regulation bell-bottom trousers and tops, which were to be worn 23 hours a day. We were required to wear skirts for dinner from 7 to 8pm, and on retiring, pyjamas were to be worn with the bell-bottoms, jumpers on top, and shoes 'at the ready'.

One evening, while the others were playing bridge, I was chatting with a Wren friend when we noticed and deciphered a morse-code message flashing from another vessel in the fleet. It warned that enemy submarines had been detected close by. The radio operator would have received this message and alerted the ship's captain, but my friend and I had to maintain silence and keep this information from our fellow travelers. It was an anxious night as we experienced the full meaning of the war time phrase, 'loose lips sink ships'. Fortunately the entire fleet reached its destination safely, and the forces disbanded and were dispatched to their consigned bases. Our whereabouts were still top secret. All letters were censored to ensure no names or military plans and positions were mentioned. Correspondence was limited to three small aero-gram forms. Knowing my parents would be anxious about where I was stationed, I disobeyed orders, sending them a cryptic letter. Back in England, a young military friend of mine had popped in to visit my parents, and when he asked how I was, and were I was posted, Sue offhandedly replied that my letter said absolutely nothing and all I'd done was mention people they didn't know. The young man asked to see the letter, which told about my new friends Bill Lakes and Mary Bitter. Looking at an atlas of the Middle East, he was able to point out where I was stationed on the Bitter Lakes between Port Said and Suez.

The first few days at my new post were very awkward. Previously, none of the male military staff had actually worked with a woman before and were unsure how to treat me, and found it difficult to assign me a task. However, a Petty Officer was struggling with the new Naval accounting system and asked me if I knew anything about it. Fortunately I was familiar with this system and was able to teach him the new methods, and so became a useful and accepted member of the team.

A new friend, a Nursing Sister, engaged to an RAF Engineer, invited me to her wedding. Five Wrens, several sailors, and RAF personnel attended the wedding one hot Saturday afternoon in a small stone church, followed by a reception in a bare hall at the Officers Mess. Time passed too quickly and suddenly I realised I had missed the Liberty Bus back to Ismailia. This also meant I would not be able to make my date that night! The RAF men I had just met offered to drive me back. Over two hours late, my date, had long since gone. But not to be defeated, four of the RAF chaps jumped out the truck and set off around the local bars to look for him. The RAF Engineer driving waited in the car with me and we chatted together, until, eventually, the other four chaps returned, along with my date! Later, back at Base, the other Wrens were getting into bed, when I returned and told them we all had an invitation for the next Saturday. The RAF lads would pick us up in cars and take us to the RAF Base for lunch and then onto the French Club to swim and for dinner.

This was the unexpected beginning of my flying adventures. While most of the girls liked to swim and dance when they were off duty, I delighted in discovering new places and exploring the many fascinating historic sites in the surrounding regions. My new friend, the RAF Engineer, would let me know if there were any planes scheduled in for maintenance or for return to other bases, and I was able to 'hitch a lift' if available flights fitted in with my scheduled time off duty. I took many trips, visiting the Temple of Jupiter and other Roman ruins near Baalbek in Lebanon, and made excursions to Damascus in Syria. Here I wandered amongst the narrow winding alley ways and crowded bazaar stalls, through the 'Street called Straight', and down some ancient steps into the tiny underground Chapel of St Ananias in which the disciple, Paul, first preached as he wandered abroad spreading the word, after Jesus' crucifixion.

One momentous flight I was given a lift in an RAF 'Baltimore' bomber. I was returning from Alexandria to Elfidan and my base at Faid, thirty miles away from the Ismailiyyah Air Base. I climbed into the hold with a French girl. It was empty, except for a huge, well secured, barrel of beer – we were all headed for the same party that night! The pilot hopped into the cockpit and we roared off down the runway, noisily lifting into the air. Back in the hold, we two terrified girls clung together for dear life. The door to the hold hadn't been closed properly and was now wide open. We were holding on desperately to a strap, and one another, gazing in horror at the huge open door opposite and the land rushing past below. It was freezing cold and the French girl managed to wriggle a spare cardigan out of a bag for me. After a nightmare journey the plane eventually landed at base, and when the pilot came round to open the hold door he turned white. He was horrified that we'd actually flown with the open door, and was visibly relieved that his two passengers, now blue with cold, were still there. Apologising profusely, he hurried us off to the women's quarters for hot drinks, warm clothes, and beds. Feeling warmer after a good rest, we turned up at the party, along with the relieved pilot, and I was able to return the cardigan to the French girl, no longer a stranger after our incredible flying experience together. She was –"

The lights suddenly went out, and it was quiet. We'd become so absorbed in Mum's stories that we hadn't noticed the time. The generator had run out of fuel and shut down, throwing us into darkness. When Dad started up the generator every evening just before sundown, he put in just enough fuel to last three hours so the generator would cut out automatically about bed time. Tonight it had beaten us to it, and with the help of a torch, Dad lit the hurricane lamp, which threw shadows over the walls as Mum finished her story.

"As Jim mentioned earlier, Army, Navy and Air force personnel were sent to Lebanon for their R&R leave and convalescence. Within the city, specified approved cafes and clubs were available for forces personnel to frequent, but other venues were strictly off limits because of known connections to subversive anti British groups. One quiet afternoon, a friend and I were treating ourselves to coffee and cakes at an approved restaurant. Tasty looking chocolate cakes arrived at our table, but my friend discovered a nail nestled amongst the cream. She complained and was given a second serving of cake, which also contained a nail. Mentioning this incident back at base, we were told that this particular restaurant, even though previously approved, was currently under observation for its surreptitious anti-British activity.

Although I was able to get about and explore many amazing places, it wasn't always the easiest way to travel, even on approved military flights. Returning from leave in Beirut, Lebanon, I had spent the night in Mt Carmel Quarter before taking a bus out of Haifa to the Palestine Air Base. The bus was crowded and noisy and the trip should only have been an hour, but the bus driver forgot to stop. By the time I managed to push my way through the raucous throng to the front, and the driver stopped, the bus was out on a long straight dusty road miles from anywhere. Dust clouds appeared on the horizon, and a jeep appeared. The bus driver flagged it down and asked if his passenger could get a lift back to the air strip, but the Palestinian soldier who was driving the jeep, refused to take me, because of my military uniform. The exasperated bus driver leant forward and whispered something in his ear, and soon I was told to clamber into the jeep beside the surly driver and was whisked off to be dumped unceremoniously outside the air base gates. I realised that the only reason the Palestinian soldier eventually gave me a lift was because the bus driver had reminded him that he was driving in the notoriously hostile Haganah territory, crawling with the rebellious militant Jewish group, and if he didn't do as asked, he would be prevented from reaching his own destination, no questions asked.

As he tore off, scattering stones and dust, I hurriedly approached the British Guard on duty at the Air Base gates, but he refused to let me in. I tried to explain that I was expected on a plane and needed to get into the air base quickly. Things became heated and the arrogant soldier pushed me back from the gate, shouting and swearing at me. Suddenly he raised his rifle butt to hit me, but just as he did a Land-Rover hurtled round the corner. The driver, an RAF Officer was very angry with me for being so late and holding the plane up, and without a word he flung my bag in the back and we screeched off to the waiting plane. Later I was informed that, even though he made no mention of it to me, the RAF Officer had witnessed the guard forcefully raising his rifle butt 'with intent' to British personnel, and duly reported him for disciplinary procedures. There was some hostility amongst an element of British military men who strongly resented women holding positions in the forces and found it hard to accept the new status quo of women's equality catalysed by wartime necessity, hence his attitude.

World War II was in full spate, and in the midst of it there was plenty of subversive activity being conducted by other militant groups in the Middle East. Shortly after the escapade in Haganah territory, St David's Hotel in Jerusalem was blown up by the Haganah rebels killing 90 people, including several British soldiers."

Dad stifled a yawn, and Mum paused, "Goodness it's getting late. I'd better stop here or I'll send you all off to sleep in your chairs!"

After our goodnight hugs, Mum reached for a poetry book on the shelf beside her, took out a creased, yellowed type written page and handed it to me. "Here's a little poem I kept. It reveals a smidgen of the personal sacrifices made by so many during the war years. Individual hardship, fears, and loss, were all bravely and quietly born."

To the Men England Forgot

Far away across the ocean, lies a land so sweet and fair,
with rugged hills, and rivers cool and crystal clear.
Once a land of free and plenty, home of England's fighting sons
Now the home of Poles and French men,
Czechs and Yanks, the sons of guns.
In its towns and country places where we lived and loved to walk,
They swagger around, with boastful sound, and brag with idle talk.
What they are going to do with Gerry –
We've heard it all before.
Meanwhile in the Desert, where there's only sand and sun
with red hot guns, old England's sons
Are fighting til they're done.
Weary, thirsty, scorched and battered, blinded by the sand,
forgotten men of England, die in a forgotten land.
And their only bit of comfort, is what the mail will bring.
But will it tell of a farewell, or contain a sweetheart's ring?
Yes, there are many in the desert, you can read it on a face,
Who have had news from England
that someone else has filled their place.
So please remember wife or sweetheart, when about to be untrue,
That a living heart, in a foreign part,
still believes in you.
And all that kept him fighting, when all else seemed in vain,
Was the thought of that great tomorrow,
When he'd be back with you once again.

The Desert Rat

6. Kenya mornings and 64

We lay in bed in our little hut, watching the candlelight flicker over the *kavirondo* matting walls. Beside us Sirri slept peacefully in her cot, adrift in sweet baby dreams, while the African night serenaded her with ancient lullabies. Above us, on a wire that stretched across the room supporting the grass roof, our tiny resident shrew scampered about, oblivious to the greater world at large.

Piercing, blood chilling screams split the air and brought us all rushing to the kitchen early next morning. The room was a hub of noise and confusion as Kipsang stamped his authority by shouting in high pitched babble, pushing a woman forward. In desperation she shrieked back, while in her arms a terrified toddler wailed in pain. Mango and Mum were trying to decipher the situation, and as Mum lead Kipsang outside, she yelled that the infant had a bug in its ear. It was obviously causing terrible pain, and the young mother was distraught. Mango tried to clear the baby's ear, but Lee grabbed a torch, shining the light deep into the ear in an attempt to attract the insect out. At last an ugly worm crawled to the surface of the ear and was quickly hooked out. The mother giggled in relief and her child's sobs subsided. Then the baby started to pee. The mother simply held it out at arm's length as urine splashed into a pool on the kitchen floor. Mango caught my eye but said nothing, only cleaning up the mess once the mother and baby had left, displaying the African way where a considerate person always leaves room for another to retain their dignity.

Lee and I took Dad's picnic breakfast down to the dip. The cattle had to be put through the dip at least once a week to rid them of ticks which caused East Coast Fever. The humped, long horned, boran cattle, were driven through a stockade where they were poked and prodded to cries of "dip, dip, dip", until one at a time, with ears back, they plunged into the powerful smelling Gamatox waters. Holding their snouts and eyes up above the water, the cows swam the length of the trough, and clambered up the slope to dry off in the sun.

When we were little we'd lived on Kibabet, a large tea, maize, and cattle estate up in the Nandi Hills. We'd always loved dip days and excitedly went along to watch. The huge herds of cattle were brought in from the far reaches of the farm. The floating voices of the Nandi herdsmen drifted through the clear morning air as dust clouds from their cattle rose in the distance. The assembling herdsmen reveled in the muster, cheerfully calling out to each other between whistles and shouts to their cattle, and the odd thwack of sticks on hides.

On Friday afternoons, a beast was killed to provide meat for the labour and their families. This coincided with pay day and the distribution of maize rations. All the Africans on the farm gathered noisily around the less fortunate animal. Tractor drivers, carpenters, planters, weeders, builders, office wallahs, guards, and herdsmen, assembled eagerly. B*ebes* and *totos* - wives and children, thronged around in clouds of ever present flies. Some of the men wore shorts and shirts with either bare feet or rubber sandals made from discarded tyres, but most preferred *shukas* or a blanket flung over their shoulders. The bebes had on leather aprons and softened skin cloaks, or large cloth shawls. They were usually bare breasted and had several beaded necklaces and copper wire or leather bracelets. Almost everyone had had their ears stretched and the lobes dangled down by their shoulders, decorated with copper cones or beads. Mothers carried their babies on their backs in cloth hammocks, simply pulling the infants round to the front for feeding. Little raggedy totos ran around playing happily and seldom grizzled. Women arrived with huge bundles of firewood on their backs. The wood and sticks were secured with leather thongs. Others women balanced square *debes* and tin water vessels or gourds on their heads. The gourds were used to carry milk and had been grown, dried out and sterilised with smoke and cows urine. Each gourd was decorated with individual carved symbols, leather and beadwork. Several of the bebes had collected masses of defunct copper one cent pieces with a hole in the centre, stringing them on leather thongs around their necks. I used to think they must be very rich!

The Africans often sang while working on the farm. Without instruments, the men and women picked up a rhythm and harmonised their voices beautifully as they worked away in the fields. I loved to sit quietly, hidden behind bushes, just listening as their voices rose and fell in flowing earthy tones that drifted in the air and gently touched your heart.

As well as slipping *Arap or Kip*, meaning 'son of' in front of a name, the Nandi often named their own children according to events at birth. Babies could be called after the night of a fire, or when lightning struck a tree, or a celebration. Africans also loved inventing descriptive nicknames, and the Luo tribesmen had given Dad's nephew Struan, (Pix and George's son) the nickname '*Kegin Doro*', a complimentary term literally meaning 'he is his uncle's nephew'. Meanwhile, Dad, seldom seen without his pipe, was known as '*Bwana Kiko*', and no matter where in East Africa he went, Africans instantly picked up on this name.

Bwana Kiko was well respected and loved by his labour. He spoke the native tongues, understood the various tribal customs, and always treated people fairly, in an honest, considerate manner. I remember once seeing two tall young Nandi men honour Dad with a rare Nandi salute. It was impressive. In one movement, the young men suddenly stamped once, stretched to their full height with every muscle taut, thrusting one arm skyward, with palms forward. It was a proud salute, dignified and intense, with great meaning, and made with their whole being.

Mzee, an old man, had told Dad about a secret, sacred cave behind a waterfall in the forests beyond the farm. Mzee arranged for a couple of guides to escort our family through the trees to this mysterious place. One exciting Sunday, we drove as far as we could, then were lead along dark mossy paths, through towering ancient trees, until we could hear the distant roar of a waterfall. A river rushed through the undergrowth far below the slippery path. Suddenly there ahead was a glorious, blindingly white waterfall, thundering down to rocks a long way below. It was a wonderful sight, and frightening too, because of its height, and its might, as it crashed through the silent, ancient forests. Spray sparkled in a shaft of sunlight sending tiny rainbows dancing into the air. Carefully, holding adult hands, we children were guided over rocks and stones, through the mists, until we stepped behind the waterfall and into a cave that stretched back into the dank darkness of the earth. The noise of thunder drumming in our ears from the waterfall was deafening, and we were soon drenched by the spray, but it was a magical moment, hiding in this secret, timeless place deep within the jungle.

With the help of the Rift Valley Correspondence Courses, Mum taught us all to read and write until it was time for boarding school. At seven, Hugh went off to board at the Hill School in Eldoret, a large school with over 600 pupils. The majority of the children were Afrikaners. Their parents and grandparents had trekked up from South Africa in convoys of wagons pulled by teams of oxen, finally settling to farm the land around the Uasin Gishu Plateau. Eldoret was originally known as '64' because it was 64 miles from the last wagon station at Londiani. The trekkers' offspring were notorious for their tough, arrogant, bullying ways. It must have been a daunting experience for young Hugh, but he put on a brave face and coped well.

I managed to escape school until I was nine, and even then I had a much easier start. I was enrolled as a boarder at Kaptagat School, which I loved. It was a small country primary school adjacent to the Foster's horse ranch. We were allowed to go riding in the mornings before school, and again after lessons had finished. There was a Shetland pony, named 'Hell-for-Leather', who was blissfully unaware of the meaning of his name. He was an extremely lazy pony, aspiring to nothing more than a saunter along at the back of the pack. We all hated it when we saw our names on the list to ride him. However, one day, Hell-for-Leather and I were plodding along dreamily, bringing up the rear, when the horse in front kicked out at him. Unfortunately the kick missed the horse and connected with my shin. Hurting, and very angry, I took it out on Hell-for-Leather. Kicking his sides wildly, I forced him into a trot and then a canter, until we were up in front of the group, where we stayed for the duration of the trek, safe from errant hooves. I received unwarranted praise from Mrs. Foster who was totally delighted that someone had made the effort to get more out of Hell-for-Leather and not settle for the accepted norm of ambling along at the back!

Our classes were small and probably interesting. However Mr Jupp's classes stand out, not so much for the content, more for the sense of the unexpected. Mr Jupp had painted the entire classroom with life size figures and scenes. Every inch of wall was covered with murals à la Seurat. Ladies in long dresses, carrying parasols, wandered through landscaped parks with dapper gentlemen. Children flicking wheels with sticks, played beside tranquil lakes, where elegant swans floated serenely. Naturally all this made it difficult to concentrate and Mr Jupp would bring your attention back by suddenly, and ferociously, yelling at you and hurling either the board rubber or the box of chalks in your direction!

Other teachers took us for walks beneath the gum trees collecting gum nuts and berries for counting projects. For nature study we explored the donga, a rocky riverbed, scattered with dried grasses, cacti, and aloes, where we tried to catch cockamonda lizards as they lazed in the sun or scampered to safety over the rocks. At weekends we played in 'shacks' or dens that we hollowed out in the thick macrocarpa hedges surrounding the playing fields. My friends, Sally Bevan, Kathleen Elson with long blonde silky hair, and mischievous Angel Jones were always fun to muck around with. On certain Sundays we were allowed out for the day, and these friends, who lived closer, took me to their homes or for picnics with their families. We all joined the Brownies and collected once a week in the Foster's lovely garden by the river. There was a special meeting place, landscaped and pretty, a natural amphitheater in a dell that sloped down to a small lily pond in the centre. This little haven captured my imagination and invited fantasy, and I was always looking for tiny elves and fairies, genuinely expecting to see one peeping through the leaves in this magical place.

After only a year, my idyllic school life was brought to an abrupt end. Dad had taken a new job and we moved to Siani on the outskirts of Eldoret. Hugh was in his final year at the Hill School where he remained as a boarder, and Robin and I now joined him as day bugs. On my first day at the Hill School, I learnt about rejection, failing to make the cut over and over again. Because I had started school late and due to lack of any information from my previous school, the teachers were unsure which class to put me in. It was a large school and classes for each age were divided into A, B or C grades and students were sorted according to their academic ability. There were at least 30 pupils in each class. Initially I was taken into 5A, who were doing mathematics, and working on a method that was completely unknown to me. I sat amongst staring kids, feeling nervous and humiliated as I tried in vain to make sense of the numbers in front of me. At morning break I was removed and taken to 5B. Oh dear, the same subject, but this time I was a little luckier. I still didn't have a clue about the maths, but I had been put next to Adrian, a friend from Nandi, who helped me by showing me his work to copy! I don't know if the teacher was aware of what was going on, or whether

Adrian had done his sums wrong, but I was removed from 5B at lunch. 5C I don't even remember. Next, I was down in 4A, where I was also unsuccessful and by late afternoon I had arrived in 4B, which was to be the end of the line. It was so good to go home that night. During my year in 4B, in every weekly test in all the subjects, I was never out of the top three. I remember this simply because we used to have to move desks each week so we were seated in the same order as our placings in the weekly test results, and I was often next to a horrible, fat, bossy girl, Caroline Benson. One day she sat beside me, sharpening her pencil to a fine point. I was writing with my left hand resting on the desk, when she suddenly held my hand down and sliced across the top of my hand with the very sharp point of her pencil. Yes, it hurt, but I was more shocked that somebody could be so deliberately spiteful.

The new farm, Siani, was planted in wattle, from which bark was cut and sent to a nearby tanning factory, where an extract for curing leather was produced. The wattle bloomed once a year, and the trees were covered in golden mimosa blooms. Millions of little yellow fluffy pompoms, or 'teddy bear flowers' coloured the entire plantation and carpeted the ground below, scenting the air with a sweet heady fragrance.

When Dad started at Siani, wattle fetched £83 a ton. Only one year later the price had dropped to £25 a ton. This drastic decline was due to plastic! Suddenly imitation leather goods made from plastic, flooded the market. Leather for car seats, shoes, jackets, bags, cases, and belts was no longer in demand. The wattle bark that created the tanning for leather products became redundant. Dad's employers told him they could no longer afford his salary. Initially Mum went to work in a fruit and vegetable store to tide us through until a new plan was hatched, then Dad got a job with the Uasin Gishu County Council in Eldoret, as Assistant Social Services Manager. After discussions with the directors of Siani, it was agreed that we could continue to live at Siani and Mum would take over the running of the farm, guided by Dad, but they could only pay her a third of Dad's original salary. She was offended that she didn't even receive that, as her wages continued to be paid automatically into her husband's account, and she was never addressed directly by her employers. However, she arranged to lease pastures out for grazing beef to neighbours. Reliable herdsmen were found and the contract required Mum to do the weekly dipping of over 400 head of cattle. Unfortunately a weekly dip was not enough to keep the ticks at bay, so Mum implemented a new routine, the 'Never on a Sunday 5-5-4', which involved dipping every 5th day and then on the 4th so that everyone got to have a break on Sundays.

Meanwhile the Anderson's fourteen head of cattle had been brought from Nandi to Eldoret on hoof and were grazed near the farm buildings. The Nandi herdsmen milked the cows by hand morning and night. As they finished milking each cow, they called out the name of next cow, who, recognising its own name, obediently walk from the yard into the milking shed. All went smoothly until the last cow, Karli Mabs. She was a black cow with long horns and a foul temper, and always managed to create a great commotion before finally allowing someone to milk her. Needless to say, this was the bit us kids enjoyed most, and I suspect the Nandi herdsmen liked the challenge and excitement as much as we did! We had our own rodeo show as Karli Mabs rushed at the herders who ducked quickly out of her way, egging each other on. Eventually normality returned, Karli Mabs was milked, and the milk in the buckets was poured into a hand turned machine that separated the cream from the 'skimmed milk'. On our way to school each morning we'd call in at the creamery to deliver our small urn of cream. As Mum dropped us off at school, she'd drive painfully slowly, hoping for a glimpse of Hugh. After the first year all together at the same school, Hugh moved on to Secondary School in Nairobi, where he boarded at the Prince of Wales, travelling to and from school by train each term.

Until the 1960s when diesel was used to fuel trains, eucalyptus wood was used as the source of power. Hence the plentiful gum plantations along railway lines right across the country. Seeing that wattle was no longer a viable product, Dad and Mum decided to convert the wattle trees into charcoal for fuel, and filled a contract with a Ugandan factory to which they regularly supplied bags of charcoal. The last bark was removed from the wattle trees before they were felled and piled into pits. The wood was torched, and once it was burning well, the pits were covered in mounds of earth so that the wood smoldered and burned slowly until it was eventually transformed into charcoal beneath the ground. The charcoal was dug up, bagged and sent by train to Uganda. Now the acrid smell of smoke from the charcoal burning pyres replaced the sweet scent of mimosa.

Dad constructed a large wooden waterwheel in the swift stream behind the house, to generate electricity for the house and farm. Prior to this we used to light the hurricane lamps and pump up the brighter tilley lamp just before dark. Previously, on other farms, we'd relied on electricity supplied by generators. These were turned on at sundown, and automatically turned themselves off when they ran out of fuel, usually about 10pm. This provided an on-going source of humour to any guests we might have, who'd joke about our subtle methods of telling them it was time to go home! Having no power during the day, meant we had no freezers, washing machines, vacuum cleaners, or electric irons. We relied on paraffin fridges and battery powered radios. This was why a 'house-boy' was essential to help with all the normal day to day chores. Our house-boys usually fitted in well with our family and were happy to move with us whenever we started on another farm. We also employed a local garden boy to weed, mow the grass with a push mower, and keep the encroaching bush at bay.

Our house boy, Kipleting, a tall Nandi, stayed with us for many years, albeit in his own fashion. He was in the habit of coming and going as and when he pleased. He also worked for another European family, who we never met, and he had a couple of wives and numerous children living in the reserve. He visited his family in between jobs with both white families. We had no idea how long Kipleting would stay with us each time, before he got the notion to head off to visit his family or work elsewhere, and he gave no sign of his inclinations. He simply took off on a whim, and was always welcomed back whenever he turned up again.

The East African Women's' League, a women's voluntary organization set up to help those less fortunate, had been operating effectively throughout East African since early times. Mum had established the original Nandi Hills EAWL Branch and was thinking of joining the branch at Eldoret.

In 1960 the Belgian Congo gained its independence from colonial rule. However rioting and heavy fighting broke out overnight, and rebellion spread through the country like wild fire. There were thousands of deaths, and those that could were desperate to escape the horror. A large contingent of white refugees managed to escape to Uganda, but Uganda was hostile to them and they had to flee immediately to Kenya. Trains carrying these people to Nairobi passed through Eldoret, which was the first friendly town they encountered. Most of the refugees escaped with their lives and just the clothes on their backs. Mum and many other locals helped organize hot soup, food, blankets and clothing, to be waiting at the station to assist these poor people when the train stopped briefly in Eldoret. With haggard looks and glazed eyes, mothers reached for milk for their babies or for warm clothing, unable even to acknowledge our presence. In Nairobi, the boarders at Hugh's school, The Prince of Wales, and the Duke of York, were billeted out to Nairobi families in order to free up beds for the refugees, providing them with a safe haven for a night or two.

Mum had notes of her own involvement during this time;

In June 1960, a blunder was made during the Congo's Independence Day speeches which caused riots and unrest. The next day the Congo blew up in Civil War. Horror stories trickled out. Blacks and whites were being murdered in their thousands. Nuns were raped and killed. Priests, Doctors and Nurses butchered. Gradually people were able to escape and the odd car or truck came through Eldoret, which was the first friendly town on their route. Petrol, meals and medical care were provided for refugees at the Town Hall.

One night Jim came home and said, "When you've done the dipping tomorrow, I think you should go to the Mayors secretary and see what you can do to help her with the refugees." The secretary was delighted to have an offer of help but said she was too busy to even stop and show me what to do, suggesting I go to the Red Cross. The first train load of refugees was due in at 1.30 that afternoon, and I immediately joined two dozen men and women making sandwiches and cutting up fruit. At 1.00 pm someone shouted out "time to go" and handed out Red Cross arm bands. Everyone rushed off with the 360 lunch boxes, leaving Mr Cloete and I to clean up. We'd almost finished when Mr Cloete answered a phone call requesting a churn of milk be picked up from the creamery and rushed to the station where they were running out of milk. I dashed off to collect the milk, but there was no way I could get through the crowds outside the station. I was barred by hundreds of demonstrative Africans. Askari soldiers, as always with their rifles, were preventing the masses from entering the station. I tried to nudge through the throng. It was frightening as I was jostled about and fists waved at me, with many shouting at me, in Swahili and English, "Your turn next". Fortunately a white officer saw me and pushed through the angry crowd. I explained my mission and he asked two askaris to assist me, one to carry the ten gallon milk churn and the other to guide me through, clinging on to his belt. I then ran down the length of the train handing out food packages because none of the refugees would get out of the train. It transpired that they were too scared to leave the relative safety of their carriages. Until now, they had been treated with hostility, intimidated and abused. A baby was screaming, and a baby's bottle was thrust out the window for me to fill. It was filthy, and the only thing I could find to clean it with was a hand full of gravel. I was able to sterilize it with boiling water from an urn and filled it with milk for the desperate mother.

That night Jim gave me a message from the Mayor. He wanted me to have hot drinks ready for the trains that would be coming through every morning at 5.30 am. Someone on night duty would fill the urns and switch them on ready, and I was to ensure there were plenty of cups, milk, sugar, tea, coffee and cocoa. I also made sure I took along a bottle brush! I was also asked to do a shift for couple of hours at mid-day to help any refugees arriving by road. Gerry Adams, from the Seychelles, (whose cows I looked after), had brought a bull horn along and walked up and down the train, greeting the refugees in French and assuring them they were now in Kenya, among friends, and need not be afraid. Soon men, women and children were venturing off the train for food and drinks, and to collect warm clothes and blankets from the EAWL and Red Cross tables. The next stop for the train would be Timbarua, at an altitude of 9,230 feet above sea level, it would be very cold.

Locals registered at the Town Hall, giving the number of beds in their homes where evacuees could stay. The cooks at the Hill School prepared hot meals. Farmers brought in baskets of fruit, vegetables and eggs, and the Afrikaners slaughtered cows, pigs and sheep. They didn't just bring in carcasses, they jointed the meat into various cuts ready for preparation, and the butcher gave up one of his cold rooms. People from near and far gave whatever they could.

During the second week, an announcement was made over the radio. All boys boarding at The Prince of Wales and Duke of York schools in Nairobi were to be sent home by rail to free up beds for the refugees. The refugee numbers were swelling as planes from Europe were not arriving in sufficient numbers to fly them out. We met Hugh's train at 1.00am and I was back at the station again at 5.00am. A few days later the Kenya Girls High was to send all their boarders home too. Jim's niece, Liz, volunteered to stay at school to help with children and babies.

The Afrikaaner men formed a commando to go into the Congo to help those trying to escape, but they were stopped at the Uganda border and refused entry unless they handed in their weapons. The men refused to hand over their guns and had to turn back and disband.

Pressure eased off at the end of the third week, although cars and lorries continued to come through for another three weeks. Most got out in what they stood up in, others had cases, and a few were seen with trucks loaded with furniture.

About three months later I went to join the Eldoret branch of the EAWL. The President greeted me with pleasure, "There you are. I have been trying to find out who you were. You were so helpful just appearing like that to help us and the Red Cross that first day".

7. The champagne air of Nandi

I vaguely tried to restrain the baby's little hands from pulling Macora's tail, while Dad and I chatted about the dogs we used to have. When we lived in Nandi Hills, we had two dogs, Spider and Wrinkles. Both dogs enjoyed taunting the baboons that chattered incessantly in the nearby trees. The dogs barked monotonously up at the monkeys, who inevitably retaliated by swinging down from the trees and harassing the dogs. Terrible noisy fights ensued, and we were heartbroken when Wrinkles was killed by the baboons. Spider lived on for many years, befriending our pet tortoises, Joey and Billy. We liked to straddle Billy for short, very slow, wobbly rides. The rides were short because Billy quickly learnt that when he'd had enough, he simply pulled his head in, then his feet, and stayed inside his shell until we ran off to play with something more exciting.

"Yes, you scallywags were always so full of beans, it was hard to keep an eye on you much of the time. The other day I found myself recalling Hugh's lucky escape on the tractor."

"I don't really remember that. What happened?" I asked

"As a small lad, Hugh had climbed up into the seat of a John Deere tractor idling by a shed. Pretending to be the tractor driver, he managed to release the brake, and headed off on his own, down the slope. Alerted by shouts from the workers, a quick thinking mechanic, in true Nandi speed, raced after the tractor, hauled himself up beside Hugh, and pulled the brake, bringing the errant tractor and its young hijacker, to a sudden standstill."

"That was close! Hugh had a few narrow escapes didn't he? But he wasn't quite as bad as Robin with his nine lives though. We certainly had an adventurous childhood – and found plenty of mischief to get into as well as things to argue about. Do you remember how Hugh and Robin used to tease me and call me a '*Kitoshi*'?"

Dad chuckled, explaining to Lee, who'd just joined us, "It was after the 'Kitoshi' tribe were proscribed. The Kitoshi were an off-shoot of the Nandi tribe and generally were from the area between the Nzoia River and Mount Elgon. However the Nandi tribe refused to recognise the Kitsohi because they were not from Nandi."

"Hugh and Robin loved to tease me by calling me a 'Kitoshi', a 'non-person', someone who didn't count, because I had not been conceived and born within the district. I didn't get the conceived bit, but all three of us were certainly born at the same place!"

"Ah I must remember you don't count Babe – that could be useful!" Lee teased.

"Don't count on it – or you'll be counting yourself very unlucky!"

Tapping his pipe on the wall, Dad added, "If you'd like to see Nandi before you go Lee, we could take a run up there – drive out to Schiehallion. I need to see how things are going there anyway. Our farm, Schiehallion, is about thirty acres and lies almost seven thousand feet above sea level. It will be nice to breathe the champagne air of Nandi again. Maybe we could go tomorrow?"

Lee enthusiastically replied, "I'd love to go up to Nandi. I've heard so much about it. Do we go up that escarpment you were talking about before?"

"Yes" I chipped in enthusiastically, "You'll like the escarpment. It's rocky, arid, and isolated, and it's spectacular with its sharp bends and sheer drops. When we were little kids, going up or down the escarpment was scary and we felt like we were in a real adventure. If we ever got a puncture or the car over-heated, I was terrified that a leopard would pounce on Dad while he was fixing the car!"

As we'd spent so much of our childhood in the Nandi Hills, I was looking forward to showing Lee my old hangouts, and with Dad at the wheel, we set off to climb the escarpment. Dad pointed out the land he had farmed with his father, and the hill, where he'd worked as a student. Then we sighted the Nandi Rock. From a distance it looked like a high peak with a sheer cliff dropping hundreds of feet to the valley below, although in reality it is a prominent rock formation consisting of several massive granite boulders overlooking the escarpment. Legend has it that disputes were settled between the Nandi and Luo tribes by elders tossing prisoners over the edge. If they survived they were innocent, and if they didn't they were guilty - justice had been done, and the matter resolved. There are older legends that a Luo warrior was once turned into the rock, and hunters still visit the Nandi Rock to sharpen their spears, believing supernatural powers from the rock will flow into their weapons giving them extra potency.

There was also another legend that was the stuff of nightmares to us children. Nandi had its own mythical creature, the Nandi Bear. It was said to hunt people down in the forests at night as it had a taste for human brains. Occasional sightings in the dense forests of Western Kenya continue to reignite the folklore, and there still is a possibility that this fabled beast could actually be a large species of hyena that stands on its hind legs.

Mum reminisced, "Our early years in Nandi were good years, and the kids grew up happily playing and learning from their wonderful surroundings. I was constantly amazed by the twists and turns of life's path, as I watched our three youngsters respond to the daily excitements and realities of an African farm. Very little related to our own childhoods back in Britain. I taught all three with the aid of the Rift Valley Correspondence Course'. The boys were good pupils, but your little wife, Heather, or Andi as you call her, always wanted to be out playing, and frequently nipped off or hid before lessons. She loved being outdoors, so much so that I used to call her 'child of the sun'."

Lee grinned, "She's still the same. If the sun's out, she's got to be in it, and we always have to cross the street to walk on the sunny side."

"Well, that's my little ray of sunshine" added Dad fondly.

"What about the freckles Mum?" I teased. "When I was a baby, Mum left me outside in the mornings with a mosquito net over the pram to keep the bugs off, and we reckon the freckles came from the sun tanning me, but only through the holes in the net!"

More laughter as Lee added, "Oh I thought she got her freckles in heaven. Before she was born, there was a group of little babies destined for Kenya, and an angel began spraying them black. Another angel quickly called out "No, no, not that one – she's supposed to be white." But it was too late she was already splattered with paint!"

We all laughed, and I related an incident when an African had been genuinely shocked by my freckles. Seeing me for the first time when I was a little girl, his face showed sheer astonishment, as mortified, he gasped, "Eh! Jua na kula weh!" – OMG the sun has eaten you!

As the car laboured up the steep road, Mum and Lee resumed their conversation, "We lived at Kibabet for about six years in the early fifties. We'd moved out of the shed into the new stone house as soon as the roof was on, and I gradually established a garden with bright patches of portulaca and verbena cascading down the banks, and morning glory and golden shower stretched out over the walls in cobalt blue and orange splendour.

Roads, all over the country, were generally bad, and filled with potholes and corrugations running into the camber of the road. When the rains came, roads turned to quagmires, and we avoided leaving the farm. If we did manage to get out, our old Ford V8 often got stuck in the mud coming home. Hearing the car revving and whining, Africans would materialise out of the surrounding darkness and soon a little crowd would gather to help push the car out. Everybody pushed with one accord at the shout of *'Harambee'* - meaning all together. The wheels spun madly and branches were thrown down for the tyres to grip. More pushing, more *'harambees',* and the car would slowly ease out of the mud, amidst happy cheers, and tips all round!

"How did you cope with the isolation out here?" asked Lee, unused to such distances.

Mum replied, "Jim has always loved nature, solitude, and the open spaces, so it has never bothered him. But for me, coming from London, I found it quite hard at times. I loved the country but I missed the company of other people. It was especially trying during the rainy season when we were trapped on the farm, but gradual progress over the years has made things a lot easier. Roads improved, and after several years a phone line was connected, and along with others in the districts we were linked to a 'party line'. Our code was a short ring followed by three long rings, and whenever the phone rang you had to listen to the code to ascertain whether the call was for you. Obviously you also had to make sure the lines were clear before you called out. However the lines were notoriously bad and we only ever used the phone for emergencies."

"Yes, we know what the Kenya telephone lines are like…" said Lee.

Suddenly we were all laughing as we recalled a certain telephone call we had made to Kenya only a couple of years before from New Zealand. Although phones lines were not good and telephone calls were costly then, Lee and I booked a call to Mum and Dad in Kenya, knowing they'd be spending Christmas with my cousins who had a phone. It was ages since I'd seen Mum and Dad, and Lee had never met them, nor even spoken to them before, so it was to be an exciting call. In New Zealand, throughout Christmas Day, every time the phone rang, we raced down the passage expecting Mum or Dad to be on the other end of the line. But it was only an operator telling us, yet again, that they had been unable to make a connection and would try again in another hour. Finally we got through, but only to Mum, as Dad had gone to bed. It was late at night in Kenya, but alarm bells rang because I knew Dad would not have missed my call for anything. We eventually learnt that Dad was suffering from gall stones, and was dosed up on aspirins to dull the agonising pain, until he could be driven across the Rift Valley to a doctor in the morning. However, before we were able to decipher why Dad was not there, we had had to go through the drama of THE phone call. It is not easy to chat to loved ones overseas when you haven't spoken for years, and every second counts, so you tend not to natter on about minor things like the weather or what you did yesterday. Gripped with emotion, we stuttered out our hellos on a very static line, accompanied by an over-zealous, well intentioned Kenyan operator. He explained that with this sort of connection, you had to keep talking so the line receptors adjusted to your voice level. Well, that was pressure in itself! But now he complicated the issue by trying to guide us, "Muddah, you talk now. Come on Muddah, talk to daughter Heddah" Mum stammered out some words, then it was "OK Heddah, your turn. Now you talk Heddah. Muddah you wait. Talk to Muddah Heddah. Heddah talk to Muddah." "Keep talking Heddah, Muddah waiting, talk Heddah talk! …"

Now that Dad was fine, and we were all together, it was easy to see the funny side of what was then a very harrowing long distance phone call.

From the front seat, Mum continued, "Although we lived in fairly isolated places, we did have a social life. Anybody who travelled the long dirt roads to visit us, would always be given a warm welcome and a meal, and in typical Kenyan hospitality, would be invited to stay the night. The family became adept at the FHB system ('family hold back'). More often than not, guests arrived unexpectedly, sometimes catching us out with limited food supplies, as we only had a paraffin fridge, and no freezer and or shops to run to. As guests helped themselves to the dishes at the table, Jim or I would quietly slip the initials 'FHB' into the general conversation. The children knew to discreetly take less of everything so that there would be enough for everyone."

Joining in, I added, "We loved it when Granny and Grandad and Uncle Teddy came to visit, or Uncle Jim and Auntie Pam joined us for Christmas. Breakfasts were usually cheerful affairs as everyone lingered around the table chatting and drinking coffee on the sunny veranda. Late afternoons, after siestas, we went for walks to the dam. Hugh had a battery operated toy boat called 'Jim' which he and the men played with amongst the bull rushes, but I had more fun with Granny and Pam who giggled and squealed as they slipped and slithered in the mud, even losing their shoes. Other times we walked up to the saddle for rolling views over the Nandi Hills. Occasionally we came across African children squatting beside mounds of earth, beating the ground with sticks. Tapping their sticks rhythmically simulated the sound of falling rain which induced flying ants to emerge from underground. The flying ants were considered a great delicacy, and were snatched up and eaten as soon as they appeared above ground.

In the evenings we gathered round the fire, reading, drawing, or playing scrabble. As soon as the hum of the generator ceased, the night noises clustered round. Insect orchestras played persistently, and you were never really sure if these noises of the night were outside, or in your head. Spasmodic bird screeches, baboon coughs, or cackling hyenas peppered the darkness, and at full moon all the dogs in the area set up continuous chorus rounds of howls. We occasionally heard the drums, horns, whistles and chants of an *ngoma* or dance, just like we did the other night."

"Ah," sighed Dad, enjoying the fresh air as he wound his window down, "The champagne air of Nandi."

"That's nice," exclaimed Lee, taking a deep breath, "It's certainly much cooler up here."

"Yes, pure high altitude air; it's got to be good for you!"

We'd climbed the escarpment and were now over 6,000 feet above sea level, up in the Nandi Hills. The air was definitely cooler, and steep barren land had given way to a patchwork of maize shambas and undulating green tea plantations. I pointed out the local 'Nandi Bears Club' to Lee. The club had replaced the original club on Soyet, which had burnt down. Dad did the electrical wiring for the new club, and he and his friend Syd Outram, established the demi golf course.

"On Sundays, it was usual for local farmers and tea grower's families to meet at the Nandi Bears Club for tennis, nine hole golf, and nineteenth hole drinks. This was followed by Sunday night films. The children, in their pajamas, sat at the front on the floor, adults behind in rows of assorted chairs, teenagers in the back row, and bringing up the rear would be Fred Jackson, operating the projector. At the end of each reel there would be a mad dash for the bar, to feed children, or simply chat before settling down for the next reel. However, if the operator was getting a little well oiled, the order of the reels would become mixed up. Cries of 'we've seen this one Fred' would ring out and much merriment would ensue as everybody tried to sort out the correct sequence of the film. Occasionally there was a party or dance at the club. All the children, dressed in pajamas, would sleep in their cars outside, while a Nandi askari guard wandered around all night keeping an eye on the vicinity. One New Year's Eve, Dad parked our car by the entrance to the clubroom, so we could watch the party in progress through the door. Mum, looking beautiful, in her long, slinky, black and red satin dress, happily danced the night away. The older kids often sneaked in and out of one another's cars, until eventually everyone grew tired and nodded off. When it was time to go home, we'd stir in our blankets in the back of the car as Mum and Dad chatted in the front. I loved to lie awake, gazing up at the passing black silhouettes of trees against the starry sky. We often surprised ant bears, buck, or jackals in our headlights, and giggled as startled rabbits, mesmerized by the lights, zig-zagged across the road for ages, too scared to venture back into the safety the dark bushes on either side. If we were still awake when we arrived home, we'd suddenly pretend to be asleep so that we'd be carried inside to bed!"

"I never realised that, you scheming wee monkeys!" Dad smiled shaking his head.

"Shall we take Lee up to see the club?" I asked.

There was a pause before Mum replied, "We don't go there anymore."

I noticed a look pass between my parents, and pushed further. Eventually Mum explained, "You remember, in the late sixties, before you went to Scotland? Well in the two months between leaving school and your departure to the UK, you frequented the club a fair bit."

"Yes, I did. I often went up there to meet friends and play tennis or hockey."

"The club was usually only open at the weekends and one evening a week. We hadn't been members for several years as we couldn't afford to be. However, the committee members wrote us a letter saying that we were obliged to pay membership fees for you seeing as you were using their facilities. It was generally known that you would soon be going overseas, and considering all the time and effort Dad had given to get the club up and running in the old days, we felt insulted. So we just don't bother with them anymore."

"That's so rude. I wish you'd told me this at the time, and I wouldn't have gone up there either. I had no idea Mum, Dad, I am sorry. Fancy doing that to you."

"I suppose these things all depend on who's on the committee at the time. All it takes is one rigid person who won't think outside the square. Who uses the club anyway? Is it multiracial now?" asked Lee.

Mum replied, "Not really. Since Uhuru, integration is encouraged and expected, but in actuality it is often discouraged by those wanting to maintain the status quo. I believe there are a few African members these days, but generally only the odd high ranking officials can afford the fees, and the life style."

We turned off the main road, and followed a long straight road through Kapchorawa Tea Estate. Colourful groups of tea pickers were scattered through the green. In bright plastic vests, with baskets on their backs, the pickers worked their way across a field. Regular picking of 'two leaves and a bud' from the top of the tea bushes, resulted in a level 'tea table' that looked remarkably like the rolling manicured lawns of an English estate. We drove between the tea plantations, past the tea factory, to the end of the ridge, where our little farm, Schiehallion, nestled close to the forests. I have to say that the empty house looked forlorn and run down, and weeds and vines smothered the roads and garden, but Dad had kept a skeleton staff on to tend the pyrethrum fields, and pick the meagre tea crop. Keifer, originally the carpenter, now the foreman, was pleased to see us and took advantage of the chance to discuss farm matters with Dad.

The place held so many memories for me. We were living here when I first went overseas at eighteen, and there had been times when I felt far away and homesick, and in my mind I had revisited every detail of my beautiful distant home. Now I felt a deep sense of gratitude as I realized, I had come full circle, returning here with my husband and baby. Later, after a picnic lunch, Lee, with Sirri on his shoulders, stood beside Dad looking out over the farm. Something caught at my throat. These moments were all the more poignant as Lee and I were soon to leave all this behind to continue our trip to London. With typical, humility I heard Dad say, "So there it is. That's our little farm. My life's work. I suppose it's not really much to show for all these years is it?"

Lee answered with sincerity, "I think you should feel proud of yourself. You have a really special family, and you have guided them through unimaginable hardships and changes. I think you have done really well."

I looked at Dad fondly. Kind, wise, and courageous, he had a gentle strength and stood firmly by his own beliefs. Remarkably he seldom forced his views on anyone, and always gave others the chance to voice their opinions before any further discussion.

Dad had been one of the first Europeans to relinquish his British Passport and take up Kenya Citizenship after Kenya gained its independence in 1963. This went against the grain at the time, as most whites were wary of the future under 'Africanisation' and were either trying to get their money out of the country, or cautiously waiting to see how things would go. However, Dad had always loved the country and its people, and felt that since he had dedicated his life to farming here with his family, it was only natural that he show his total commitment to Kenya and its future.

In 1965, weary of working for others, Dad felt that at last the time had come to work his own farm. In spite of having to pay school fees for three children every term throughout our education, Mum and Dad had managed to squirrel away a little. Eventually all the years of saving had culminated in 'Schiehallion', our own small farm in the Nandi Hills. Our thirty acres of land was beyond the tea plantations, at the end of a valley, and there was already a house on the hill. The day we moved was wet, and at the end of the long slow journey, the priority was to light a fire, boil the kettle for a cup of tea, and stand the damp mattresses around the hearth to dry. A good feeling of contented anticipation washed over us that night, as Robin and I lay on the driest mattress with Mum and Dad, watching flames and shadows play as we talked about the things we'd like to do here. Robin wanted to start a vegetable patch, Mum was going to rejuvenate the garden and propagate an interesting variety of African violets, and I was keen to claim an old shed for an art studio.

Dad was eager to plant pyrethrum as it grew well at high altitude in Kenya, and as Schiehallion was 6,500 feet above sea level he felt it would be an ideal crop. First he needed to experiment with the different strains of the plant, and we constructed a nursery with posts made of branches and a roof thatched with dry grass. Dad worked enthusiastically with the various pyrethrum cuttings and seedlings as he researched which plants would produce the highest pyrethrum content. Samples of flowers were sent to the Pyrethrum Board in Nakuru where they were tested for their content. Many strains of pyrethrum have very little potency, but those with a high pyrethrum content provide a potent and effective natural insecticide. Eventually Dad was to produce pyrethrum plants that rated the fourth highest content in East Africa, but it was always going to be about quality rather than quantity.

Dad carried out his research, and planted a small field of tea bushes near the house, claiming half of Mum's garden. The Nandi squatters felled trees and cleared the allocated land for a field and another area higher up where they could build their own huts and plant maize and vegetable gardens. Soon an African village was established, a field ploughed, and little pyrethrum seedlings planted in rows. While the plants grew into healthy bushes that produced masses of daisy-like flowers, Dad turned his attention to building a solar powered dryer from an old farm building, using rolls of heavy-duty black plastic to absorb the heat from the sun. He was a firm believer that we could harness natural energy from the sun, wind, and water currents to produce power, and back then, was well ahead of his time. He studied everything he could find in books and journals, and combined this with his knowledge and experience gathered from the environment. He experimented by constructing models to determine the most effective methods. The water wheel he made earlier in Eldoret had been another of his designs that had worked perfectly, supplying us and the farm with plentiful electricity day and

Twenty Miles to say Goodbye

night. On previous farms he had always enjoyed implemented new methods and engineering machinery to do various tasks more efficiently.

Finally the pyrethrum was ready to harvest. With babies on their backs, and children helping, the African women picked the thousands of white flowers, singing while they worked. The harvest was transported by donkey to the solar drying shed and the flowers spread out on trays to dry. Once dry, they were bagged and taken to Nakuru. Unfortunately pyrethrum fluctuated in price, and in roughly twenty years it hit rock bottom three times. This was mainly due to the introduction of chemical insecticides. Just after the war DDT was promoted, but years later this was proved to be harmful, so natural pyrethrum became more popular again. However other types of synthetic insecticide were produced, sending the prices plummeting again. Eventually the demand and prices evened out as it was discovered that even in chemically produced insecticide, pyrethrum provided the best base.

Our trips to Nakuru were planned around when another bag of 'pye' would be ready. Two sacks of dried pyrethrum flowers were loaded into the car with us, and there was a good chance we'd arrive with headaches. Muttering that we should have kept the windows open for the entire trip we thought no more about it. It eventually came to light that some of the Africans were unable to work with pyrethrum, or 'bransom' as they called it, as it caused respiratory problems. They'd named and known about this complaint long before Europeans discovered the side effects of dealing with large amounts of pyrethrum it in its powerful raw state.

One year the rains were late. We had long since passed the phase when you expect rain. It had let us down, time after time. The land grew dry, the air hot and empty, and the earth cracked and turned to dust. Without a supply of rainwater off the roof, our household water tank dried up quickly. Once a day our donkeys, Sue and Neddy, carted water up to the house in tin *debes* from a merciful stream at the bottom of the valley. Unable to flush the toilet, we used the long-drop outside. Occasionally we had a bath and shared our bathwater. Mum always had the first shallow bath, followed by the rest of us in turn, and whoever got the last dirtiest water, had the first bath after Mum next time!

Every evening the hornbills returned to roost in the spreading thorn trees at the bottom of the garden, and night after night we'd accompany Dad outside to gaze up into the starry sky, but there was no sign of rain. We'd breathe deep every morning, but there was no moisture in the air. Plants wilted and died, creatures were sluggish, and people became listless, edgy and irritable. Hopelessly we watched crops give up the ghost, and listened to the rustle of brittle leaves. Where there is life there is hope, but hope was dying all around. Dad and Mum were anxious and tense, the Africans sighed deep knowing sighs. Even the parched earth seemed to hold its breath. Every part of our being cried out for rain. The farm became suspended, immobile. One afternoon large banks of clouds appeared on the horizon, but they were not for us. Day after day the clouds formed again, only to float off elsewhere. Even diagonal streaks of rain slanted from distant clouds, tantalizing and teasing. Greyish clouds eventually drifted our way, but we continued to look up at a barren night sky, and wait.

Reading quietly in the lounge one evening, we heard a minute noise on the roof, then another. We looked up, our eyes locked. Could it be? Was it? There were a few more soft sounds, a slight pattering. We rushed outside, faces and arms held out to the sky. Tiny sweet rain spots kissed our skin, whispering promises of things to come. It was not much, but it was enough. Relief passed through us in tangible waves, and cheerful chatter skipped about. That night we went to bed with a lightness and new hope in our hearts again. Much later, the wind stirred and rain beat a smooth, steady rhythm on the roof. The dry spell had broken. The rains had come at last.

In the morning everyone, everything, was bursting with joy. The rains had come! *'Nvua na kudja!'* Smiles and sighs of relief flowed in abundance. Little children splashed in the puddles, the birdsong was brighter, a thousand new scents filled the air, and African chatter and laughter rippled through the valley. The farm picked up its rhythms, and a new cycle began.

One day, in a simple meal, I was given an insight into the intricacies of racial integration. I suddenly realized that it wasn't just a matter of accepting people of another colour or race, it was more about a meeting of the ways. One dominant race expecting another to adapt and fit in to its own culture could never be enough. An American consultant had been visiting the farm, and Dad invited him to stay and have lunch with us. The American said he'd like that and immediately called his African assistant to join us. At this point Dad suggested the assistant would probably prefer to have lunch with Mango in the kitchen. This was what normally happened in these situations, and everybody ate were they felt most comfortable. However the American, perhaps trying to show there was no room for any discrimination, insisted his assistant should dine inside with us. The poor assistant had obviously never been in a European house before, never mind eaten with *mzungu,* white people, and had no idea what to do. We hurriedly tried to spoon vegetables onto his plate for him, but he had already picked up a bowl of beetroot tipping the contents over his plate and everything else. Butter and the use of knives and forks presented more problems, and he dolloped huge portions of mayonnaise over his entire meal, which must have tasted awful. We tried to help him feel more at ease and drew him into the conversations, but really we were embarrassed for the unfortunate man, who, I am sure felt completely humiliated and out of place.

Us kids had always lived in short shorts and faded cotton shirts, spending our carefree days wandering freely around the farm and through the bush, but one day that changed for me. Dad had mentioned to Mum that while the men were working and chatting amongst themselves, he increasingly picked up suggestive comments about his daughter. So Mum duly had a word with me and told me to wear less revealing clothes and that it was no longer safe for me to wander far from the house or go into the bush alone. Until this, I had been very naïve and unconcerned about any effect my body might have on others, and now suddenly my freedom was being taken from me. I was furious! I just couldn't understand how the boys and men were OK but I was to be restricted and confined. Needless to say a huge argument with Mum followed and I stomped off out of the house. Smoldering with anger at the unfairness of it all, I marched towards the hills in defiance. My objective was to go as far away as I could. I would not be restrained, and they'd just have to accept it. I would show them!

Much later I climbed to the top of a hill, where I sat looking back over lesser hills to our distant house. The house and workshop looked tiny and I was so far away that I couldn't see any people or movement. I imagined that by now everyone would be really worried about me, and that they'd be rushing around frantically looking for me. Rolling over onto my tummy, I toyed with a stick, absently watching industrious insects scuttle about in the long grass. The wind whispered, and blew across the grasses, but soon it gathered strength, becoming increasingly insistent. Gusts of wind swirled dust and twigs about. Large dark grey clouds flocked across the sky, growling and grumbling. The world grew dark, and suddenly the heavens opened with flashing lightening and crashing thunder. The rain pelted down in torrents and the thunder and lightning were so loud and vivid that I grew anxious. Normally I loved a storm, but I suddenly realised how vulnerable I was out in the open, a lone target for lightening to strike. I peered through the sheets of rain, looking for shelter, but there was only one spindly tree nearby. Panicking, and fearful now, I became muddled and was unsure if I would be a better target for lightning strikes by the tree or where I was in the open. I could be hurt or killed out here and nobody would even know where I was. So, already drenched, I set off down the slippery slope for the long walk home. When I finally arrived back, everyone treated me like normal, and I was told to go and get dry if I wanted something to eat. No one had missed me. No one knew I'd even been gone. All my rebellion and frightening adventures had gone totally unnoticed!

However it all stood me in good stead, and several years later, Dad and I sat on a rock overlooking Schiehallion. I was 18 and shortly to leave Kenya to further my studies in the UK. Dad tried to explain that things would be different to how things were in Kenya. Here, if a European stopped to help it was usually because he simply wanted to lend a hand. In the wider world I'd probably find all sorts of people may try to take advantage of me. I was very trusting and would have to be much more cautious in the UK. It wasn't until later experiences overseas that I fully understood the meaning of our conversation.

We pondered the difference between being alone and being lonely, before drifting off into our own thoughts as we enjoyed the solitude of the morning together. From out of the blue, we picked up the clear floating calls of Nandi tribesmen relaying a message through the hills. The message is always brief – maybe someone's son has returned, cattle have been stolen, or there's been a death. Scant words are pulled together, and stretched into a cry that echoes sweetly across the land, until it is picked up by someone else far away who relays it further into the hills to another, and another, until eventually the message is delivered to its intended destination. To those of the tribe, the simple message arrives intact and promptly, but to us it is indecipherable, abstract, and timeless. You are never sure when a call begins, but once you have become aware of it, you drift and flow with it until the calls fade and taper off into the distance. Although it is a message, it seems wordless, an extended silver note that plays with the bird song and the earth's sighs, as clear and as pure as the air it travels through.

While I was overseas, Mum and Dad had to move again. The farm was struggling and there was not enough money coming in to pay the workers and cover expenses. Dogged by random obstacles – too much rain, too little rain, thrips in the pyrethrum, or plummeting prices, Dad acknowledged he'd have to work elsewhere if he wanted to keep the farm. He found a challenging job with an international Sugar Company down in Chemelil, where they lived in a residential compound and Dad worked for a couple of years until he was offered a more suitable job managing Maraba.

8. The Coast and Zanzibar

Tea companies operating at high altitude stipulated their employees spend at least ten days of their annual holiday at sea level. We all looked forward to our holiday at the coast, which was taken during the quietest season on the farm. Up before day break, we'd travel the seven hour journey to Nairobi by car, and all going well would manage to catch the 6pm train leaving for Mombasa. There was a wonderful air of excitement at the station. The platform was crowded with a seething mass of humanity, a crazy kaleidoscope of shifting colours, smells and sounds. Chaotic calls bounced around in so many languages you couldn't actually understand a word. Groups chatted gaily, while others rushed around with luggage, loading it into carriages through windows and doors. Porters and passengers balanced great loads on their heads. Crates, boxes, and bundles wrapped in cloth, hands of green bananas, and chickens squawking in baskets, all found their way onto the train.

The train lurched, and hissed. A sudden silence, then everyone rushed forward, making more noise than ever. People scrambled to climb aboard, stopped for last minute hugs or to shout final messages. The train hissed again, shunted back and forward a couple of times, then waited. At last the whistle blew, shrill, sharp and final. We lurched forward and the train pulled out of Nairobi Station. The steam engine began its journey to the coast, dragging behind it a long snake of carriages.

At last our real safari was underway. The train gathered speed, steam trailing out from the engine as the tracks rattled beneath us in a steady comforting rhythm. We crowded round our cabin window to watch the world rush by as we flew through industrial estates, factories, and shanty towns with shacks of mud, tin and cardboard. Gradually the outskirts of the city gave way to dried grassland with stunted thorn trees and rocky outcrops, and we were soon spotting grazing herds of buck and zebra. Our eyes stung from staring into the gloom as the darkness gathered and we searched hopefully for a lion or elephant. Orange and gold splashed across the sky, and moments later the sun set quickly, as it does on the equator. Pitch black outside, we pulled the shutters down and turned to eat our sandwiches, while we squabbled about who would sleep in the top bunks.

Outside in the corridors, a gong chimed enticingly, calling passengers to the dining car for dinner. Friendly stewards brought our bedding in rolls and we tried to help them set the bunks up and prepare the beds. We lifted the semi-circle table by the cabin window to discover a wash basin with a tap. We brushed our teeth and climbed into our bunks. We were allowed to read on our own while Mum and Dad went to have a drink in the dining car. After they returned we switched off our lights and snuggled down between stiff cotton sheets. We lay listening to the rhythm of the train on the tracks and an occasional whistle, before drifting contentedly to sleep, while the train sped south through the night. From time to time we'd become aware of the train slowing, or stopping at mysterious little stations in the middle of nowhere. In a sleepy haze we'd hear voices and doors slamming, and then the train hissed and heaved forward and onward again.

As soon as it was light, we crept to the end of our bunks and peeped out the window at a changed world outside. The scenery was different. The earth was dry and reddish, and large towers of termite mounds climbed out of the tawny grass. Huge curiously shaped barrel trees with sprawling branches and no leaves were dotted about. Dad told us these were the ancient baobab trees, and travelers and hunters collected fruit and water from their large trunks during the hot dry seasons. He added that the Africans told tales that the baobab tree got too full of itself because it was so beautiful, and Mungu (God) grew angry at this foolish pride, so he pulled up these great trees and stuck them back in the ground upside down. It certainly looked like it!

Soon we were up and dressed. The boys in khaki shorts and open neck shirts, and Mum and I in pretty sundresses and sandals, as the air was now much warmer. The bunks folded away, we gazed out the open window, or stood outside our cabin in the corridor, balancing as we swayed to the motion of the train as it hurtled along. We chugged past clusters of huts with thatched roofs, and friendly children waved and called out. There were more and more trees now, and the villages were surrounded by huge spreading mango trees, tall pawpaw trees and the odd coconut palms. The wind in our faces was hot and salty. We must be near the coast. We could smell the sea. Who would be the first to see it?

The closer we got to the coast, the more we noticed the way the Africans dressed. Most wore kikois or kitenges, rectangles of cloth in bright patterns and stripes wrapped simply around their middles. Women carried large *debes* or buckets of water on their heads, others dug in their vegetable patches and maize *shambas*, while old men sat chatting in the shade of sprawling fig trees. Little markets were scattered about with fruit stalls displaying pyramids of green skinned oranges, pawpaw, mangoes and coconuts. Suddenly there was a startling glimpse of the sea, brilliant, blue, and inviting. Then it was gone, lost amongst the tropical trees as the train rattled on.

Mombasa Station was hot and humid, bustling with colour and noise. Like young warthogs, we followed our parents through the teeming crowds. We were

Twenty Miles to say Goodbye

surrounded by people of every shade, wearing bright clothes and uttering strange words. Muslim women, draped in black burkqas, strolled past mysteriously. Young dark haired girls, red dots on their foreheads and rings in their noses, giggled and chatted together in gay saris. Giriama men, and bare breasted women, with kitenges tied round their waists, sat and gossiped in the shadows of a huge spreading tree. Old men spat crimson splotches of betel nut juice onto the ground, others loitered, while slim bare topped porters bantered as they hurried by with heavy sacks on their heads. Vendors sold bananas, samosas, and young green coconuts. They scalped the tops off the coconuts in one swipe with a sharp *panga*, before passing them to customers to drink the cool white milk. Longing for something to drink ourselves, we had to mill about, hot and sticky in the blistering sun, searching for a taxi. Eventually we located a rusty old zephyr, with rips in the back seat and tinsel and plastic flowers hanging from the rear view mirror. Dad bartered with Sayid, the smiling sweaty taxi driver, until an agreement was reached, and we all piled in. With windows wide open, we hurtled through the busy Mombasa streets, honking loudly and swerving to avoid jay walkers and bicyclists along the way. We pulled up beside a street stall and bought large baskets of mangoes and oranges, papaws, pineapples, tomatoes, potatoes, and a huge bunch of green bananas. Then we drove across the causeway, and from high above the inviting water, we viewed the proud ruins of Fort Jesus, the ancient 16th Century Portuguese fortress that had protected Mombasa from invaders for hundreds of years. Clear of the town now, a white dust rose behind us as we rattled along the coast road, past little villages nestled amongst coconut plantations. Sayid swung onto a bumpy track that led towards the ocean, and, after several minutes of shuddering jolts, we arrived at a coral cottage with a thatched roof of palm fronds. Kicking our shoes off, we raced across the wide white sandy beach, hurling ourselves into the clear water. Heaven!

The banda was basic, with shutters that allowed the cool breeze to flow through the house. There was a front veranda and an outside kitchen, which was adequate as we lived simply, on fish and fruit. After siestas through the hot afternoons, we'd enjoy a thick slice of Mum's fruit cake and tea with tinned milk, before a family swim as the tide rolled in. At night, we lay without covers and cocooned beneath mosquito nets. We watched geckoes and long black millipedes scale the plaster walls, serenaded by the distant boom of the surf crashing eternally onto the reef.

Our biggest treat was when Mum handed each of us a mango, and we'd sprint off across the scorching sands, throwing ourselves gleefully into the translucent shallows. Can you just imagine a child's pure delight, sucking juicy orange mangoes in a warm turquoise sea?

The days were long and lazy. Mum and Dad said the humidity relaxed them and they spent hours reading on the veranda or strolling along the deserted beach. Meanwhile we'd explore the rocky coves, sandy bays, and splash in the calm waters when the tide was out. The sun beat down mercilessly, and we always had to wear hats and shirts to protect us from its fierce rays. Sandshoes or *tackies* were also essential to avoid cutting our feet on sharp jagged corals, or treading on urchin spines, or squelchy sea slugs.

There were so many strange creatures to discover; prickly sea urchins, crabs, jelly fish, sea slugs, red starfish with zippers, and a myriad of fish and shells. Always, in the distance, perhaps a mile away, was the constant boom of huge ocean waves breaking on the coral reef in a permanent line of white breakers. Beyond was the wide dark blue of the real Indian Ocean, stretching out to the horizon. Inside the reef the waters were a translucent turquoise, chequered with patches of darker greens and blues. When the tides were right, Dad arranged for a Swahili man to take us out to the reef in his dugout canoe. His canoe had been hollowed out of a single tree trunk, and was propelled and steered by a long pole. We were warned to avoid large clams, which could close quickly, clamping over your leg or arm, holding you tight. Unable to prize the clam shell open to free yourself, you would be trapped by the rising waters of the incoming tide, and drown. Time ceased to exist as we snorkeled in the large deep pools on the reef. It was like floating in a beautiful garden of coloured corals, where butterfly and sunfish darted amongst endless exotic tropical fish, and amazing, unimaginable sea creatures curled and wriggled between branches of coral. Always was the added excitement, or fear, of seeing a shark or large octopus. We kids, oblivious to the incoming tidal waters sweeping across the corals, were disappointed when we had to clamber back into the dugout to return to the beach before the deeper waters submerged the reef. As the dugout glided over the clear waters, we investigated star fish, sea snakes, and small octopus that shot inky blue clouds at us when we disturbed them. We arrived back at the banda with a haul of cowrie and leopard shells, and small delicate branches of pastel coral that soon faded into a dull dirty white.

Once local fishermen knew there was a family staying in the bay, they would guide their dugouts, through the shallow waters, beach their boats, and approach us with baskets filled with their catch. The fish were always large and of varied shapes and colours. They were so fresh, the scales were shiny and the fish eyes still bright and shining. Further out, beyond the reef, occasional Arab dhows, with triangular sails, silently slipped up and down the coast, carrying exotic cargoes of ivory, chests, carpets, copper ware, and spices.

Mum and Dad on holiday had so much more time to do things with us and we really enjoyed their company. When the tide was in they swam and played with us in the warm waves, or we enjoyed ball games on the sands, playing skittles with coconuts, or taking leisurely evening walks along the deserted beach. As we approached, little creatures disappeared swiftly into holes. Hundreds of small crabs scrambled sideways towards the water in search of morsels deposited by the last wave. Suddenly they'd all change direction as one, and, microseconds before the next wave broke, they'd scamper sideways up the sand, just ahead of the racing water, only to return to search again as soon as the wave receded.

A cool evening breeze stirred as we ate our fish supper on the veranda, watching the stars sprinkle the sky. Sometimes a fat full moon slipped above the horizon, sending magical moonbeams dancing over the dark waves like a giant's torch.

In later years, when we lived at Makuyu, instead of taking the overnight train, we travelled down to the coast by road, leaving home long before dawn. When the sun rose, large, red and round, we'd join Dad reciting a verse or two of the Rubaiyat of Omar Khayyam.

"And lo the might hunter of the east has caught the sultan's turret in a noose of light, and flung the stone that put the stars to flight"

This was usually followed by an enthusiastic rendition of the old KAR song, *'funga safari'*, and the rest of our repertoire of folk and sing-along songs. We had a welcome pit stop for a picnic breakfast and cups of safari tea with tinned milk, before continuing our long dusty safari south. As the day wore on, we became hot, thirsty, and quieter, as the fine white powder dust settled on every surface. Weary of looking for wildlife, we silently absorbed the straight dirt road ahead. Mteto Andei appeared like an oasis in the desert, and we revived ourselves with sandwiches and cold bottles of coke under umbrellas around a pool for a half an hour before clambering back in the car. The next excitement came mid-afternoon, as we pulled into a petrol station in Voi, where an Indian lady at the duka made the most glorious granadilla - passion fruit juice. The delicious fresh golden juice slipped down our dry dusty throats like honeyed nectar. We managed to clear the duka out of their entire daily supply as they filled and corked several assorted bottles for us to take with us. Nectar to go!

Once we'd arrived in the tropical coastal belt, we drove between the plantations of coconut palms until we reached Mtwapa Creek. The ferry here was little more than a raft, which we carefully drove the car down onto, and then three or four operators on each side of the raft took up a song and began hauling at the ropes to pull us across the creek. The song became louder as they stamped their feet on the wooden deck in rhythm, pulling in time to their beat. As each man stomped his way hauling on the rope, to the front of the raft, he'd pick up a conch shell and blow a few blasts of the horn, and then dance to the back, picking up the rope to resume pulling. Nobody ever missed a beat and the entire crossing was superbly synchronized. Every so often the chorus stopped and one of the men would pick up the tune, making up the lyrics on the spur of the moment. It was usually about one of the passengers. I didn't understand what they were singing about but Dad always knew and laughed along with them. The singers enjoyed it immensely and there were shouts of laughter before they took up the chorus again. We would have happily gone back and forth across the creek all day! Baksheesh were given to everyone and we all waved goodbye as we chugged up the slope on the other side.

At the end of our wonderful holidays at the coast, we had one more treat in store. We liked to drive back through Tsavo Game Park. One year we spent the night at Amboseli by a windy damn where the elephant, lion, zebra and buck came to drink. However we preferred to cross over the main Mombasa Nairobi road, into Tsavo West, where we spent a couple of nights at Kitani, in self-catering 'rondavel' huts near Mzima Springs. From our beds we could hear the strange loud rumblings of elephant stomachs as they cavorted in the rock pools surrounding our cabins. Up at dawn, we drove around the area looking for game before returning to breakfast on the veranda. We idly passed the hot midday hours watching little ground squirrels scampering about amongst iridescent glossy starlings, serenaded by the constant twittering from weaver bird communes in the thorn trees. In the background beautiful snowcapped Mt Kilimanjaro serenely stole the show. Later we drove along the river, and sat beneath doum palms, warding off curious monkeys and fast footed ticks, as we watched hippo laze and grunt through the hot afternoon. The beautiful Mzima Springs lured us to its crystal clear waters. A window had been constructed in the banks of the pool so you could gaze into the translucent water at silver tilapia fish, and the occasional hippo below the surface. Underwater, these huge ungainly beasts took on the streamlined movements of greyhounds drifting past in slow motion.

Towards evening we clambered back in the car and drove further afield 'game spotting'. We all enjoyed the plentiful herds of zebra, gazelle, gnu, giraffe, and monkeys, and the odd lion or gerenuk. The gerenuk was a buck, more common in the drier areas of the Northern Frontier District. These deer balanced on their hind legs while grazing at thorn bushes, enjoying a supply of leaves that were above the level of most grazers. Mum loved the majestic water buck. However, our favourite had to be the elephants. We were always lucky finding small herds of elephant and had some wonderful close encounters with these huge, gentle creatures. We came upon a young bull standing guard on the dusty road. We edged forward hoping he'd wander off into the long grass, but instead he flapped his ears and trumpeted as he pawed the ground before charging. Dad quickly slipped into reverse and we beat a hasty retreat as he chased us away from his domain. Elephant were usually accepting of our presence, as long as we kept our distance and didn't threaten them in any way. We were happy to watch these enormous fascinating mammals as they grazed or bathed, or simply basked in the shade lazily throwing clouds of dust over themselves or their young.

***

I had asked Dad about his sister, Pix, my favourite aunt, who now lived in The Isle of Man. Dad replied, "She's keeping well and is very happy in her wee cottage by the sea. It's a far cry from the life she lived out here, but she's had an interesting innings and is content to take it easy now."

Keen to hear more about Aunt Pix's life in Kenya, I pressed Dad until he succumbed.

"In the early days, when George had taken possession of his one thousand acres of 'soldier settlement' land, it was uninhabited bush, and no local tribes lived in this area due to ongoing conflict with neighbouring tribes. It transpired the British Government originally put this land up for European settlement in order to keep the warring Nandi, Luo, and Kipsigis tribes apart.

When Pix married George and came out here as his bride, they lived in grass huts and worked hard to establish an income. By a long process of trial and error, George learnt that his land was not overly productive due to the climate, soil conditions, and limited water supplies. Most crops did not do well in the area. The exception to this was sugar cane, which thrived here, but there was no outlet for it. Cane seeds had initially been transported from Queensland by one of the Mayers boys from Australia, who later planted the first tea in Kenya. However, over the years, George built up a decent herd of indigenous cattle which provided milk, butter, and cream. European breeds tended to be susceptible to disease, while the native cattle were hardy and adapted to the conditions although the milk yields were lower. George and Pix planted an orchard, which eventually produced a large variety of fruit, including pawpaw, oranges, bananas, mangoes, avocado, tangerines, lemons and guavas.

Pix and George had twins, Struan and Norna, born in 1928, and followed a few years later by Elizabeth. The twins went to boarding school in Nakuru and later to segregated secondary schools in Nairobi. On special Sundays parents were allowed to visit their children at Nakuru Primary. Living over a hundred miles away and working on a farm, George and Pix weren't often able to make it, but they did occasionally manage to see the twins. By filling the car up with fresh fruit from the farm and selling it to Indian shops along the way, they were able to get money for their petrol!

Eventually a proper house was built, and leopard skin mats dotted the wooden floors. Norna became Head of School at the Kenya Girls High in Nairobi, but Struan left school as quickly as possible. He loved the outdoor life and took an interest in mechanics and, at 17, he volunteered to join the Kenya Regiment, where he was able to study and further develop his engineering skills. Towards the end of 1947 Struan was summoned home to assist his father on the farm. The farming situation was still difficult due to post war austerity, and basic materials and spare parts were hard to come by, but Struan was able to help considerably by using his technical maintenance skills to improvise.

The farm workers had been erecting a dry stone wall alongside the long road up to the house when George died. As a mark of respect, his workforce continued to build this wall, bringing to it the biggest, heaviest stones they could find. Struan took over the running of the farm, with Pix as an able assistant. They continued to send fruit and dairy produce up to Nairobi by train, and Pix would be up at

1am to prepare the butter for its early morning delivery to the station in time to catch the 4.30 am train. She baked dog biscuits which she sold by the sack, and also made 'doggy dawa', a sticky combination of cod liver oil and malt, which all you children devoured greedily.

Struan married and his ambitious young wife was determined to quickly move into the main house as its mistress. Pix felt it was time to think about an alternate life and purchased an acre on the slopes of Menengai Crater, overlooking Nakuru. However medical problems also contributed to Pix leaving Kwisos, as she had been advised to live at higher altitudes. Unable to turn her head and in order to get around, Pix was now obliged to employ a full time driver.

Meanwhile Struan did a great job on Kwisos and substantially increased the water supply to the farm by divining for water and digging a borehole. Recognising that sugar cane was really the only crop that thrived in this area, Struan specialised in cane seed. In the early 1960s an international company, Chemelil Sugar, began buying up land in the valley in order to establish large sugarcane plantations, and build a factory. Struan sold Kwisos to them for a good price and took his young family down to Natal, where they lived for a year or two before moving permanently to Kent, in England. Things went badly for Struan in England, and his wife left him taking their three children with her. After a very difficult period, Struan met Tricia, and they spent his last years happily together."

"I'm glad Struan found someone special in the end. He was a good sort, a kind gentle soul. The last time I saw him, we passed away a couple of hours companionably with only the occasional conversation as he played his guitar."

We were thoughtful for a while, until I added, "But I remember Aunt Pix's wee place in Nakuru, and I loved going to visit her, and riding her horse, Gypsy. Do you remember when she built the little cottage, comprising of two round huts connected by a small rectangular passageway that became a dining room? How when the roof was thatched, the walls plastered, and the floor concreted, it was suddenly a delightful little home full of music, laughter, and discussion. The view from the cottage was expansive and beautiful. Looking out over the tawny grasses, your eyes settled on the pale blue satin sheen of Lake Nakuru, fringed delicately in pinks spun by the movement of hundreds and thousands of flamingo."

"It was an idyllic little place" agreed Dad, "and we had some great times there. But eventually Pix made the decision to move to the UK to be closer to Norna and Struan, who had both settled in England, so she bought the cottage in Laxey in the Isle of Man. Did you know that before leaving Kenya, Pix bought some land for her driver? She wanted to make sure he'd be alright after she'd left, and thought a little land for him to retire on was a nice way to thank him."

"No, I didn't know that Dad, but it's the sort of thing she'd do. She's a pretty special person."

Dad paused and smiled. No doubt fond memories swirled round him. Then he was talking about the township of Nakuru.

"Interesting changes evolved in Nakuru, which is a Maasai name, meaning 'the place of swirling dust'. Prior to the 1950s it was common to see great clouds of dust billowing up from over 60 miles away. Two proposed secondary schools were initially abandoned as it was considered such an unhealthy area due to the constant dust created by the wind on the dry lake bed. At one time your Uncle Jim and I, and probably all the young men of Nakuru, used to race our cars around the great soda flats at weekends. I think Mum's got a photo somewhere. However, now, on this exact site, is the renowned Lake Nakuru Bird Sanctuary. The rains came in the mid nineteen fifties, the lake filled up and vast numbers of flamingo and pelicans arrived. In 1960 Sir Peter Scott officially opened the bird sanctuary. Hippo settled in nearby fresh water streams and water buck and buffalo moved into the area permanently. In 1976 giraffe, zebra, impala, rhino and warthogs were transported into the park and a chain wire fence was erected around it. However, within 10 years the herbivores had multiplied so prolifically that lion and leopard were brought in to keep the balance, and an electric fence was added to the existing barricade. Lodges and restaurants have been established as Lake Nakuru Sanctuary became increasingly popular with birdwatchers and tourists from all over the world."

There was a sudden shout as Kipsang appeared and Dad was called away to the coffee factory, where there was a problem with a leaking pipe. Bringing her sewing, Mum sat down beside me, as I watched Sirri splashing in a basin of water.

"Wasn't Aunt Pix over in Zanzibar during the Revolution?" I asked.

"Yes," Mum replied, "That was quite a while before she went to England. She was over in Zanzibar staying with Norna when the coup occurred."

"What happened exactly?"

"I'm not too sure about the actual events now, but I think I had notes about it in the box. I'll go and have a look."

As I waited for her to return, I recalled a holiday we had taken in Zanzibar in 1962.

We'd travelling down to Mombasa by train, and boarded an overnight ship to Zanzibar Island, one hundred and forty miles into the Indian Ocean. In the cool of the evening we sat around on deck listening to Arab sailors yarning about their days at sea. One told a chilling tale of an upturned yacht they had come upon. It was drifting in calm waters, and a lone shark lazily circled the capsized boat. There was no other sign of life, only an eerie silence, and a little girl's red shoe drifting on the swell.

Mum and I leant over the salt crusted rails at dawn, gazing at a pearly sky. We caught a hint of spice in the air. Tantalizing, beguiling, scents of cloves wafted in the gentle sea breezes, promising us of something new and exotic. Land was still out of sight, the odd seagull floated above, and the delightful fragrances played in the wind.

Zanzibar was all it promised to be. The harbour and Stone Town teemed with life, as traders and hawkers shouted and beckoned, while young men heaved sacks from donkey carts. Women in burqas passed by like shadows, revealing only their dark eyes, and toes that peeped from sandals. Arab men, dressed in *jelebas* and embroidered skullcaps, strolled past chatting together.

The bazaar was surrounded by ancient, cracked buildings with hefty wooden carved doors, decorated with solid brass studs. Narrow dusty alleyways lead to tiny intriguing shops. Little curio stores with carved ivory, miniature dhows, and carpets, competed with tables stacked with shoes, and vibrant fabric stalls displaying silks, brocades and saris. Beautiful melodious chants floated above as Muezzins called the faithful to prayer from delicate mosques and minarets. Pavement cooks squatted over small braziers preparing food, and pungent smells sizzled in the sultry air. Spices, and garlic aromas wafted through the souk, mingling with the stink of fish, ripe fruit, and incense. Sidewalk coffee sellers called out enticingly, pouring their thick bitter sweet coffee from Aladdin copper kettles into tiny china cups.

Norna and Aubrey's house was in a quieter area, nestled amongst shady trees. We played with our cousins on beautiful palm fringed beaches and swam in tropical seas. Norna took us for a drive through the coconut plantations to visit an artist, Aileen Belcher, who was making small clay pots on a wheel. Norna filled Aileen's little pots with lime, clove, and vanilla plants to sell to the tourists visiting Zanzibar on ocean liners.

The cloves grown on the islands were exported overseas, as well as being used in combinations with other local plants, as a base for lime juice, perfumes, and soap. One afternoon we toured a copra factory which harvested the dried husks of coconuts for manufacture. The owner, a sheik, had invited us to tea. In the courtyard, a long table was laid out with tempting spicy treats and startling canary yellow sponge cakes. We sat down to afternoon tea with the Sheik and his sons, drinking endless cups of sweet spiced chai, as silhouettes of coconut palms swayed against a citrine sky.

Aubrey was Superintendent of Police, and Head of the Police Training School. He took Hugh with him one morning, when he popped in to the Police Barracks. Hugh was told to wait in the entrance hall, and watched a policeman labouring over the disassembled pieces of a sterling sub-machine gun spread out on a table. Intrigued, Hugh wandered over and asked to help. Within minutes, he had the gun back in one piece while the policeman watched in astonishment. Smiling, Hugh explained that he had learnt to assemble Bren guns and Lea Enfield 303s as part of his Combined School Cadet Core training.

Mum had returned during my reveries and was glancing through her notes. She paused for a moment, looking out across the garden, before describing the events of the Zanzibar Revolution to me;

"The revolution erupted violently in January 1964, only one month after Zanzibar's independence from Britain. Approximately 700 African revolutionaries attacked the two police barracks, broke into the armouries and appropriated the machine guns, rifles and revolvers. Now that they were the most heavily armed force on the island, they quickly took control of the local radio station and telegraph communications department. The insurgents proceeded to Stone Town to depose the Sultan Jamshid bin Abdullah and his government, as well as taking over other strategic buildings and the only airstrip on the Island. Reprisals against the Sultan's guards, and Asian civilians followed and thousands of Arabs were massacred. Hundreds were herded into the bay where they were machine gunned or hacked to death.

The Coup d'etat ended 200 years of Arab dominance in Zanzibar, and resulted in changing the island's social structure since British and Indian residents fled from the archipelago, and so many Arabs were killed. A dubious interim government took over under a local opportunist, and many years of tumult followed. The Sultan, who escaped with his life, was banished and took exile in England.

At the time Aubrey and Norna's children were away at boarding school in Nairobi. Aubrey, Norna, and Pix had spent the Sunday morning on the beach, and were unaware of the uprising. As they turned into their driveway they were met by three policemen waiting in a Land-Rover. Aubrey was quickly told of the troubles and informed that the two police stations had been attacked. Norna and Pix scrambled out of the car and Aubrey sped off with the Land-Rover following. Entering his office, Aubrey glimpsed one of his students, a police trainee who had been a star pupil and a favourite of his. Suddenly this student rushed at him with an axe. Aubrey had to shoot him at point blank range in self-defense. It was a traumatic moment, and one that changed Aubrey's life forever.

A government representative appointed four houses for citizens to gather in. One of these houses was Norna's and she had thirty people staying there. The men slipped out in twos and threes under cover of darkness to collect food from their various homes. Aubrey's car was sighted once. The boot had been ripped open and two thugs with machine guns squatted in the boot, as it hurtled past.

Meanwhile a small group of police, reserves, and local whites, did what they could to keep the rebels away with a few long range rifles. Eventually the police commandeered a launch in the harbour and managed to transfer a contingent of dignitaries onto the launch and out to a government ship, the Salama. On seeing that they did not return with the launch for others, local, Bill Belcher, swam out to another launch with an African volunteer. They managed to start the boat and transported the remaining people on the dockside out to the Salama. The Sultan had been escorted to the safety of the ship earlier and Belcher now transferred him, and his retinue, to the royal yacht, Seyyid Khalif, waiting in deep water. Belcher then returned to rescue the remaining police still holding fort in the police station.

An American navy destroyer in the area, arrived to rescue American citizens on the Monday. However the US had not sought the Revolutionary Council's permission for the evacuation and the ship was guarded by an armed gang while docked in the harbour. After two days, permission was granted, and American citizens were taken to safety. The British considered this incident to be the cause of much of the ill will and subsequent confrontations between Zanzibar and the Western powers. Britain took longer rescuing their citizens because they believed that the presence of government personnel on the island might help to stabilise the volatile situation. It is questionable how many government personnel were actually still on the island.

It wasn't until Tuesday that Norna heard, over the radio, that three Police Superintendents had got the Sultan and his family to safety. Several government ministers, along with their families, were rescued with them, all escaping on the Royal Yacht 'Seyyid Khalifa'. The yacht sailed to the nearest port, Dar es Salaam in Tanzania, but President Nyere refused sanctuary, so the Seyyid Khalifa sailed north up the coast towards Mombasa. It was again was refused entry, this time by Kenya's President Kenyatta. The yacht headed out to sea but Nyere suddenly changed his mind and it was now granted permission to dock in Dar es Salaam.

On the Thursday, Norna and Pix were informed that a British frigate, the HMS Rhyl was approaching Zanzibar to evacuate British citizens. Mothers and children were taken below the decks, and Norna and Pix remained up on deck with other adult evacuees."

We heard voices out the back, and Mango approached to tell Mum that there was someone waiting to have a wound bandaged. As she got up to go, Mum added, "During the rebellion, Dad and I were extremely anxious about Pix, Norna and Aubrey out there on the island." Passing me the pages, she said, "Here, you read the rest."

"We heard of the coup in Zanzibar, the Sultan's escape, and scant details of the unrest and evolving situation filtered through on the radio. We drove into Nairobi and spoke to the Headmaster at Nairobi Primary and explained who we were. We thought it would comfort Norna and Aubrey's children to see someone from the family and to know that their parents were safe. Once she knew that her parents were OK, Morag's thoughts went to their pets. We told her that the monkey would be alright as he'd escape quickly into the trees, and that the cat would be fine because there would be so many mice to eat.

The British Army were preparing a camp at Nyali Beach to receive evacuees, but then on the Friday the HMS Rhyl disappeared. We were concerned as to what had happened to Norna and Pix. On Saturday there was still no news broadcast about the ship's whereabouts. Jim came in from work. "Sorry I'm late, I've been trying to phone the British High Commission all morning". Just then our 'party line" started ringing. I swayed towards the phone, then knew that it was not our call. Jim said, "Are you on tenterhooks too? Why don't we just pack a bag and go down to the coast. I'll let the boss know". We stopped only once, for fuel. Late that night we arrived in Mombasa and managed to phone the army who told us that the evacuees had arrived safely and had been given a meal and were now sleeping. Those rescued were beginning breakfast the next morning when we arrived at Nyali hotel. Jim went straight over to Aunt Pix, and I towards Norna. I will never forget her face – a look of sheer surprise, joy, and utter relief. We hugged each other and she was so grateful to have someone who cared there. Soon after, Norna was summoned to the phone by a soldier. It was Aubrey making contact from the yacht, the Seyyid Khalifa, now in Dar es Salaam. It was great to know everyone was alright. Jim and I had to get straight back to the farm as it was a busy time. We thought Pix and Norna would want to come with us, but they preferred to stay and wait until they were reunited with Aubrey, and agreed to come up by train later. So by lunchtime we were driving north again.

Apparently the arrival of the HMS Rhyl in Mombasa had been delayed as the captain had taken the ship further out to sea because bad squalls and rain storms were forecast along the coast, and he was considering the many people up on deck with no protection.

For a few days, Aubrey and fellow officers were heroes but then the British Government recognised it had been a coup d'etat and due to several international issues and confusions, the policemen were suddenly dismissed. Pix and Norna arrived at Punda Milia a week later, and were soon joined by Aubrey, who had a week with us before he was summoned to London.

Aubrey, Norna, and the children moved to England, and settled at 'Kitani' in Haywards Heath. Aubrey commuted daily to London where he worked with Barclays Bank until his retirement."

9. A bullet in the heart

Later that same afternoon, I asked Mum to tell us about Granddad. Granddad's story about the 'bullet in his heart' had sounded exciting when we were children, but now I wanted to know more, and I knew Lee would find it interesting.

"Well, my father, Arthur Chapman was a budding photographer with his own box brownie camera, and he enjoyed riding around on his bicycle taking photos. He was nineteen at the beginning of the First World War in 1914, and like all the young men of his time, he immediately volunteered to serve his country. He initially enrolled in the Battersea Labour Corp, and became a Lance Corporal in the London Cycle Brigade, but was quickly assigned to the Queens Royal Rifles and sent to France to fight on the front, in the trenches of Ypres.

It was a living hell. The soldiers, constantly drenched and freezing cold, endured endless months in open trenches, amongst the sickening stench of death, blood, and excrement. The deafening din of gun fire and exploding bombs was splattered with the cries and moans of the wounded and the dying. Bewildered and shell shocked, the men waited for orders to shoot and kill, or were shot at and killed. The troops suffered the discomfort and monotony of long, cold, lonely nights in the trenches, unable to sleep, in the eerie harrowing silence while they waited, and waited. Images of bloody scenes, severed limbs, and bodies flung into oblivion flashed through tired minds. Cries for help and last words uttered by young mates echoed round and round. Thoughts on the insanity of war, its futility and degradations, and loved ones far away, were hurriedly pushed aside as dawn split the sky and volleys of gunfire split the air. Another day of hell had begun.

Arthur was shot and wounded in his chest and right hand. Semi-conscious, he was transported back to England and taken to a military hospital in Brighton, for treatment. His hand healed but his chest didn't. In those days, there was no sympathy for soldiers who were shell shocked or psychologically damaged in anyway by the horror, trauma and deprivation they had experienced fighting on the front. Wounded soldiers were treated in hospitals and as soon as their wounds healed they were quickly returned to the front lines. Those who were slow to heal were automatically under suspicion, as it was assumed they were putting off their recovery to avoid going back to fight for their country. Soldiers who were expected to have recovered, but hadn't, were charged with 'malingering'. The punishment for malingering was execution by firing squad. Arthur's chest still caused him a great deal of pain and there had been no improvement. He was due to be court marshalled for malingering. After all he had experienced on the front, he now had to suffer the injustice, the stigma, and the utter hopelessness under the pending Court Marshal for malingering. My father was an agnostic all his life, but what happened next he always referred to as 'my personal miracle'. A new colonel was transferred to the hospital. He was a surgeon, specializing in chest and respiratory problems, and brought with him a radical piece of equipment – a portable x-ray machine. An x-ray of Arthur's chest revealed a 303 bullet lodged in his heart. He was told that the bullet's position in his heart meant it would be too dangerous to operate - even a tiny shift could be fatal. Arthur was warned that any sudden movement, perhaps a coughing fit, a trip, a laugh, or sneeze, could dislodge the bullet causing instant death.

After living under the fear of an impending execution, Arthur Chapman now received an honourable discharge from the army on the 15th April 1917.

After his 'miracle' and further discussions with the surgeon, Arthur became determined to train as a radiographer. His love of photography helped his understanding of the x-ray process and he gained experience working at both the Royal Free and Great Ormond Street Hospitals in London.

Over 50 years later a bill was passed to pardon all those unfortunate soldiers who faced the firing squad during the 1914 -18 War. Far too late, but perhaps bringing a smidgen of dignity back to their poor families.

Meanwhile Arthur met a young nursing auxiliary in a military hospital. She was Sue Baynham, a lively girl from Birmingham. With laughter in her eyes and gypsy in her blood, she stole Arthur's heart. Arthur and Sue married in March 1918, and I was born in March 1920. The necessary six years of radiology study were not easy for Arthur with a wife and daughter to support. However he worked at the hospital during the day and spent his evenings studying for various medical diplomas. Arthur and Sue had two more children, both sons. My brother Jim was born in 1926, followed ten years later by Teddy.

In early 1939 Arthur replied to an advertisement and secured a job as a radiographer in South Africa. He was to be employed by a diamond mining company in Johannesburg. This necessitated leaving his family in England, finding the fare, and several weeks of travel by ship from England to South Africa. On his arrival in Johannesburg, Arthur was shocked to discover that he was not required to x-ray patients for medical reasons, but to x-ray the black miners coming off their shifts, in case they had tried to smuggle any diamonds out the mine by swallowing them. He was incensed that radiology was being used for non-medical purposes, and was staggered by the blatant discrimination towards the black indigenous people, while the white miners, 'some the scum of the earth' in his opinion, were exempt from these x-ray searches. Arthur resigned and left within a week and for the rest of his life he would never differentiate between black and white.

However, South Africa then practiced a system of segregation and discrimination on the grounds of colour, and the black majority were treated as inferior beings. The 'blacks' were constantly humiliated and deprived of basic human rights and freedoms, and it was only marginally better for the smaller populations of Indians and people of mixed race, known locally as 'coloureds'. White supremacy was dominant in all areas of life and 'blacks' were only permitted to live in certain areas, had to carry passes, were given the most demeaning jobs, paid pittance, and were continually harassed and insulted. It was many years before South Africans and the rest of the world looked honestly at their apartheid system, and long before the fight for freedom and equality began in earnest.

Meanwhile Arthur found employment at the famous Groot Schuur Hospital in Capetown. [*In later years this was where Dr Christian Barnard performed the first ground breaking heart transplants*]. Arthur lodged in a guest house with young university students, who took him out with them as often as they could, and insisted he climb Table Mountain with them - just for the experience!

The plan had been for Sue to sell the house and furniture in England and take both the boys out to join Arthur in South Africa. However, Europe was now under threat of World War Two, and by the time Sue had organized the sale of their house, it was impossible to get a passage. All shipping had been commandeered for the transport of artillery and military equipment for the impending War. Rather than risk being apart from his family during war, Arthur managed to procure a single berth back to London, vowing to return to South Africa when the war was over.

Reunited with the family, Arthur resumed work in a London hospital, where efforts were focused on training staff, organising facilities, and compiling stocks and medical supplies, in preparation for the advent of war.

Arthur did return to South Africa, many years, countries, and adventures later, and was employed as a radiographer, working tirelessly at the East Street Clinic in an African and Asian township in Pietermaritzburg until he was 83. He had been trying to retire for ten years before this, but had been unable to get a replacement. South Africa was still dominated by Apartheid and it was impossible to get medical and staffing assistance at a 'coloured' clinic. In fact Arthur seldom took a holiday because he always had so much difficulty getting a locum to cover for a couple of weeks. There were only two occasions when he took time off, and they were when I visited South Africa, but each time the X-ray Department had to close down while he was on holiday. When Arthur was 83, and the doctor and nursing sisters were all in their seventies, they had to admit that enough was enough, and the East Street Clinic closed down for ever. This would have been a sad blow to the hundreds of patients who would now have to walk several miles to the nearest hospital for treatment."

"That's a fantastic story Peggy. Your father sounds like a man of principal, and an interesting person."

"Thank you Lee. Yes I have always been proud of him, and we enjoyed a special relationship. I spent a lot of time with him when I was a child as I was so much older than my brothers."

"I never appreciated what a narrow escape Granddad had. Did the bullet bother him and cause much pain?" I asked.

"No, I believe the pain lessened with time and he adjusted psychologically to the knowledge that he could die at any time. In spite of it all, he lived to 89. Over the years he had x-rays taken of his chest, when he was required to provide medical checks for employment or insurance purposes. He had a dozen x-rays in his briefcase, showing progressive pictures of the bullet gradually being covered by a build-up of fatty tissue and muscle until the bullet in his heart eventually became immobilized."

Ironically, before finally settling in South Africa, my grandparents and uncle had also lived in New Zealand for several years, and Lee asked her where they'd been.

"They were on the east coast of the North Island. Jim and Pam had ventured off to explore New Zealand in the late 1950s, and were joined a couple of years later by Arthur and Sue. The four bought a Tip Top dairy at Ohope Beach."

"A 'dairy' in New Zealand is like a modern duka." I added, although Mum probably had a pretty good idea anyway. "It's an all-purpose shop, providing locals with groceries and house hold necessities, fresh milk, bread, newspapers, and ice-cream. The ubiquitous Tip Top ice-cream, in a delicious assortment of flavours and colours, served up in large scoops loaded onto a cone, is by far the most popular product! In the summer months, Kiwi's flock to 'the beach' for their annual holidays. Families pile everything they need into their cars and travel to the coast where they stay in basic *baches* along the shore, or in caravans and tents."

"Yes, I'd imagined it like that, and I believe Arthur and Jim were quite partial to those ice-creams too! Supermarkets had not come into being when my parents were there, and Ohope Beach was a long drive from Whakatane, the nearest town with large shops. The dairy was open from sun up to sun down, seven days a week. The four shop workers were run off their feet during the peak holiday season over the Christmas and New Year period. On Christmas Day they didn't get a chance to have a bite to eat until they finally sat down to Christmas dinner at 10 o'clock that night, by which time they were too exhausted to enjoy it!

Oh I am so cross with myself for not saving my father's letters. They were always so interesting and full of detail," said Mum, "But I do remember him writing about the trouble they took to sail their boat. When things were quiet in the shop, Jim, Pam, and my father, took every opportunity they could to go sailing. The surf was usually too rough along the beach to launch the boat, so they travelled to the harbour in the next village to do this, which entailed a fourteen mile drive along a rough metal road and through the mud flats before they could get the boat out for a sail. Meanwhile Sue was happy to man the shop. She still didn't really trust small boats!

However, it was only a matter of time before Africa called everyone back. Pam and Jim returned to South Africa, while Arthur and Sue came to Kenya, setting up a Bed & Breakfast in Nairobi. However Sue was unsettled, and in April 1961 the plague of green army worms that covered every surface, followed by a severe drought, convinced her to move to South Africa. They packed up all their belongings, booked a passage on a southbound ship in October, and came to stay with us for a few weeks. However, a week before they were due to sail, the heavens opened and floods began. Over five inches of rain fell the first night, and soon roads and bridges were being washed away. Arthur and Sue were fortunate to catch the last train to Mombasa. After that there were landslides and more bridges were swept away by the flood waters. There were no more trains for three weeks and access by road was also seriously hindered. Once in Mombasa, high waters caused Arthur and Sue to be marooned in the Palace Hotel until it was time to board their ship. From the hotel, they had to step into a boat instead of a taxi for their journey to the docks. I think Sue was more than happy to finally be leaving the country!

On arrival in Natal, Arthur and Sue bought into a partnership, running The Rob Roy Hotel, which overlooked The Valley of A Thousand Hills. They managed the hotel for two years, catering for locals as well as visiting cruise liners which sent parties up for lunch and afternoon teas. A huge fire destroyed the entire complex, along with it everything Arthur and Sue possessed. The only things saved were Arthur's briefcase of documents and his typewriter which he snatched off a chair by the bedroom door as he ran out. Ever resilient, my parents, both in their sixties, moved into an apartment in Durban, near Jim, and Arthur took up work as the radiographer in the East Street Coloured Clinic in Pietermaritzburg that I mentioned earlier.

As well as being agnostic, Arthur was also a strong anti-royalist. When they were still in Kenya, he ignored the clamour of Princess Elizabeth's visit to Kenya, when she became Queen. On honeymoon, with her new husband, the Duke of Edinburgh, she spent a couple of nights at 'Tree Tops', a small exclusive hotel built on a concealed platform high up in the tree branches. From there you watched the wild animals drinking and splashing in the pool below. It was during her stay here that the princess heard that her father, King George VI had died, and she was now the Queen of England.

Princess Margaret also visited Kenya several years later, when you children were small. We'd all piled into the car and driven down to Kisumu, where we waited for ages with others lining the route. Arthur muttered away, refusing to get involved in all this nonsense. He withdrew to a field behind us, and sat on the car bonnet reading a paper. You kids sat on the curb in the hot sun growing irritable, until at last the royal cavalcade drove past. Hugh looked at me blankly and said,

'Is that it?' and Heather was bitterly disappointment that the princess did not look like a princess at all, 'she was just an ordinary lady!' Meanwhile Princess Margaret, had noticed a solitary man away from the crowd. He was sitting on his car reading a paper and she gave him a special wave!

My mother, Sue was the 13th of 14 children, and was born on the 13th. She considered herself a lucky person, and was a small gritty bundle of energy, with psychic ability. A lively sense of fun balanced her determination and strong work ethic. Always spontaneous, she spoke her mind in no uncertain terms, and was often a bit too bossy! Sue and Arthur complimented each other well.

Arthur was tall and calm with a dry sense of humour. He spoke little, but his words were kind and wise. Not long ago, Hugh told me that he was in an English hotel. He'd noticed photos of the East African Safari Rally on the walls, and commented on these to the owner. It transpired that the hotel manager had also lived in Kenya, in Nakuru. Hugh mentioned that his grandparents, the Chapmans, once lived there, and had he known them? "Oh yes", said the man, "I do remember Arthur Chapman, a tall man with auburn hair, who worked at the hospital. He was a decent sort, a real gentleman". Hugh relayed this back to me, and I felt so proud that after all these years, in another country, someone still remembered my father so well."

I recounted how Granddad Arthur had given me my best art lesson when I was quite small. "Sitting beside me as I drew and coloured, he abruptly said, "Ducks, what are you drawing trees that look like lollipops for? Do trees really look like that? Look at a tree to see how the trunk and branches grow, notice where the leaves bunch together, and then draw what you see. Every tree is different. Make it interesting."

Mum smiled, "I didn't know that. It's nice to hear snippets like that about your parents."

After a brief pause to count stitches, she continued, "Back in Durban, Jim and Pam parted ways. They had been a happy couple, but there was an underlying sadness in their relationship. Jim had always longed for a family but Pam was unable to have children. Jim met someone else in Durban, and during the affair his lover became pregnant. After much discussion, Pam unselfishly insisted that Jim take this chance to have the family he'd always wanted, and felt it would be best if they divorced. She wanted Jim to be free to marry his new love, Denise, and be able to bring up their baby in a happy family environment. So Pam bravely walked away from the love of her life. She still lives alone, and we keep in touch with her, and I'll always remember her lovely sunny nature and her kindness to Jim. I am also eternally grateful to Pam's mother, Wynne Cashmore, who did so much for our family when Teddy was killed and we were all away overseas.

Jim and Denise were blessed with a daughter and then a son. Living so close to Arthur and Sue, the children, Sandra and James, were able to grow up enjoying the company of their grandparents. Sandra told of an amusing incident when, as a teenager, she popped in to visit her aged grandparents. No one answered the flat door, so pushing it open she was surprised to see Granddad Arthur fleeing for his life behind the couch, with Granny Sue in hot pursuit, waving the frying pan, shouting "Hanky panky? Think you can just waltz in here expecting hanky panky! Hmph, I'll give you hanky panky alright!"

10. Triptych

Our lovely long holiday in Kenya had come to an end and it was time to continue our journey to London. There was one last hitch at Nairobi Airport when officials insisted we needed a permit to take our souvenir zebra skin drum out of the country. Either a bribe or a long stale mate situation loomed, until Dad asked whether musical instruments normally required permits. Having ascertained that no permit was required, he wrote 'DRUM – musical instrument' across our form, settling the dispute. We received an official stamp and were on our way!

We were met at Heathrow by dear friends, Mick and Susie, who gave us the shelter of their home while we found our feet. We had stepped off the plane to a very different world. Not only was it winter, but Britain was under the grip of a serious economic depression and it certainly was not the best time to arrive in London with a baby. New laws had come into place making it difficult for landlords to evict tenants with children. Consequently landlords were not keen to take on new tenants with families. We eventually found a flat to rent by agreeing not to mention we had a baby unless asked.

Britain was caught up in this severe recession during the first half of the 1970s. They were trying times. There was petrol rationing, car-less days, and intermittent shortages of items like bread, canned food, loo paper, and sugar. Some stock piled grocery items which exacerbated the situation. We gave up meat, and there were times when I had to choose between half a cabbage and half a loaf of bread for supper. Lee quickly got a start with Fords at Dagenham, who advertised nightly on TV that you could earn £40 a week with them. But when he applied for extra work and wages more in line with what they were advertising, Lee was told that you had to be employed for a long period of time before you could even ask for overtime or shift work. His wages were £25 a week, our rent £17, and it was costing £5 to get to and from work, which left us £3 to live on. Needing to earn more, Lee left Fords, bought a little bomb for £15, and started selling life insurance, but this was on a commission only basis and a hard slog in the current climate.

However, in spite of the conditions, we were a happy little family, and had some wonderful times with friends. After the isolation of New Zealand, it was fun to be in London, the crossroads of the world, with friends coming and going, and it was great seeing my best friend Hon, who popped in whenever she could. Our flat was in a row of houses similar in appearance to Coronation Street. One Saturday, as I was painting psychedelic faces on a friend's minivan, Hugh and Linda pulled up behind us. They had just flown in from their stint in the Cayman Islands. It was great to meet Linda, Hugh's cheerful friendly wife, and Hugh enjoyed getting to know his wee niece.

Hugh

Hugh and his 'Sunshine Girl', Linda Wood met in London, and were married in Linda's home town on the Isle of Sheppey on 25th July 1971. Not long before their wedding, Dad, out in Kenya had been chatting with a work colleague at Chemelil Sugar Company. He mentioned that his son, Hugh, was getting married soon. Asked if he was going to the wedding, Dad replied that he was afraid it was out of the question as the wedding would be in England. The colleague was shocked to discover that because Dad was employed locally, he received less than half the salary of the overseas employees and was entitled to no perks, no paid home leave every two years, nor any assistance with school fees for his children. So, unbeknown to Dad, this man kindly went to his superiors, who in view of Dad's excellent work ethics and invaluable local knowledge and skill with the labour force, decided that the company would give him a bonus by way of an overseas trip for two.

Dad and Mum were thrilled that they could be at Hugh's wedding after all, and had a truly wonderful holiday in England. Whilst staying with Aunt Pix in the Isle of Man, they were joined by Dad's other sisters, Wynne and Anne, making it the first time in over fifty years the three sisters and their young brother had been together.

Ever since Mum heard they were going to the wedding, she had been scouring the shops in Kenya for something special to wear. Nothing had stood out, and once they arrived in England, this had become the mission everywhere they went. At long last, in a small shop in a little Manx town, Mum found two outfits she loved. Unable to decide which to buy, she had gone to join the others for a cup of coffee. Enthusiastically everyone suggested she 'get both!' However she had gone back in to the shop and made her choice, delighted to finally have something nice to wear for her son's wedding.

Linda's parents, Owen and Jeanne Wood, welcomed in Mum and Dad into their home in Sheppey, and on the morning of the wedding, as everyone gathered to leave for Minster Abbey, Mum came down stairs and gasped. There stood Linda's Mother, looking gorgeous, in an outfit of exactly the same material as the dress Mum had come so close to buying. An amazing co-incidence considering the vast range of materials, patterns, and colours, available across two continents, and fortunate that the two new mother in-laws weren't in matching ensembles!

The wedding reception took place in a marquee in the Wood's garden and was a real family reunion for both families. Hugh accompanied his beautiful happy bride, looking resplendent in full tartan regalia, accompanied by his best man, Robin, dapper in top hat and tails (or monkey suit as he preferred to call it). Just before the speeches, a surprise telephone call came through from Lee and me in New Zealand, linking the family together for these special celebrations.

A few months after the wedding, Hugh and Linda set off for a wonderfully happy year working in George Town in the Cayman Islands. Now they had returned from this assignment, and, as it had been several years since we'd last seen each other, we sat around chatting and swapping stories, while Sirri clambered happily over her new uncle.

Hugh related an incident which had occurred in Nigeria, "Our survey team was working on the Hadeja Irrigation Project in the North East of Nigeria, close to the Niger and Chad borders. The distant Tiga Dam breached due to heavy rains, and, after a flash flood, we were unable to get the four Land-Rovers across the raging waters. We raced our vehicles overland ahead of the deluge to a place we could cross downstream before the flood waters arrived. We just managed to get three vehicles to the other side, leaving the fourth where it was so we could continue using it for getting to and from our accommodation. The waters didn't recede for many days but once the force had lessened, we were able to cross the river to work and use the three Land-Rovers on the other side. We built a ferry out of poles and empty 44 gallon drums, and when the waters subsided a little, were able to 'wade' the Land-Rovers back and forth across the river using our 'Irish bridge'. One evening, returning from the day's work, we eased the Land-Rovers across the ford, and noticed a Peugeot taxi pull up on the bank. Seeing the Land-Rover travelling through the water, the driver assumed he could do likewise. Unfortunately he chose the wrong crossing point and taking a run at the river, aquaplaned to midstream. Then he simply sank gracefully into the water until only the roof of his vehicle was visible. With only his pride hurting, the bemused driver emerged from his submerged taxi, coughing, spluttering, and scratching his head."

During his secondary school years at the Prince of Wales School, in Nairobi, Hugh had helped form and run the Geographical Society, and together with a friend, founded the Mountaineering Club, which led to the mass ascents of Kilimanjaro in the early 1960s by groups of secondary school children. Both Robin and I were able to join these fantastic expeditions up Africa's highest mountain.

On leaving school, Hugh immediately found a job with a survey company, J A Storeys. He worked with them for nine months until he left Kenya in September 1965 to commence his land survey course in London. During his time with

Storeys in Kenya, Hugh camped with the work gangs in basic caravans at sites in wild remote parts of the country. They worked on a project at Kindarooma where a dam was being constructed for hydro-electricity, then in West Pocot, mapping an area where platinum was supposed to have been discovered. Later he worked in Tanzania on a Transmission Line to the south east of Kilimanjaro from a dam at Numbia Ya Mungu and Moshi. Here there were no roads and Hugh had to sit on the Land-Rover wing looking out for hazards such as ant bear holes and termite mounds. The Land-Rover broke down while they were collecting water, so Hugh hiked the couple of miles back to camp to get the Peugeot pickup. Whilst walking along a very narrow path through tall napier grass, a black mamba slithered across the path, actually passing between Hugh's feet. Not long after, he nearly sliced a chainsaw through his left knee, but managed to throw the machine away in time so it just nicked him, leaving only a scar to tell the tale.

Hugh was able to pop home one night, bringing with him a tiny dikdik buck. Its mother had been caught in a trap and Hugh was caring for this delightful little bambi. A member of a dwarf antelope family, Dikdik have tiny slender legs no thicker than a pencil. The adorable wee buck struggled to stand as his legs splayed out on our slippery floors, so we had to rush around laying towels and mats down so it could walk about inside, safely away from the eager dogs at the door.

All too quickly the time came for Hugh to leave Kenya for his studies in England. In order to train and qualify as a Member of the Royal Institution of Chartered Surveyors it was necessary for him to study in London for the next five years. To us younger siblings it seemed an improbable eternity without our big bro around. We set off at dawn on our safari over dusty rutted roads to Mombasa, where Hugh was to join the Union Castle liner, the SS Kenya Castle, to South Africa. He planned to spend a few days in Durban with Uncle Jim and our Grandparents, Sue and Arthur, before they would drove along the Garden Route to Cape Town where Hugh was to join the SS Edinburgh Castle for the remainder of the journey to Southampton. This part seemed all very exciting, but it was very sad when the time came for us to say goodbye to Hugh. On the afternoon of departure we wiled away a couple of hours at the Oceanic Hotel, high up on the cliffs overlooking the Indian Ocean, and Robin and I were rather impressed that Dad had ordered a beer for Hugh. Our last hours together were spent in a small motor boat, chugging through the murky harbour waters around the Mombasa port, gazing up at the huge prows of ocean going liners, cargo tankers, and ancient wooden dhows. Finally we boarded the ship and checked out Hugh's shared cabin. Putting off the imminent farewell, we lingered on deck, drawing out our last moments together before we had to part. It must have been in Dad's mind, that he himself, had set sail from Glasgow as a young lad, to start his life in Kenya. Now, here was his son, heading in the opposite direction, embarking on his own life. Subdued, we watched sadly and silently as the ship slipped out of the harbour. Mum's shoulders shook with quiet sobs as her son disappeared towards the horizon. She too had once sailed off to her new life, while her father stood watching her sail away into the unknown.

The years ahead would prove difficult ones for Hugh, compounded by lack of funds, and certainly no trips home to his family. Term breaks and holidays were spent working with survey crews, gaining work experience and meagre wages to see him through the next term. However, Hugh did his best and made the most of the experiences along the way.

Hugh and I met up for a day in London in 1967, when I was on my way to Scotland to begin my own training course. Hugh had borrowed a friend's old convertible MG TC and we were driving through central London in heavy traffic. The wee green MG was wont to stall when moving off from a stand-still, so every time we stopped at the lights the engine ticked over fine, but the second the lights turned green and Hugh put his foot on the pedal, we stalled. Exposed in the open top car, we were well aware of our lack of cool and the impatient drivers tooting behind us. We both turned red, looked at each other, and burst into giggles, while Hugh tried valiantly to get us started again. Off we'd go – until the next red light, and it would happen all over again!

In the 1970s, Hugh and a colleague, Roy, were sent to Yemen to survey the position of several boreholes, which had been drilled in order to study the geology of the area with the aim of building a new dam. Using a Wild T2 and Wild Electronic Measuring Equipment, the young men were required to map the boreholes in order to produce an accurate geological chart of the Marib area.

Marib, where the Mountains of Yemen meet the sands of the Rub al-Khali, is thought to be the location of the Sabaean Kingdom, mentioned in both the Qur'an and the Old Testament. Ruins of the ancient city and temple, believed to be the home of the Queen of Sheba lie at Mharam Bilqis. In the 8th Century BC, an ancient dam was constructed using very advanced engineering technology for the time. Its waters were diverted into a network of irrigation canals, creating a vast fertile oasis over 25,000 acres. The area became a mecca for the camel caravans crossing the deserts along the trade routes which connected Africa, Arabia, India, Persia, and beyond. The city was a haven of culture and commerce, and prospered greatly with its control over the trade routes and mighty army, but it was to fall into decline. Evidence remains that some of the original dam walls were heightened in 115BC, and the dam was breached twice in the 6th Century AD, bringing devastation, mass migration and an end the great Saba civilisation which once thrived here.

Hugh explained, "In more recent times, because rain is such a rare commodity in Marib, the local people used a system of small dams and channels in an attempt to control the waters of the Marib River when rains up in the mountains caused it to flood. They were building large, 3 metre high, sand banks, around their fields to retain as much water as possible. A new dam, upstream of the ancient dam, was much needed.

Early one morning, I was driving the Toyota Land Cruiser across one of these large earth banks when I heard a sharp crack – it was like an iron bar being broken, and a whine followed. I initially thought I had broken the chassis as I had been using the Land Cruiser in rather extreme conditions, but then realised I'd heard the report of a rifle being fired at the vehicle. A man, with robes flying, bounded over the top of the bank about 20 metres in front and threw himself to the ground with the barrel of his American WWII rifle aimed squarely at the bridge of my nose. I quickly placed the palms of my hands against the windscreen to show I was unarmed."

"Wow! That must have been scary Hugh!"

"I don't really remember any particular emotions. I had already had a gun pulled on me in this rather lawless place."

"So what happened?"

"After an endless moment, this man got up and ran towards the car, opened the door and proceeded to jump in and then work the bolt of his rifle, spewing bullets over the floor of the vehicle. At this point I actually got quite angry with him. He did not speak any English and my Arabic is very limited, but we managed partial communication. Eventually, following his directions, we drove to one of the boreholes where he had dug a well some seventy metres deep, and had actually found some rocks in this 'sand sea'.

Locals gathered, some with a spattering of English, then Roy arrived, and communication improved. The man believed that the borehole was to get water (rather than look for it) and was angry that he had dug such a deep well and found no water. Somehow I managed to convey to him that we had been sent to measure where the boreholes were and had nothing to do with choosing where they were placed, so we all ended up the best of pals drinking the local coffee.

Using a glass prism as a point to measure to, we placed one on top of the borehole to record the position, and drove off to continue our survey. When I returned to collect the prism in the evening, I found him guarding it with his rifle across his knees. He greeted me enthusiastically and more coffee drinking was required."

Hugh paused a moment before continuing, "Being a nomad in foreign countries, and amongst different cultures, we had many strange and interesting experiences. I actually stole back my passport in Saudi Arabia, and I once flew with a Saudi prince to Bahrain. Oh yes! And another bizarre little incident occurred in Yemen. We had travelled a long way south from Sanaa towards the South Yemen (Aden) border. Yemen was two countries then, and we'd stopped for the night at a camp where a German Engineer was building a road. All his staff were locals or Indians who did not drink alcohol, and I suppose he was just pleased to have someone he could drink with. This German Engineer had bribed the authorities into letting him import quite a large quantity of alcohol – no deal or I go home and you have no road kind of thing. All of his alcohol was of the highest quality and we enjoyed pre-dinner drinks, wines with dinner, then after dinner champagne, which he opened rather flamboyantly by cutting off the top of the bottle with a samurai sword. Why he had a samurai sword in Yemen I do not know! Interestingly, in spite of all the alcohol we consumed that night, we didn't feel particularly intoxicated, nor did we feel any the worse for wear the next day – perhaps it was the exceptional quality of the liquor?"

Robin

Robin, the youngest in the family, was the most out-going, cheeky, exasperating, and lovable. As a little brother he was often annoying, as he managed to scarper his way out of all sorts of situations, leaving us older siblings to take the blame. But we all loved him dearly, enjoying his unlimited love of life, great sense of humour, and easy going manner. At school he was an integral part of every sports team, excelling at hockey, tennis, and rugby, at which he became more proficient through the years, representing his clubs, districts, and country.

I recall Hugh, a senior at The Prince of Wales in Nairobi, coming home and joking, "Fame at last, and in my final year at school!" Apparently Robin's sporting prowess and social reputation had preceded him to secondary school, and on passing junior students, Hugh would hear them say "That's Rob Anderson's bro!"

When we were young kids, the family went to England for a holiday. We easily adapted to our new surroundings, happily exploring the fields and lanes, and befriending the local villagers, donkeys and dogs. One day we picked some apples from a bough in a country lane. We returned with bags the next day to collect more. Climbing higher and higher, the boundaries became blurred, and suddenly an angry woman appeared in her garden below, waving her fists and shouting at us. We quickly shinned down the tree and raced off down the lane - with our apples! It didn't take Mum long to get to the bottom of this little story, and the next morning she sent us off to apologise to the lady. So there we stood, the three of us with hands behind our backs, listening politely to the lady's tirade about stealing. She concluded her stern lecture by saying "If you want some apples, all you have to do is ask." No sooner had she got the words out of her mouth when Robin piped up, "Please can we have some apples". There was a stunned silence. Hugh and I squirmed in our shoes, embarrassed at the audacity of our cheeky young brother, while the lady recovered from her shock at this blatant impudence. Then, to our astonishment, she uttered a curt and dismissive, "Very well, you may pick a few on your way out!"

Soon after this incident we went to London to visit Mum's relations in Putney, before driving north to Scotland. Several weeks into our Scottish holiday, we were in a men's outfitters in Kilmarnock. Dad had been pressganged into buying a new jacket, and we kids, chattering away as usual, were helping him choose from the range of tweeds. Mum was waiting at the counter when another customer approached her and asked, "Excuse me but weren't you in London recently?" Mum affirmed that we had been in London, but only for a couple of days in Putney. "That's it!" exclaimed the man, "I knew I'd seen this family before. I was in Putney too, and noticed you all getting into a car. The reason I remember you is because of your strange accents!"

'Three's a crowd' was certainly true with us kids, and we were always ganging up two against one. We had some fearful rows and Mum or Dad would have to come to the rescue, putting a stop to our wild brawls. On one occasion, after intervening to prevent us strangling each other, Dad shook his head in bewilderment, "I just don't understand you people. You fight tooth and nail, so fiercely that I have to stop you. I go away feeling down in the dumps that my children behave in such a heathen manner towards each other, then, not ten minutes later, I look up and see you out the window playing happily together as thick as thieves!"

As a boy, Robin loved to 'go round the shamba' with Dad, and most mornings he'd tag along as Dad attended to the planting, harvesting, labour, and other farm duties. Robin had written an essay describing his boyhood experiences of cane fires.

When Dad was working in sugar, as a kid I would often accompany him on his field rounds, and sometimes we had to rush to a cane fire. The sugar cane fires were quite something. Of course terrifying and dangerous, but Dad was extremely careful where he parked the Land-Rover, and I with it. Usually the vehicle would be parked upwind and on the other side of a fire break or road.

The fire sweeps across the fields, flames leaping higher and higher. Yellow, orange and black tongues. Flames fighting to reach the sky first; and all the time the heat, getting hotter and hotter, allied with the angry crackles of flame and fire, plus the nasty choking and cough-making smell of smoke and burning. I was not on my own, feeling, sensing, and hearing these things – so did every living creature there, but they of course, could not remain there. Get out, get out, and thus the panic and chaos set in. All living creatures, so mobile suddenly in their haste to escape – mice and rats, squirrels, skunks, scorpions, and spiders, bush buck, water buck and duiker, plus all the various snakes – all heading in the same direction. Everything moving as fast as it can, oblivious of, unaware and unconcerned with each other, as they rush headlong in their mad chaotic scramble to get out. To see them all come scurrying out of the burning cane and scuttle across the fire breaks into the safety of the other side was quite amazing and a sight not to be forgotten easily.

Robin seemed to have the luck of the devil and we often joked about his 'nine lives'. He'd been seriously bitten by the "Kili bug", and had climbed Mt Kilimanjaro with a school party, and at the time he was the youngest ever to climb the highest mountain in Africa. A little later Robin climbed the mountain again with a group of friends, but following this, he and two others attempted to climb the mountain from the other side. The 14 year old boys had not discussed their plans with anyone, intimating they would be with a school party. It was foolhardy as these youngsters had no experience, no guides, or proper maps, not even a porter to help carry their kit and meagre rations. Consequently the boys suffered exposure and altitude sickness, and finally frostbite set in. They were extremely fortunate to make it back to civilisation at all. Parents were notified and the boys were hurried back to Nairobi. Once Robin was home in Nandi Hills, the full impact of the severity of his condition was revealed. Peeling off his socks, Mum saw that Robin's toes looked as though gangrene was setting in. She immediately rushed him to Kapsabet Hospital, where a Canadian doctor was standing in as a locum. Miraculously this doctor had been in Alaska and was familiar with the treatment of frostbite. On doctor's orders Mum kept a fire roaring day and night, and Robin, ensconced in rugs, with legs raised on cushions lay alongside, sipping brandy four times a day! Mum became concerned that this was training her son to become an alcoholic. However, this method proved very successful and Robin recovered remarkably quickly, and with little damage to his toes.

The latter years of Robin's schooling were affected by the integration of African students into local secondary schools. It was a necessary move, but in the early stages, pupils of all races were drawn into constant conflict and fights. There were several gangs and quite a lot of bullying incidents. Mum and Dad decided it was not conducive to a good education, and, as they hoped Robin would go on to university, they arranged for him to complete his schooling in the Isle of Man, boarding with Aunt Pix. However, having gained his university entrance, Robin decided against further studies, electing instead to return home to Kenya to work on the land.

In the early 1970s, those born in Kenya with overseas connections were entitled to retain 'Dual Citizenship' - British and Kenyan Citizenship, until the age of 23 when they were obliged to select one or other. However, while Robin was on a flight home from the Isle of Man, the rules suddenly changed for him. Mum and Dad had purchased him a 'one way ticket' back to Kenya, and had travelled up to Nairobi to meet his plane. However, The Department of Immigration, in its infinite wisdom, threatened to send Robin back to UK on the next plane. Apparently at the time, only passengers with return tickets were welcome (as tourists, bringing well needed revenue to the country). Barring professionals like doctors and lawyers, immigrants were a threat to the employment of local people. So in effect young Robin, who was returning home to the country of his birth, was not welcome in his own country, unless he had a return ticket. Robin was in the air, looking forward to coming home, and oblivious to all the fuss. Meanwhile Dad was staging a sit-in in the Immigration Department at Nairobi Airport, protesting the farcical and ludicrous situation. Eventually sense prevailed, or more probably, the Immigration Officer just wanted to knock off and go home, and it was decided that they would allow Robin to stay in Kenya, but he was forbidden to work while he remained in the country. Work permits were required for non-residents, and could only be obtained by bribery, or purchased at astronomical cost.

Due to this absurd officialdom, Robin would become an illegal citizen as soon as he got a job. Having completed his schooling, he needed work and was looking forward to getting a job as a farm assistant, with the eventual goal of progressing to Estate Manager. Robin's own records take up the story;

For my first, full time permanent employment, I moved down to Kiambu to work for Loresho & Kiora Plantations Ltd. They had five or six coffee estates in the Kiambu and Ruiru areas and I was taken on as the trainee / relief manager, and began on the mother estate, Kiora, helping out in the workshops, working under, and living with my good friend Brian Haworth. I was clueless as to what I was really supposed to do, but attacked whatever task I was given with enthusiasm and energy, in the hope that this would overcome my inexperience and lack of qualifications. This seemed to be a good starting point and stepping stone to a secure future, as the company had some switched on young managers, all of whom I would work under and run their 'shambas' when they went on leave – an ideal way to pick their brains and study methods to sort out my own formats for when I eventually managed my own shamba. This was to my advantage, coupled with the knowledge I had picked up as a youngster from Dad as we went round the farm, and Dad used to refer to me as his driver – any excuse to get behind the wheel of a car even then!

At Kiora, one of my jobs was to drive the twenty odd miles into Nairobi for farm purchases, spare parts, chemicals, banking etc. Here was my next legal problem, for although I had been driving since I was ten, I did not actually have a driving license. This in itself was a minor problem, but unfortunately there was about a three month waiting period for driving tests. It was virtually guaranteed that no first time youngster, let alone a white one, would ever be passed until at least the fourth attempt. If my maths was correct this meant about one whole year without a license for me! Without a driving license there was no way the company could use my services. Never to fear, one of the assistants, Peter, was a 'cousin brother' of one of the examiners, and for a small bit of 'cha' all could be arranged within the week. I was so naive and ignorant, the morals of the matter did not come into it, and I was soon the owner of a Kenyan Driving License. Looking back on this, all these years later, the amazing fact now remains that in spite of thirty odd years of driving experience, over thousands of miles, including all the rallying I have done, on and off road in every conceivable surface, and in several countries, I still have never passed a driving test!

Robin was dismissed from his first job as soon as it was discovered he was working illegally. However he was quickly taken on by a positive Greek, who considered that since Robin was still a dual citizen, he must still be a Kenyan, and therefore did not require a work permit. So Silon Spyratos employed Robin on his coffee estate, and life was sweet for several years. Robin enjoyed the Thika / Nairobi social scene, playing rugby for Thika, and venturing into his true passion, rallying. He and friends would spend every cent and every spare minute, as 'grease monkeys' doing up their cars, driving in local rallies, and arranging sponsorship from local businesses for bigger rallies. Eventually, as Robin's name became more familiar within the rallying fraternity, he was asked to co-drive or navigate with more experienced local rally drivers.

Heather ~ Andi

In January 1967 I set off to Scotland for my training. I left Nandi Hills with mixed feelings, sad to be leaving home, my family, and boyfriend, but excited to be going overseas. Dad's sister, Aunt Wynne and Uncle Jimmy welcomed me off the overnight train from London, and I was able to meet my cousin June. June and her husband, Tom Shanks, were artists who had studied at The Glasgow School of Art. Tom had also spent eight years working as a designer at the Edinburgh Weavers Dovecote. He was renowned for his beautiful water colour paintings of Scottish scenes, which completely captured the atmosphere of the misty moody highlands. Tom and June were a really kind, happy, down to earth couple. June told me that as a teenager she had been holed up in a small hotel one very wet day, and made friends with an old Polish guest. He had taught her to say, "Isn't it lovely the sun is shining" in Polish. After that, whenever June met people from other countries, she always asked them to teach her the same phrase in their own language. She obviously had a good ear because she regaled me with about thirty different languages, slipping easily from one to the next, changing her accent, voice, expressions, and character accordingly with each new language.

Life suddenly became more serious for me as I commenced my course. The Edinburgh Home for Babies, was a large stuffy Victorian institution where we trained as children's nurses, and at the same time manned the orphanage day and night. The wards were full of terminally ill children, babies with congenital disabilities, tiny 'illegitimate' babies waiting for adoption, and toddlers unable to live at home due to extreme poverty or violence. Students started their shifts at 7am, working through the day to 5.30 pm, with a brief lunch and tea break. It was a bleak, cold, hard place, run with strict discipline and few pleasantries. Coming here from my carefree life on a remote farm in Africa wasn't easy, but I did my best to adapt and settle in.

During the course, to enable students to gain hands on experience in all areas, it was mandatory that we each work three weeks in every department. You might be rostered to do three weeks in 'Milk Kitchen' preparing babies' feeds, then three weeks in the ward caring for older babies, or with premature babies. I was dismayed to find my first shift was in the kitchen, where I was required to cook meals for the toddlers. I was to work amongst the institution staff who prepared meals for the students, Matron, and nursing sisters. Back at home, Mum had done the cooking, but I had always been too busy outside to learn anything from her. I could only put together scrambled eggs or make the odd cake. Now, on my first day in 'Kitchen', well aware that Toddler Lunch was served promptly at midday, and with only half an hour to go, I was still struggling to cut up swedes and neaps (turnips). I had never come across either of these rock-hard vegetables before and had no idea how to prepare them. Asking the other kitchen hands resulted in shrugged shoulders, as they scurried around with their own tasks. Observing my ineptitude, they shook their heads or raised their eyebrows. I was well aware that everyone knew I had come from the colonies, and I heard the odd dig to the effect of 'she's a spoilt girl who doesn't know how to do anything because she had servants who did it all for her'. Feeling very embarrassed and totally humiliated, I was extremely relieved when Ruby, the head cook, finally came to my aid. She was a small Scottish woman who tut-tutted incessantly as she bustled about at odds with the world. Her broad accent was not easy to understand, and she sighed in exasperation when I looked at her blankly or asked her to repeat herself. But somewhere behind her austere exterior, Ruby had a kind heart, and between her own chores, she taught me the rudiments of cooking. Every evening all the students and staff collected for 'Hand-over Reports' where details of children's health or medication was read aloud. The reports concluded with a review from 'Toddlers' on the content and nutritional value of meals served that day. The fact that lunch for the wee bairns was served over an hour late, was unthinkable! Again rumours of the indulged girl from the colonies swept the place. I had to wise up smartly, and realised that a little creativity was needed to get me out of the jam. Preparing the simplest of meals, I began presenting them in fun, attractive ways, giving them exotic names. Ordinary mince became Monkey Mince or Coconut Curry, served with oranges and banana, while basic custards and semolina puddings became tropical island desserts with a little flower, fruit, or hundreds-and-thousands. Suddenly 'Toddlers' were giving glowing reports at Hand-over since the children were tucking in to novel smiley-faced plates and pretty puddings.

After completing my duties, I went to help out with the babies, and then, being one of the most junior juniors, the last hour of the day was usually spent in the sluice room washing the dirty nappies or 'niffs' as they were called. A disgusting job, and the only way I could stop myself retching was by mentally blocking out what I was doing (it didn't require much attention anyway) and with my imagination in overdrive, I escaped to Kenya and played with my memories until the buckets of nappies were empty.

I began to make friends with the other students and we'd watch 'Top of the Pops', go out to the pub or to see a film. Following my stint in 'Kitchen', I was rostered to 'Laundry', which was easier to handle and not so stressful. There was only one washing machine, a dinosaur dryer, and wooden scrubbing boards were still in operation. One glacial February morning, I glanced up from my duties to see a watery sun peeping through the window. Ah the sun! The sun's here! How happy I was to see it. I rushed outside, holding my hands and face up to the sunshine. But there was nothing – no warmth at all. There was no heat in the sun whatsoever, absolutely none. I was stunned at this cold hard reality. It was akin to a slap in the face, and I felt the distance acutely. Naturally I was already well aware that I was thousands of miles away from my home and loved ones, but now I realised just how far. So far that even the sun's rays couldn't reach me.

However the cheery smiles of the little children and my new friend, Hon, lifted my spirits again. Hon Perry was born in India, and grew up in the Lake District. She was also eighteen, a senior at the babies' home, and we quickly became friends. With flame red hair, a happy caring nature, and a great sense of fun and adventure, Hon got on well with everyone, and had a way of making people feel instantly at ease. It was 'the 60s' and outside the babies home everything was alive and 'happening'. Young people everywhere had suddenly broken free from conventions and were high on the sheer enjoyment of living. The times were changing, and great music, laughter, discussions, bright colours, and creativity abounded. Ideas, customs, and clothes came in from foreign lands, and we broadened our horizons and became aware of hardships and injustices in other places. There was a spirit of togetherness, of freedom, of hope, and it was all laced with our own youthful exuberance. We thrived on it all, exploring the lively old city, and frequenting pubs and university parties. The Scots were warm and friendly, with a great sense of humour, and often welcomed us into their homes, sharing meals or giving us a place to stay. Hon's family also made me feel very welcome, and every few months we'd head 'home' to Cockermouth, in the Lake District to stay with the Perrys. Meanwhile we continued our training, with theory classes and hands-on experience with the babies. Unlike the university and college students, we weren't granted the usual holidays, but the up side of this was that we completed our courses quickly. Almost two years later we were released from the babies home, and Hon and I headed straight for London to take our diplomas, earn some money working as Nannies, and to enjoy 'the scene' in London. We had a brilliant time, and it was here our dream to hitchhike through Europe was hatched.

But first, after two years away, I felt the need to go back to Kenya. I was overjoyed to be with Mum, Dad, Robin, and my boyfriend, and it was heaven to feel the sun's heat again. I was lucky to be offered a job teaching at Pembroke House, a boarding school for young boys, close to Lake Naivasha. Although I loved it here, I probably never really appreciated at the time that this was the best job I'd ever have! I taught seven to ten year old boys in tiny classes of less than a dozen children. Most of these boys were from up country farms. They were cheerful adventurous children and their school days were filled with interesting activities, including weekend sailing safaris, when the entire school camped, fished, and sailed, around Lake Naivasha. At school the boys were encouraged to grow vegetables or flowers in their own little gardens anywhere within the school grounds. During one afternoon class, the heavens opened. One of the boys asked, "Why does it always rain in the afternoons Miss Anderson."

Before I could answer, another little voice piped up, "It's because I always pray to God for rain to water my vegetable garden."

Then young Bongo, a game warden's son, joined in, "I don't need to pray to God. I've got a watering can!"

After class, teachers took the boys for soccer, hockey, swimming and athletics. The school was in the habit of taking a coop of homing pigeons with the team in the truck when they went to play away matches at other schools. At half time the score would be written on a slip of paper and tucked into a ring around a bird's foot. Half the pigeons were released, and flew back to school with the up to the minute score. The same thing happened with the final result, and the homing pigeons always found their way back. However, there were occasions when the truck with the team arrived back before the full time pigeons!

There was an interesting mix of staff, from original old timers, Ray and Sue, to a lively group of young teachers. The new House Mistress, Anne was a courageous young Irish girl, whose husband had died very young, leaving her with three small children. Even though she knew no one in Kenya, she applied for a job as a House Matron, and left Ireland to begin a new life with her three children in a remote boarding school in Kenya. She was a lovely, spirited person, who fitted in well and we all had some great times together. Several nights a week we'd find ourselves over the road at the Club where we played tennis, ping pong, or had mammoth darts tournaments with the few local residents. Other times we'd all squash in a car and drive to Nakuru for hockey matches and socialising, or do weekend trips to Nairobi to dances and parties. We had an open invitation to ride Sue's horses, and early one magical Sunday morning, Anne, Dick, Dave, and I, saddled up and rode off over the hills. It was a beautiful clear day and the country stretched peacefully out into the blue distance. When the sun was high above us, we dismounted beside a rocky splashing river, tethered our horses, and enjoyed the cool clear water and a picnic in the shade, before trekking higher up the walls of the Rift Valley. We eventually turned our tired horses homewards, down steep slopes, as the sunset faded in the sky.

I often received kind invitations from parents to stay with them on their farms or at the coast during the holidays. But I liked to freewheel, and enjoyed going back to stay with Mum and Dad at Chemelil. From there I would catch up with friends in Nandi, or stay with my old friend, Jan in Kericho, where we'd go water skiing or flying. Two young American pilots were employed by the large tea companies, to fly up into the hail clouds and disperse the hail by lighting flares. One fall of hail on the tea plantations would damage the top growth on hundreds of thousands of tea bushes, resulting in huge financial loss, as the current crop would be wiped out and it would take several months for the plants to recover. A radar detected potential hail clouds amongst the rain clouds on the horizon, and the pilots would phone us if they were going up. Rushing out to the airstrip, we'd find the Cessna Cherokee and Comanche two-seaters warming up. We'd each leap into a plane and we were off! The pilots flew straight into the dense dark grey clouds and once we were bouncing about in the thicket of the hail producing mass, they'd ignite the flares that dispersed the hail. It was exciting flying blind amongst these huge grey clouds. The engine's roar echoed around us and was peppered with crackles from the radio as the pilots kept contact. Once the task was done, the rest of the flight became a joy ride. The two little planes frolicked happily in the huge wide skies. We'd do loops and dives, or fly in synch, while communicating by radio. The planes were fitted with dual controls, so Jan and I, in our respective planes were at the controls and the skies were our limit! The pilots were good teachers and of course drew the line at us landing and taking off. On one occasion we ended up above the sugar plantations of Chemelil, and taking the controls, the guys swooped down, skimming the treetops above our house. We buzzed over a few times, and as everyone ran out to see what the commotion was, we tipped our wings, and flew off into the blue. At least Mum knew where I was!

Another time Jan and I went to stay with Angie at Elburgon, and along with several Peace Corps friends, decided to go camping at Lake Baringo. It was during the dry season, and the journey was long and dusty. The weekend trip hadn't been planned properly, and we didn't take enough spare water or petrol. The water level of the lake was unusually low and the water a thick dirty brown. We'd pitched our tents beneath a clump of sparse thorn trees, but the days were uncomfortably hot. Unable to drink the filthy lake water, we had to depend on the few crates of beer we'd taken with us, which had to be rationed. There never is enough to drink when you are really hot and thirsty. Jan and I also had a terrifying encounter with a camel whilst walking along the wide cracked lake shore. We'd noticed a nearby herd of goats, and a couple of camels slowly making their way back from the water's edge. Suddenly we looked behind us to see a camel tearing towards us. It seemed to be flying across the ground. We ran! There were no trees to climb, or rocks to shelter from this angry beast, and desperately we threw ourselves behind a straggly bush. I shut my eyes, expecting to feel the crushing weight of the camel upon me. Shouting and shooing, and frantically waving his spear and stick, a herdsman rushed towards us and the camel veered away at the last moment. We hadn't even seen the herdsman before, and we were unable to speak his language, but I think he knew how grateful we were. It was a narrow escape, and very frightening to be on foot in the open with an angry camel bearing down on you. Meanwhile a Peace Corp couple had taken one of the Land-Rovers up into the hills exploring. They hadn't returned and it was getting dark. The hours passed, we'd eaten supper and sat nursing our beers, while we discussed what to do. The guys had driven round looking for them, and eventually it was decided there was not much more we could do until morning. They could be anywhere, and would probably be alright if they stayed with the car, and we'd search for them in daylight. Fortunately they arrived back early next morning. Their vehicle had broken down and an African family had welcomed them into their hut, giving them food and a place to sleep beside the children on the floor. Two of the guys went off with them to locate and repair the Land-Rover.

We had other, easier camping trips with Angie and her group of young Kenyan, Italian friends, on the shores of Lake Naivasha, a beautiful, large, fresh water lake, with an abundance of fish and fascinating bird life. We chatted and listened to taped music around our camp-fire, beneath a starry sky. All night, lion grunts and growls could be heard, but we were unafraid because we knew we were in no danger. The lions were descendants of Elsa, the feline star of the film 'Born Free', and were housed in a secure compound under the thorn trees, where we could visit them during the day.

One special weekend we flew down to Malindi, on the Kenya coast. My boyfriend's brother worked as a crop dusting pilot, and the three of us chipped in to hire a small plane from his boss for the weekend. What a great time we had. As we took off in an unbelievably loud engine roar, I watched the dried grass below through spaces in the floor boards. It was all so exciting. We had decided to follow the Athi - Sabaki River, from Nairobi down to its mouth at the Indian Ocean, two hundred odd miles away. We flew low, above the Athi as it tripped and meandered through the rugged hills and plains. We gazed down at herds of zebra, buck and wildebeest, hippo in the river, crocs basking on rocks in the afternoon sun, and herds of elephant. Sometimes we'd buzz down for a closer look. It was thrilling. Passing over a lonely campsite, we tipped our wings saluting the unknown campers waving to us in the middle of nowhere. All too soon we reached the ocean, which lay below in enthralling transparent shades of turquoise and blue. After landing at the local airstrip, we hitched into the quiet Malindi town and knocked on the door of friends. Our weekend in paradise passed in a haze of beautiful starlit walks along the beach, days beside a pool under palm trees, and round after round of irresistible fresh orange sling gins. Sunday afternoon appeared out of nowhere and we had to sober up for our flight home before nightfall. Totally shattered, and too exhausted to plot a course, we simply flew the plane south along the coast to Mombasa, turned right and followed the main Mombasa Nairobi Road homewards. It was still a spectacular journey, and the beautiful terrain stretched out in golden hues beneath a wild red sun set, as we prepared to touch down, tired and happy.

Obviously I was having a wonderful time, and already a year had passed while I was teaching. Hon wrote from London quite often, always ending her letters, 'When are you coming back to do the Europe trip?' I was so happy where I was, but a promise is a promise, and I had definitely been bitten by the travel bug, so I started seriously thinking about going back to London. I had been squirreling away a percentage of my pay and had enough for my flight and a little extra. That's all I ever seemed to save up over the years, enough for the fare, and a little extra.

Jim, Ian Barbour, sister Pix & George Martin, Sunday in Songhor, 1927

Cheetah

Jim, 8th Army   Peggy, Woman's Royal Navy

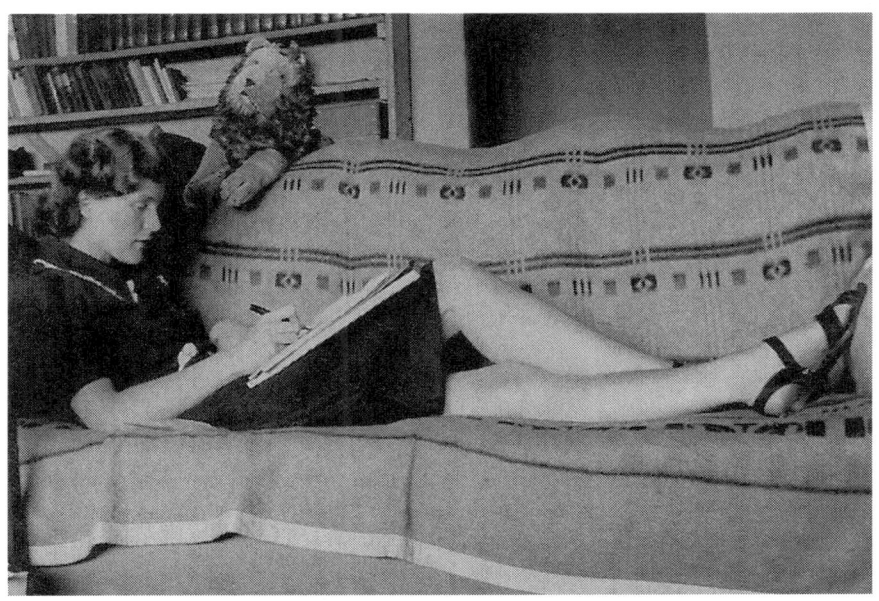

Peggy at home

Peggy (left) watches the first TV in 1936

Savani home

Youth prepares for tribal ceremony, Savani

Heather, Hugh and Robin, Nandi Hills

Arthur, Teddy, and Granny Sue, a week before Teddy died

The family at the coast near Mombasa

Hugh   Jim, Bwana Kiko, Maraba

Robin, Maraba

Hugh & Linda's wedding,
Isle of Sheppey

Lee & Andi, Karehana Bay, NZ

Mango with Sirri and Margaret the chicken, Maraba

Vervet monkey in thorn tree

On our neighbours
parched farm, Songhor

Boran cattle and herdsman
on dip day, Maraba

Maasai family, Longido

Giraffe with attendant tick birds

Peggy and Robin, Australia

Gold for Kenya, 400m relay, final event Commonwealth Games

Supporting Kenya's marathon runners in NZ, when Mum in England saw us 'live' on TV.

11. That Summer

It was exciting to be back in London, at the start of what Hon always referred to later as 'that summer'. When I arrived, Hugh, who based in London, was away doing survey work in Panama. So I headed up to Liverpool, caught the ferry to the Isle of Man, and stayed with Aunt Pix at 'Ballapeg'. She was a lovely free spirit and we had a great time exploring the island during the days while Robin was at school, and when he was released we made the most of our time together, meeting friends and checking out various haunts of his. Driving over the island, he instructed me to say hello to the fairies as we crossed the 'Fairies Bridge'. Superstition demands that anyone crossing this bridge greets the fairies, or bad luck will befall them. We giggled as we called out "Hello Fairies", and Robin assured me that it never failed to amaze and amuse him when en route to rugby matches in a coach full of strapping great rugby players, everyone still calls out to the fairies! Apparently even motorcycle riders and crews visit the bridge to say hello to the fairies to ensure good luck rides with them throughout the TT Races.

Luck had it that I'd arrived in the Isle of Man for the TT Races. There was no racetrack, or even a broad straight road, so all the races took place on the normal winding lanes throughout the island. The roads were usually lined with dry stone dykes, metre high rock walls. It was thrilling to watch the skill and courage of the riders as they hurtled along the narrow twisting lanes at incredible speeds. Leathered bodies missed the walls and road by inches as they roared round corners and negotiated the sharp s-bends. It was an amazing experience just to watch, and it was easy to appreciate the expertise of the riders. Bikies, petrol heads, and supporters invaded the island in their thousands, and the roads and car parks outside pubs were cluttered with bikes of every description, and a lively, carefree atmosphere pervaded Manxland. As soon as the TT Races were over, the island quickly resumed its peaceful charm. It was also time for me to leave, and I set off for Cockermouth in the Lake District to stay with Hon and her family. It was super to see everyone again, and Hon, her brother Brendan, and I spent endless hours chatting in their sunny garden while Brendan strummed his guitar and we played 'Bridge over Troubled Waters' over and over again. We hitched over to Manchester and Birmingham Universities to see friends, and I was able to catch up with Angie, who was now studying drama at Manchester University. My 21st

birthday came and went, spent at a pub with Hon's friends. The birthday girl got to ride in a sports car and wear the 'little black number', which was a gorgeous black mini dress, a sort of sexy slinky safari style creation. We shared this dress, both loved it, and of course always wanted to wear it at the same time. Whoever missed out on wearing the little black number, got to wear my black and white Mary Quant dress, or just to be bloody minded, put on a pair of jeans and tee shirt, so that 'she' in the little black number felt overdressed!

    Reality soon kicked in and I took the bus back to London to earn some money. The plan was for Hon to join me in London in a couple of weeks and we'd take the ferry over to France for the start of our hitchhiking trip through Europe. Hoping to pick up a live-in job for a few weeks, I had joined an agency that found and filled vacancies for temporary nannies in London. However, it wasn't working out well, and after making an unsuccessful call in a noisy Brompton Road phone box which reeked of stale cigarettes, I decided to wander into Harrods. I spent the rest of the day there, scouring the 'Situations Vacant' columns in the much nicer, quieter phone booths. But nothing fell into place, and at closing time I was still without a job and homeless. Feeling despondent, I felt an urge to ring Hugh. It was a silly idea, as I knew he wasn't even in the country. A bell rang through the store and Harrod's staff ushered people towards the exits. On impulse I quickly dialed Hugh's number. Sure enough Hugh was away, but Drew, his friend from Nigeria, who I'd met years before, was called to the phone, and suggested I go out to their flat for supper, and that I could stay the night as the late trains weren't good. It suited me just fine and I caught the tube to Leytonstone. I was having a beer with Drew, when a nice looking guy walked in smiling. He looked as though he was ready to go out. I hoped he wouldn't. He didn't! His name was Lee and he shared the flat with Hugh and Drew.

    Had I made that impulsive phone call to Hugh a day later, Drew would not have been there either, as he flew out to Nigeria the next morning. So fate had decided Lee and I should meet, and there was only a tiny sliver of time in which it could happen. Later I learnt that Lee only came to be there by a series of coincidences too. A few months earlier he had noticed a minivan in his street with a New Zealand emblem on the back. Needing to borrow some tools, and since his family lived in New Zealand, Lee thought this might bode well. He wandered over to chat and ask the owner of the minivan if he was from New Zealand. The answer was no. Did he have any tools? Again, the answer was no. Days later this young man, Drew, approached Lee, explaining that he was going overseas for a couple of weeks and could Lee look after his minivan? The use of the car was good, but it also entailed taking Drew to the airport, picking him up on his return, and letting him shack up as he had let his flat go. Drew eventually found a new flat, but needed two others to share the rent. The flat mates became my brother Hugh, and Lee. And so we met.

Twenty Miles to say Goodbye

Lee and I hit it off instantly, but I had to leave next day as a temporary nanny job in St Johns Wood had come up. We said goodbye and I checked in with my new charge, a seven year old girl, whose American parents were off to a golfing weekend at St Andrews. We were playing games after supper when the doorbell rang. There, unexpectedly, stood Lee, with a sleeping bag he'd bought me for the European trip. The rest, as they say, is history! How sweetly we fell in love. We spent a couple of wonderfully happy weeks together. After an evening at the pub with friends Mick and Susie, we returned to the flat to find Hon waiting on the doorstep. Wow! London – Life – Laughter – and Love! We all had a great few days and on our last night we ended up in Piccadilly Circus wandering around the lively streets, enjoying the atmosphere and the music. On a whim, in a lively sounds shop, we decided to buy a current '45' record each to mark the occasion. We returned to the flat with the Lola by the Kink's, Dylan's 'Lay Lady Lay', and The Moody Blues great song, 'Questions'. The next morning was difficult, and I was torn in two. Half of me was excited that we were off on our hitch-hiking trip, while the other half wanted to stay with my new love. But Hon needed to get away, so we bid Lee a fond farewell. Taking off 'the millstone' the enormous black plastic cross she wore over her tee shirt, Hon presented it to Lee telling him she'd be very disappointed if he didn't keep it on – no matter what. We all laughed and headed off to the station.

The Janis Joplin / Kris Kristofferson song 'Me and Bobby McGee' captures the mood of our freewheeling, hitchhiking days through France, Spain, and Switzerland. It was an amazing time and our days were filled with new places, tastes, languages and people. We slept out in the woods, in quiet parks, or occasionally splashed out on a night at a Youth Hostel. Here we enjoyed the luxury of a shower and the company of other young travelers from all parts of the world, and the evenings were often filled with guitar music and sing-alongs. In retrospect I am aware of how fortunate we were to have travelled around then, before the era of package tours and mass tourism invasion. TV documentaries, the Internet, and cell phones had not yet come into being, so our sense of discovery and expectation had not been dulled. It was easy to become absorbed by different cultures and ways of life in naturally friendly times, and it was a wonderful carefree adventure.

Hon had a Scottish friend, Sase, whose parents owned an apartment in the south of France. Several of her friends were meeting here during the summer. Meanwhile Lee was going to hand in his notice and join us here in Sanary sur Mer as soon as he could.

The ferry across the channel and our first lifts were uneventful and we arrived in Paris as it grew dark. We had been dropped off in central Paris, and decided to splash out on a cheap hotel room for our first night. The tiny attic room, several stories high, was slightly bigger than the bed. This creaking old bed had an interesting inner spring system, and every time Hon moved on her side of the bed, my side would spring into action with a loud 'boing' and I would be popped up like a slice of toast. Likewise, if I turned over, Hon would be bounced skywards with a loud 'boing'. After an hour of helpless giggles and vague attempts at sleep, we got up and went out to enjoy the lights of Paris. What a beautiful city. The L'arc de Triomphe was particularly fascinating at night and I was astonished at its size, design, and the intricate relief over its entire surface enhanced by the floodlights. We wandered along the boulevards, amongst the tourists and Parisians, as traffic flowed past late into the night. Our first morning in France began with a stroll up the Champs Elysee. Stopping at sidewalk cafés we soon learned that the only drink within our budget was tonic water. Even water was too expensive in Paris! We had a magical day ambling along the Seine and through the cobbled streets of Paris. Unfortunately economics dictated we get out of the city fast and we took Le Metro to the outskirts where we picked up a lift immediately. Clambering into the back of a van we discovered our travelling companions comprised of a goat, a tortoise, a spinning wheel, and two nice German guys!

Arriving somewhere very late, we shared our food and kipped down beside a lake. We got on well with Hans and Peter, who were heading for Grenoble and on to Italy, and we allowed them to talk us into splitting up for lifts. It seemed sensible and we arranged to meet up at a particular Youth Hostel in Lyons. The lifts should have been easier, two couples, one with a pretty red head, the other with a little blonde, but we all had a long hot day getting small lifts that took us a only a few miles further each time. We'd clamber out, wave and call out *'merci beaucoup'*, then begin hitching again. It was often ages before anyone stopped for us. Very late that night, Peter and I finally reached the city of Lyon. We gazed over a bridge at the city lights reflected in the Rhone, well aware that it could take a couple more hours to get to the hostel. Suddenly we lightened up and began tossing small stones at the colourful neon reflections in the water. We laughed like children as the colours split, rippled, and danced in errant patterns and swirls below us. Eventually we trudged on, until completely exhausted, we decided to call it quits and get some sleep. We snuggled down in our sleeping bags on a little patch of grass, but, as day broke, we realised that we were in a small square surrounded by towering blocks of flats, with people calling down to us from their balconies! Not the place for a sleep in, and looking forward to joining up with the others, we were soon on our way. But when we arrived at the hostel, there was no Hon waiting. It had taken us so long to get to Lyon that it had never occurred to me that the others would not be there before us. After hot showers we sat around chatting with other travellers while we waited. It was late afternoon now, and still no sign of Hon and Hans. I was very worried and started wondering how on earth I'd explain to Hon's Mum that we'd split up, that Hon hadn't turned up, and there was no way of knowing where she might be, and if she was OK. There were no means of contact, and all we could do was wait. Finally, to my great relief, Hon and Hans stumbled into the hostel. We celebrated togetherness that night, but alas, the lessons learnt were soon forgotten as next day we set out in the same fashion for Grenoble. Hon and Hans got the first ride and sped away in a classy BMW. Much later, a little French Citroen kindly stopped for us. Hon would be really jealous! She loved these cute little cars. I squeezed in the back with the rucksacks. The canvas sunroof was open and we chugged along chatting happily. Up ahead were two hitchhikers, a red head and a blonde guy! Getting into the spirit, our driver tooted at them as we approached. We hooted, hollered, and whistled, and standing up I waved manically from the open roof at Hon and Hans laughing and gesticulating as we passed. Having arrived at Grenoble Station, Peter and I again sat around waiting for the others. Hours later I put myself through the same torture, wondering why I hadn't I stuck with Hon. Once again, I was totally relieved as they walked in. We all had a bite to eat, accompanied by the usual cheap red wine, and settled down to sleep in what appeared to be a sports field. We awoke in the morning to find a market had sprung up around us! Stalls had mushroomed up while we slept and we were welcomed into a vibrant market day atmosphere as friendly locals offered us coffee, bread and fruit. We said goodbye and parted ways with the guys. They set off for Turin, and we for Le Cote d'Azure.

The country we drove through was so beautiful, and of all the lovely places we went in Europe, I will always remember the road south from Grenoble through the Alps. It was truly spectacular. Arriving in Cannes, back-packers told us about a good place to spend the night, in the dried out moat of an old ruined fort. As evening faded, we sat on the rocks, munching bread and cheese, gazing along the bay to the twinkling lights of Monte Carlo. In the depths of night we were woken by headlights and the gendarmes asking to see our papers and passports. We noticed other small groups were given the same treatment, and a couple were even driven away in the police van. It was to become par for the course on our travels. Everywhere we were stopped by the police who asked to see our *'papiers'*. I was eternally grateful for Hon's French savvy. She spoke French fluently, while I was hopeless. Not wanting to become reliant on her French expertise, I became responsible for asking directions and for items in cafés and shops, but it was good to have someone who knew what was going on in difficult or unusual situations.

Sanary sur Mer was a lovely coastal town and we located our friend's flat in a smart block of stylish apartments. It was sheer luxury. No one had arrived from Scotland yet, and I was delighted to find a couple of letters from Lee in the letterbox. We spent our first morning down on the beach but by the end of the day, had decided that it was an anti-climax. We loved being 'on the road' so much that lying on a sunny beach on the Cote d'Azur didn't quite do it for us! That night, studying the map in the luxury apartment, we elected to hit the road again, journeying along the south coast of France to Spain.

In France hitchhiking on l'auto route was prohibited, and we tended to follow more scenic but still direct main roads to towns ahead. While waiting by the roadside for lifts, we'd print the town we hoped to reach that evening in large letters on the back of our map. Underneath our sign we attached a card saying *s'il vous plaît*. Holding up the destination and saying 'please' seemed to be a winning formula for us (possibly being two girls together had something to do with it too!) However, taking notice of those distant lessons Mum and Dad tried to teach me, we never wore shorts, minis, or revealing tops. We had had a couple of nasty experiences with men veering off the main road, taking us into quieter areas, stopping, and trying it on. On one occasion, this happened with three young guys who drove off with us, into a maze of vineyards, but when they realized they weren't going to get anywhere, they became very angry, pushed us out the car and roared off. It was a pathetic situation to find ourselves in, as our rucksacks were still in the boot of their car and we were now stranded in the middle of nowhere. Fortunately for us, they roared back about ten minutes later, slammed on the brakes, threw our rucksacks at us, hurled some abuse, and screamed off.

Another time we were given a lift by two business men, who, along the way, suggested we stop for lunch at an attractive open air restaurant. C'est la vie! On being asked how I was enjoying France, young and blonde, I looked across the table and sweetly said, "I love you." Well *je l'aime* (I love it) and *je t'aime* are very similar. We all laughed and tucked into our steaks, salad, and white wine. However, these men hadn't treated us to a posh lunch for nothing, and things became nasty when they turned off into a secluded wood.

You can't choose who stops to give you a lift, but we had to wise up to the consequences. We naturally relied a lot on our intuition and if we felt at ease with someone and trusted them, we were more relaxed and would just go with the flow. Now, along with our 'dress sensibly' and 'stick together' rules, we added another precaution. We agreed to ask to stop and insist we get out as soon as anyone turned off the main road, even if they said it was a short cut, or they wanted to show us some scenery. We also both carried a small knife and kept our heavy glass water bottles filled and at hand; just in case.

We fell into an easy rhythm, travelling in the daylight hours and sleeping in the woods at night. We survived on a regular diet of baguettes, the long loaves of French bread, dipped into delicious gooey cheese, washed down with a bottle of local red. Occasionally we were able to wander in to the nearest village in the morning, order a *café au lait et du pain'*, disappear into 'Les Dames' to brush our teeth and have a quick wash, before our breakfast was served. In some villages, cafés served an evening meal on long trestle tables for the locals. We loved these and would always be warmly welcomed, and were able to enjoy hearty cheap meals of local fare with friendly company. On one of these occasions I had my first taste of eel, sautéed in garlic with a herb sauce, and served with chunky bread, it was just fine.

The feeling of space and the tawny golds of the dry marshland grasses of the Camargue reminded me of Kenya, but sadly the wild horses were illusive. We travelled on, through fruit growing country, reaching a small town at twilight. Here a group of boys started hassling us and following us about. Not wanting them to see where we settled for the night, we approached a house beside large greenhouses. Knocking on the door we asked if they'd mind if we stayed in their greenhouse for the night. This foiled the boys and in the morning the lady invited us over for coffee. She had a lovely large wild flower garden that needed attention, so we gave her a hand weeding it, before she drove us out to peach orchards where she'd heard fruit picking work was available. Left here, we eventually located the boss in the fields, but he told us he already had too many pickers, so we began the long walk back to the main road through the orchards. With an endless blue sky above, hot sun on our shoulders, simply happy to be, we wandered along enjoying this fantastic day, and tucking into the largest, most delicious juicy golden peaches I have ever tasted. Later that evening, relaxing in a field overlooking a small gypsy camp, I suddenly realised I had lost my watch. Presumably it had fallen off when we were weeding. I had been so touched when Mum and Dad gave it to me for my 21st when I left Kenya. Now only a few months later, I'd managed to lose it. I was cross with myself and sad, but with the loss came a new found freedom. We hadn't known what day it was, and now no longer knew what time it was. We ate when we were hungry, slept when tired, and woke with the sun. Time had no claim on us, and I have never worn a watch since.

Passing through Perpignon we headed towards the Pyrénées and Spain. A lovely family gave us a lift, even though it meant rearranging their holiday luggage to find space for us and our rucksacks in their tiny car. The little boy rolled around in fits of giggles as I'd addressed him intimately as *tu* instead of *vous*, and we all laughed at my attempts at French, which although improving, still left endless scope for amusement. The small car laboured up the winding mountain roads with its heavy load and we alighted at a youth hostel in La Molina. The young couple had driven out of their way, insisting we spend the night there where we'd be safe. We were extremely grateful they had. The sole residents in this wonderful old stone hostel nestling amongst the mountain pines, we watched for hours as lightening flashed through dark, rolling clouds, and thunder grumbled through the hills. The rain was hard and heavy as the wild storm raged, and we snuggled up inside, safe and warm.

Washed clean, the mountain scene sparkled clear and beautiful in the early morning sunshine. All too soon we were whisked away, and with only one quick lift, arrived in Barcelona at lunchtime. We learnt our first Spanish lesson. Everything, simply everything, stops for siesta! Needing Spanish cash, we were marooned in the city centre for a couple of hours waiting for the banks to open again. Drifting along to a pier, a popular place for young people to hang out, we were approached by a young boy who wanted to show us a place to stay. This was deciphered with the help of a nearby long haired translator as neither of us knew a word of Spanish. The little lad led us to his modest home, where his mother rented us a cheap room for a couple of nights. We explored the amazing bustling city and visited Maria Rosa, a Spanish friend I'd met in London in 1968. Together, we'd been on a Peace March, singing 'Stand by me' and chanting 'LBJ, LBJ how many kids have you killed today?' over and over as we marched to Speakers Corner with thousands of others.

Now we travelled with Franz, a philosophical Austrian guy, who, as a boy, had been in the Vienna Boys Choir. The three of us hitched a lift up into the mountains with a lorry driver delivering supplies to Montserrat. Once a Benedictine monastery, with buildings built into the rocks, it was quite spectacular. However, it was no longer simply a religious retreat and the place was swarming with tourists, and vendors trying to flog plastic statues of Mary, gaudy rosary beads, and other cheap trinkets. I disliked the feel of the place and was anxious to leave. Eventually we trundled down the mountains towards Zaragoza where we spent that night in a vineyard. Plagued by mosquitoes, we had to cover our heads with light clothing, which made us extremely hot and irritable. This part of Spain was flat and dry, but we enjoyed Franz' company and the friendly people who made us welcome wherever we went. Most villagers didn't speak French or English, but a smile is the same in every language.

Waving goodbye to Franz, we jumped into the cab of a huge haulage truck and set off for an unforgettable trip across Spain. Our larger than life driver was completely over the top, singing his heart out as he thumped rhythms on the steering wheel. We frequently stopped at *tavernas* along the way. He was obviously a regular on this run, and friendly locals appeared at our table with tomatoes, tapas, and bottles of wine. As the day wore on, with all the attention he was getting, our friend's ego had become a bit over-inflated and he was now ordering champagne, and getting pretty inebriated. Hon and I became concerned at the state of our driver, and our requests for coffee were brushed aside. Perhaps foolishly, we attempted either to spill, or drink as much of his glass as we could, which only really resulted in three of us being unfit for the road. However we continued, and as we approached the next town, he changed down to pull over at the *taverna*. We protested and a massive argument developed. Our driver was furious and it became apparent he expected far more than just our company. Things were now becoming very hot and unpleasant as he pulled over, screaming and shouting at us. Our amazing happy journey had gone sour, and as the driver's temper soared we hurriedly grabbed our rucksacks, leapt from the truck, and hid amongst the bushes, waiting with baited breath until his truck finally graunched into gear and thundered off into the night.

We eventually emerged on the Atlantic coast where we met up with five cheerful American surfers in a VW Kombi. We travelled via the coast road through La Coruna and along the Bay of Biscay to San Sebastian before re-entering France and cruising up the west coast. In due course we needed to veer eastward and parted company with the carefree surfers, leaving them to their joints, and their eternal quest for the perfect wave. The next part of the journey was to take much longer than anticipated.

Meanwhile, unbeknown to us, Lee had hitched down from London and arrived in Sanary sur Mer. When he located the apartment, he found letters he'd written to me still in the mailbox. None of the other visitors had arrived, and apparently he spoke to a gorgeous blonde in a tennis dress. The blonde called the caretaker, and together they took him to Sase's apartment. Lee's French was worse than mine, and the caretaker must have assumed Lee was the first of the expected visitors from Scotland, and handed him the keys! Lee now had a luxury apartment in the South of France all to himself. He had anticipated meeting up with us in Sanary sur Mer, and because there were no signs we'd even been there he became concerned. Joined by a young French couple he befriended, Lee spent the next few days searching for us, but there was little to go on as we hadn't hung around or stayed in any hostels on the Cote d'Azure. As he hadn't received any of my letters, he had absolutely no idea where we were, or if we were alright. It occurred to him that we might not be coming back for our rendez-vous? Disillusioned, he started thinking about moving on.

There was a little bar on the beach, and he'd sometimes go there for a drink and some company, playing the jukebox, and belting out 'the long and winding road'. One afternoon, in only swimming shorts and the black plastic cross, he waded into the sea clutching a bottle of wine. He remembers waking up much later, on some rocks, hot, hung-over, and sunburnt. He was red all over except for a large white cross on his chest where the black plastic 'millstone' had shielded him from the sun! How Hon enjoyed it when she heard the story. She giggled and laughed for ages as tears ran down her cheeks.

Fate was not going to let another chance go by. We'd turned up a day later, and after lots of happy hugs and tales, we headed back up from the beach to the apartment, where Sase and a contingent of Scottish pals were just arriving. We all squashed into the apartment that night, and when we had some time alone, Lee asked me to marry him. The very next day, we had our first row. Wandering through the village, we passed a church, and Lee spontaneously said to me, "Come on let's go and get married". Even though I had told my Aunt Pix that I wasn't going to think about getting married for at least another five years, I'd said 'yes' to Lee without a moment's hesitation. But tying the knot the very next day was out of the question. I couldn't envisage sending my family a postcard telling them I'd just got married – it was definitely not a spur of the moment thing. Later that afternoon Lee, Hon and I bid farewell to the others and headed off for more hitchhiking exploits as we wended our way towards Switzerland. Our plans had changed as Lee's Mum was unwell in New Zealand and he was anxious to get back to her. It was on the cards that I'd join him and we were taking Hon to Berne where she'd stay with friends.

Almost déjà vu, we arrived late in Lyon that night. We found ourselves under a bridge looking for somewhere to sleep. This idea was quickly thwarted when we noticed the banks were seething with huge ghastly rats. They really were the size of cats! We progressed to a park, which was equally unsavoury, with every type of weirdo stopping by while we slept fitfully and Lee kept watch.

On the road again, we were given a lift by the amusing, eccentric, Maurice, who continually peppered his speech with colourful words and imagery. He entertained us in his throaty French accent, 'She was too nice, yes, but her friends, zey were, how you say? Zey were not my circus, not my monkees. So I hit ze road, but ze storm is coming, ze trees bend over backward for ze wind, and ze rain is like ze cow pissing on ze flat rock …'

We crossed the border into Switzerland early afternoon. Below us lay a beautiful Swiss scenic paradise, a clear tranquil lake with snow-covered peaks in the background. A swim in this heavenly setting was definitely in order. Hon declined and waited for us while we braved the icy cold waters. Alas there was a very strong current that was sweeping us along too quickly. Freezing cold, and a bit frightened, we laboured towards the bank. It was a great relief to get out of the powerful current. Trying to clamber up the slippery muddy bank resulted in us doubling up in hysterics as Lee hauled himself up the slope, only to slither helplessly down again, looking more and more like a chocolate coated sloth! Once out, dry and changed, we finally translated a nearby warning notice, "*Achtung,* There is danger when the dam gates are opened and strong currents can drag you to the outlet."

In the beautiful city of Berne we were made very welcome by Hon's friends, the Wyss family. We stayed with them for several days and Lee and I were given a wee attic room. Everyone gathered round the table at lunchtimes for huge bowls of delicious Swiss bircher muesli made with fresh cherries and yoghurt. We played boule in the garden, wandered through the woods looking for bears, or strolled along the immaculate pretty streets. All too soon it was time to leave our beautiful friend Hon and hitch to Zurich, from whence we were to fly out to New Zealand. Mr and Mrs Wyss, keen mountain climbers, had always dreamed of climbing Mt Kilimanjaro, so I was able to give them details about this, along with an open invitation to stay with my family in Kenya. Less than a year later we heard they'd travelled to Africa, climbed Kilimanjaro, and had driven up country to spend a week with Mum and Dad. Everyone had got on really well and it was wonderful to be able to return their generous hospitality.

Unlike the swallows, we flew from summer into winter. Gale force winds bucked the plane which teetered over Wellington until the pilot was able to ease us down through the hills onto the slick runway. Despite the weather and our delayed arrival, Lee's best friend, Brian, and all Lee's family were at the airport to welcome us to New Zealand. From the unprotected gangway, I blew into the terminal in a wayward mini that responded eagerly to the whim of the wind. Despite this, I think there might have been a little disappointment when I appeared, small, windswept and white. An exotic black girl was expected since

Lee's phone call saying he'd be bringing his girlfriend with him, and that she came from Africa!

I felt instantly at ease with everyone. Not so the 107 steps up the steep hill to the house. Lee's Mum, Char, was a lovely warm-hearted soul, who took me under her wing. She called me 'her little hippy', as we turned up the music and danced around while we did the housework. It seemed all she ever wanted was for everyone to be happy. Several weeks after our arrival, talking to Lee about his Mum, he confessed that he felt sad I would never really know his Mum, not the way she used to be. Life had changed her he said, there was only a sense of her original spirit left. It was strange. For me she was just beginning, yet for Lee she was already ending.

Wellington, in 1970, was like a small town. Situated on the southern tip of the North Island, above Cook Strait, it nestled amongst the hills which slope steeply down to the harbour. Although beautiful, it was cold, incredibly windy, and after coming straight from Swinging London and Europe, it felt extremely slow and isolated. I felt a long way from anywhere. I was.

Char understood this. She knew how it felt to live so far from home, in a small place on the other side of the world, with no family or friends around. Part of a large family, she had grown up in Ireland, in the port of Cobh in County Cork. As a young woman, she had lived in London, where she remained during the war years, eventually coming out to New Zealand to join her husband in the early fifties. It would have been even more isolated then. Worse still, Char's husband had taken up with somebody else. At least I had the love of my man. Although people were friendly, they were pretty conventional and no one was particularly interested in the larger world beyond. There was little curiosity or interest in where you came from, or what it was like there. Topics of conversation tended to cover the three Rs, rugby, racing and rearing, and you were expected to quietly fit into the world of New Zealand, putting your former life on the shelf. Fortunately all the young people loved music.

However on a sunny day Wellington was charming. The hillsides were cluttered with unique colourful wooden houses, studded with gables, trellised verandas, pointed roofs, and leadlight doors and windows. The houses twisted haphazardly along angled streets or perched en masse on impossibly steep slopes and cliffs. All the houses were painted in interesting colour schemes at the whim of their owners and contrasted wildly with next door's décor. The overall scene of bright creative houses crowding hillsides looked like a vibrant child's painting. I believe the majority of similar houses in San Francisco are built from New Zealand timber. Wood being the desired construction material, because both cities, Wellington and San Francisco are built on fault lines.

I had been pleasantly surprised to see the racial harmony between the Maori, the Pacific Islanders, and the Europeans. Many marriages were mixed, and people of all colours and cultures accepted one another, working and living together with an apparent ease. This tolerance intrigued me and it was heartening to see a country that didn't appear to discriminate and was adapting so well to diversity. Having grown up in Africa, I was always conscious of the on-going difficulties between tribes, cultures, and races. At this time, racial friction was evident in many parts of the world, from South Africa with its apartheid system to the problems in UK as the English and influx of immigrants struggled to live alongside each other.

After our rough and ready travels in Europe, we had arrived with all our worldly possessions in our rucksacks. My wardrobe consisted of a pair of faded jeans and jacket, tee shirts, two tight lacy tops, one black and one white, and my tiny red mini skirt. I went straight to the Education Department to see if I could get a job teaching, but they were not interested in me as I did not have the required qualifications. So I started at an electrical supplies office in Taranaki Street. I appeared at work every day in the red mini, alternating my black and white tops on a daily basis. I had come down to earth with a thump. No more carefree days travelling through Europe. The brakes of normality had locked my freewheeling spirit. I suddenly found myself with airfares to pay off, a boring office job, cold windy weather, and I felt completely isolated from the rest of the world. Wellington's wind is legendary, and Aussies frequently make jokes about its horizontal rain! The wind used to tunnel down Taranaki Street, shrieking and wailing through the telephone wires like a demented banshee. On particularly wild days, it was no mean feat to get to work. I would leave the safety of one lamppost, hurtling myself into the howling gale, and rush headlong to grab hold of the next post before I was swept off my feet by the whirling gusts. The antics of the red mini were no longer a priority!

Lee's family were Catholic, and we arranged to be married in The Church of Our Lady of Mt Carmel in Haitaiti, overlooking the beautiful expanse of Wellington's harbour. We duly went to meet the Priest, Father Donahue, and over cups of tea, enjoyed an interesting philosophical and religious discussion. But when it came to the request that we christen our children as Catholics, Lee wouldn't accept that the reasoning for a christening was to remove sin from the baby's soul. As far as he was concerned, an innocent baby wouldn't have any sin on its soul to be removed. Meanwhile I couldn't promise to bring my children up in a faith that I did not believe in myself. We told Father Donahue that we would bring our children up with love, and leave it to them to choose their own religion when they were older. He wisely let this ride for the time being, but later was to make many visits to Lee's Mum in an attempt to influence our decision.

Meanwhile, as we left to go, Father Donahue suddenly said, "You'd make a good teacher". I laughed and told him of my unsatisfactory visit to the Education Department, to which he replied, "Come to my office on Monday. I'll give you a job teaching." I couldn't believe my luck. It transpired that Father Donahue was also Head of Catholic Primary Schools in the Wellington region. At the time they were short staffed, and I was able to choose the age group and area in Wellington I'd prefer to teach. But before that I was asked to fill in immediately at St Ann's in Newtown, a poorer part of the city. This particular classroom had already had no less than six different teachers, and I was to take them through the next two months to the end of the year. It was no easy task as this junior class was like the League of Nations, with children from Poland, Belgium, Samoa, Fiji, Noumea and Chile. Several of the youngsters spoke little or no English, and they were an unruly little bunch. I worked with several kindly nuns, who suggested that I tell the children my married name, even though our wedding was weeks away, so that the children would not have to get used to any more names. The Nuns, happy to have a full time teacher at last, accepted me whole heartedly and never complained at my smoking in the tiny office at tea break, where I sat amongst them, teetering on a bar stool, cigarette in hand, and the little red mini barely covering any leg.

Lee had taken up with the same telecommunications outfit he was working with in England, and spent days suspended in bucket cranes in gale force winds wiring high-rise buildings. He soon moved to another job as a diesel mechanic for a company extending the airport, which gave him the opportunity of lots of overtime so we could pay our fares back and start saving for our next trip. In the New Year I commenced work at a primary school in Lower Hutt. I was given a large folder with the year's syllabus to follow, and as long as I taught the children everything the syllabus required, and respected the Catholic Church, the nuns were perfectly happy for me to run my class as I liked. What faith they put in me, and perhaps because of the freedom they had given me, I taught with total enthusiasm and commitment. The children responded accordingly, and we all had a wonderful year. We were a radical class for 1971 and worked without a timetable. Instead we had noisy, active lessons when the children were restless or excited, and concentrated on maths and English when they were bright and alert, and if they got bored we'd start up lively discussions about the pros and cons of war, or how we'd run our own island. Our classroom was decorated with 'happy pictures', which the kids created one afternoon. With music playing, the children painted their abstract creations, with colours, shapes and movements expressing their own joyful delight, and covered every inch of wall with these beautiful bright works of art.

One little girl, Margaret, was painfully shy and unable to utter one sentence in front of the class without stuttering and blushing profusely. She reminded me how it felt to be shy at school, and gradually we were able to draw her out. At first it was slow and tenuous, relying on simple things, like only asking her a question in front of the class when I knew she knew the answer, or placing her with kinder more positive kids for group activities. Gradually she started to relax and enjoy what we were doing until eventually she blossomed into an endearing little girl, happily involved in all the classroom activities. There were three particularly bright boys and it was a continual challenge to keep them stimulated and busy while the rest of the class needed my attention to finish their tasks at a slower pace. One of these boys, Richard, appeared quite aloof, almost superior, and I could imagine him thinking 'who's this twit trying to teach me?' If I asked him to do anything, he always quietly applied himself to the task, but again, I could almost hear him thinking, 'I'll do it because I have to, but it's not what I'd do'. He was a little detached from the general hub.

Towards the end of the year, I was leaving as our baby was due. On my last day at school, Richard gave me a wonderful gift, one that remains tucked in my heart. It was a total surprise. He put on a farewell play for me. He had written the play himself, and everyone in the class was involved and had learnt their lines and rehearsed without my knowledge. Richard had co-ordinated the entire show, down to all the eight year olds bringing costumes and props from home, and keeping it all a secret. I was very touched.

We saw the children once more, along with Sister Maria Joseph and Sister Anna. It was a weekend and they'd all turned up at Wellington Airport to see us off to Kenya. It was another beautiful and special surprise, and why, on our first morning in Kenya, we were down at the markets buying 30 wooden animal carvings to send back to our little New Zealand friends.

12. The Last Christmas

We'd been back in England almost two years, and were living in a tiny one bedroom flat, with a bath in the kitchen. We depended on one small electric bar heater to keep the winter chill at bay. The heater depended on us feeding shillings into its hungry, bottomless meter. There were many occasions when we had to pick the meter, leaving I.O.Us for our landlords, Mick and Susie. Sirri was now two and a half, and while Lee was at work, Sirri and I took the bus to a play school for 3–5 year olds, where I worked every morning and Sirri quietly amused herself. Alas, one morning we arrived 'at work' to find ourselves fired. Sirri had bitten another child, and we were shown the tooth marks on the arm to prove it. We had to go. Being a petit little thing, Sirri was constantly surrounded by older girls who loved to 'mother her'. They were always picking her up and lugging her about, pretending she was their baby. I think Sirri just got so frustrated with constantly being held and dragged around in tight little arms, that one day she retaliated in a way that worked.

Now we were caught in November's cold grey grip. We were on the wrong side of another long English winter. The chill seeped through the walls and into our bones. I found myself day dreaming about being able to go home to Kenya. I could see us playing in the garden under the jacaranda tree, feel the crisp dry grass between my toes, the warm sun on my skin. It was a secret dream, an impossible dream. Here we were, struggling to get from one week to the next, and I was entertaining thoughts of fun in the sun. I'd imagine taking Sirri to watch the cows swim through the dip, evening walks with Mum through the flowering coffee bushes, and days spent with Dad on the farm. Home. How I longed to go home. Yet we carried on happily and I remember thinking that my dreams were probably a kind of mental fuel to keep me warm through the long cold winter months, so I continued to dream.

Out of the blue, Lee suddenly said, "Why don't you go home to Kenya for Christmas!"

I couldn't believe I was hearing this. How strange that even though I'd said nothing, Lee had been thinking along the same lines. But how could we possibly go home? Realistically we didn't have enough for the metre, never mind airfares.

"You and Sirri could go…"

"Oh no, I couldn't go and leave you here, to this…. Anyway how could we afford it? Let's just wait until one day when we can all go out for a holiday together".

"Somehow we'll find the money Babe. We'll find a way", said Lee.

Now the dreams were positively bubbling. Then they'd evaporate into steam that clung and dribbled slowly down the grey-green wall. But Lee never gave up. He was working hard at the insurance, so he started doing that in the evenings only. We invested our weeks grocery money on a pair of work boots, went out the back yard and scraped them on the concrete and smothered them in mud, so he wouldn't look like the new kid on the block. Next morning Lee got a start as a brickie's labourer. During the day he worked as a builder, came home, chatted to me while he scrubbed up in the bath and I cooked supper, then he put on his suit and went out to do the insurance.

One euphoric afternoon, a few weeks later, we three took the tube to Soho. Lee had scraped together the fare for a ticket home for me and Sirri. It was going to happen. Dreams do come true. Excitedly we turned up a back alleyway, looking for a particular travel agent. We climbed some dark, dodgy, creaking stairs into a tiny windowless office.

Oh, but there was a spanner in the works. The travel agent explained that non-residents were not allowed to travel one way to Kenya. They had to have a return ticket. This was law and the customs and immigration would not let anyone into the country, without a ticket out again! Raising the fare out had been all we could do, a return ticket was quite out of the question. Our hopes slithered to the dusty wooden floor, retreating under the piles of discarded dreamers' pamphlets and brochures.

Then from out of the cobwebs came a vague memory. I remembered hearing about Dad, a few years earlier, staging a solitary 'sit-in' in the Immigration Department at Nairobi Airport. Now I recalled the details. Mum and Dad had gone to meet Robin, who was returning home after completing his schooling in the Isle of Man. Robin was on his way home, to the land where he was born, the country he grew up in, but they were not going to let him in because he only had a 'one way ticket'. Foreigners were not allowed to stay on in case they took jobs from the locals.

Now, here I was, years later, in a crazy fog of déjà vu. How could I have forgotten this? Our hopes were totally dashed. Then, as we got up to leave, the kindly agent tentatively told us that there was a loophole. They could arrange a return ticket that was invalid. To all intents and purposes this ticket would look exactly like any other return ticket, however, only other travel agents and flight personnel would be able to recognise it as null and void! Customs and Immigration, apparently, were unable to tell the difference. Well this was exciting! We would be able to fly to Kenya after all, and it was agreed that when Lee got the fees for the return flight, he would pay the travel agents, who would then provide a valid ticket for our journey back to England. How remarkable. Others had obviously been in this situation too.

We went ahead with it. Although we must have been slightly concerned because we decided not to tell Mum and Dad that we would be flying over, in case it didn't work out and they'd be disappointed. Instead we sent a telegram to Robin telling him of our E.T.A. and asking him to keep the secret.

We flew from London to Vienna, where we were treated to dinner and a free hotel room for the night, compliments of the airline, as we had to wait for a connecting flight to Rome then onto Nairobi. Little Sirri and I spent a wonderful day exploring Vienna, enjoying a spectacular practice session of the Lipizzaner Stallions as they were put through their paces, to strains of beautiful waltzes in an enormous baroque hall. We wandered the ancient streets, marveling at the magical assortment of Christmas displays decorating shop windows. There were fairy tale scenes with exquisite miniature turreted castles in snow-covered wonderlands, with twinkling lights, music and small folk dancing or skating on icy mirror lakes.

Stepping off the plane on a balmy Kenyan morning we were welcomed by Robin's warm smiles and hugs. It was the 12th December, Uhuru Day, a public holiday, and Robin was free to drive us straight home to Maraba. We squashed into his blue dusty, rally car, with roll bars and no back seat, and roared off, dazed and happy. A quick stop at Agip for cold drinks and fuel, then we thundered off on our safari. Kenya still looked so beautiful, even in the grip of a severe drought. The vast, dusty plains blended into hazy blue layers that dissolved into smoky mountain ranges. It felt so good to be back. We hurtled down the escarpment, raced across the shimmering plains of the Rift Valley, roared up the highlands and through the tea plantations, before descending into the hot, parched dustbowl of the Songhor Valley. It was now late afternoon and Sirri, after all this travelling, was tired, hot, sticky, and covered in dust from the red murram roads. She was understandably peeved and getting fretful. Fortunately we only had half an hour to go as we zoomed past endless fields of sugar cane, humpy hills, and sausage trees, leaving huge clouds of dust suspended in our wake. Inside the car, soft dust seeped into every imaginable space, coating our teeth and hair. At last, Robin changed down, hung a right at the Maraba post, and we growled up the hill, past the dip and coffee sheds. We turned into an oasis. Amongst trees and shrubs, a little wooden house, with Mum and Dad coming down the steps. Home!

Mum and Dad had been enjoying the peace of a public holiday. In the quiet of the country afternoon, having heard the distant roar of the rally car twenty minutes earlier, they knew Robin was on his way to visit them. They were outside waiting for him. Then suddenly they realised I was with him, and their little granddaughter too! It was a truly magical moment. There was so much joy as we all hugged and laughed and hugged again. Finally we all sat down to a priceless cup of tea together while Sirri ran around the garden with Macora, the dog. Robin needed to be back for work in the morning, and couldn't stay long as he had to drive the 300 kilometres back to Nairobi and on to Thika. He said goodbye and roared off into the dusty dusk.

Dear old Mango woke us in the morning with a cup of tea and a fond welcome. He was delighted that Sirri was now able to talk with him. Later we ventured off to the coffee factory, and Grandpa held his finger out for Sirri to hold as they walked off down the track together, chattering happily. My heart was too small for the happiness I felt. Africans were singing as they spread the beans out in the sun to dry, but work stopped as soon as they saw us and everyone crowded round to say jambo and to hold and touch Sirri. So many familiar faces, so many friendly smiles. There was the old headman, Kipsang, Daniel the mechanic, Kijana, Arap Koskei, Kip Lagat, and Cherop, all laughing and chattering at once! Then Otunda came hurrying over, his smile as warm as the African sun. He vigorously shook my hand, telling me *Mungu* was good, because he'd brought us home. God was indeed good. Reminding me of the baby's bottles we gave for his tiny baby after his wife had died in childbirth, Otunda happily told me that Margaret was now running around and talking. Here we were, two years later, sharing better times together.

Dad and Mum set off early for Eldoret the next morning. They had appointments with lawyers and banks as they'd just sold our farm, Schiehallion. They had been trying to sell for several years, and a Nandi syndicate had recently purchased it. Dad had worked his heart out on his dream, but after a few years it became necessary for him to work elsewhere, and now at 69, he concluded that he was too old to keep the farm going and it was time to sell.

Sirri and I sat down to draw, and write a letter to Lee. The mail still took a lifetime, and phones were best left for emergencies only. So it was much later that I learnt Robin had sent Lee a telegram to say that he had delivered us home safely, and that he wanted to pay our fares back to England. A couple of weeks later I also learnt that Hon, on hearing that Lee's girls were overseas, had invited him up to the Lake District for Christmas with her family.

The shamba boy dug a rectangle, a foot deep and Dad lined it with plastic, and hosed some precious water into it so Sirri could have a little paddling pool under the purple shade of the jacaranda tree. The sunny days on the farm were as close to perfect as you get. Mum's singing filled the air, as she baked and we all looked forward to Christmas. With my unexpected arrival, our little family would be complete. We were only a small family, Dad, Mum, and us three youngsters, yet one or other of us had always been away overseas. Now, for the first time in ten years, we would all be together. Hugh and Linda were flying up from Malawi, and Robin would be joining us, along with my cousin Liz and Bruce from Mau Narok with their two girls.

On the farm, and throughout the country, the drought was quietly causing havoc. Everywhere the temperatures soared and the land grew parched and brittle. Dust devils lazily swirled across the plains. Scorched dry grasses covered the hills, and snakes came out of the undergrowth in search of water. Mum accurately described the cows as 'looking like coat hangers', their humps and skin hanging loose over scraggy ribs. Several cows died of snake bite, simply because they were too listless to move out the way of snakes in time. Dad continued to dip the cows twice a week to get rid of the abundant ticks.

Walking up the hill from the dip, Dad stooped to pick up a seed. Smaller than a peppercorn, the seed was surrounded by transparent wings so it could fly and hover in the wind. Nothing was ever too small to escape Dad's attention. We wondered at the seed's construction, a tiny miracle that one day, given the right conditions, would become a huge shady tree. The *barakah*, the spirit, or blue print, of a particular type of tree was already within that tiny seed, and eventually it would grow into exactly what it was meant to be. We continued to enjoy a philosophical discussion and I felt grateful that I was the recipient of so many of Dad's seeds of wisdom and love. I hoped that I could do justice to the seeds he had scattered and that they'd grow and flourish wherever I went.

We were having lunch in the cool shade of the house, when there was a knock at the back door. Dad warned me that if it was Otunda, he wanted to give us something, and that I should accept it. I went to the door, and there stood Otunda with his ever present smile. Under his arm he held a chicken he wanted to give us.

"This chicken has eggs inside," he said, "It is a laying one." In Africa a man places far more importance on his livestock than on money. His cows, goats, or chickens ensure his family's survival, and are his riches, his wealth. He may have nothing else, but as long as he has a beast or two, he is doing fine. Now here was dear Otunda, struggling to feed and clothe his own three children, wanting to give me this truly generous present. I was overwhelmed, but I graciously took this precious gift, as he had once accepted our little gift to him. Sirri was very excited and immediately christened her chicken 'Margaret' after Otunda's little girl. Every evening, when she heard Margaret squawk and cackle, she'd run round the garden looking for her own newly laid egg.

At last the Anderson family was complete. Hugh and Linda flew in from Malawi, and Robin drove down from Thika for a few days over Christmas. We were all young and had been travelling, and doing an assortment of interesting things, and there was much to catch up on. It was all so special, and dear Mum and Dad were enjoying every single moment too, as was little Sirri. With all these Uncles and Grandparents to play with, she was in paradise, and certainly needed her wee siestas! Sirri also had two new companions, the imaginary 'brudders' (brothers). These brudders came everywhere with us, and we had to be mindful, getting into the car or sitting down at the table, as she'd suddenly say "Careful. Don't sit on de brudders!"

In Malawi, Hugh and Linda were living in a humble cottage on the lake shore in Chinteche, at about 1,500 feet above sea level. Lake-flies were a real pest, and Linda told us that everything, including underwear, had to be ironed. Fly larvae lived on the bottom of the lake and at the pupae stage floated to the surface where they hatched en masse, creating enormous dark spiraling insect clouds that actually looked like storm clouds rolling across the lake. Hugh was surveying a route for a road that would transport paper pulp from a proposed mill near the forests in Chikengowa at an altitude of 7,000 feet. One Friday afternoon, at a nearby site, the driver of a cement mixer rushed off for the weekend without first emptying and hosing out the huge drum of his machine. Monday morning presented the problem of a cement mixer filled with rock hard cement!

Christmas Eve at Maraba was hot, with dry gusty winds. We'd all slumped into chairs after lunch, when the dreaded cry went out. "*Moto* – Fire! *Pese, pese,* quick, hurry!" There was a bush fire up the hill above the house. Without a moment's hesitation, Hugh, Robin, and I raced off up the hill, along with the Africans from the farm. The fire was raging, fanned by the swirling wind. Wild orange flames leapt twice as high as us, roaring and changing direction at the whim of the wind. The heat was intense, and the fire was spreading rapidly. Somebody was hacking down branches with a *panga* - machete. We grabbed the branches to beat at the frightening flames. The task was forbidding, the heat unbearable. It was exhausting. Without a single word between us, Hugh, Robin, and I, stuck together. Helping each other with the ferocious flames, we'd change shifts every couple of minutes, so one of us could catch their breath, and get more branches. Occasionally I'd glimpse other fire fighters through the flames and the dense smoke. Everyone was giving every ounce of energy they had. No one had been asked, or organized, to do this. It was just the way it was. Out here there was no water, no fire-fighting equipment, only the combined efforts of each individual, beating down the flames with branches. The fear was that the fire would work its way down the hill towards the house, the farm sheds, the African villages, and the coffee factory. Crazy crackling flames wolfed up the dried trees and grasses, leaping to new places with each undecided gust. Eyes stinging, lungs screaming, throat scraping, I choked and spluttered in the thick swirling smoke. My body, sapped by the overwhelming heat and the constant beating, was completely drained. I swayed, feeling I couldn't go on. But everyone else was battling on, fighting that fire with all they had, and they would be feeling every bit as exhausted. Shouts recoiled though the smoke, reinforcing the knowledge that we were all working together, and I pushed on. Roaring flames devoured the tinder dry undergrowth with a wild insatiable hunger. Momentarily the wind blew the smoke away, but then it whirled the blazing fire back towards us. More branches, more beating, more effort, and then gusts that sent the blazes back. The wind changed direction. Now it blew up hill, turning the fire back on itself. The burnt patches acted as a fire break, and soon we were able to get the fire under control, and eventually out. The camaraderie as we all headed down the hill was fantastic. Dad was there to thank everyone and give the Africans *baksheesh*, money for their help. I headed straight for Sirri's little paddling pool! Minutes later Hugh appeared from the house with an enormous glass of orange for me, and Mum and Linda brought us out more jugs of water. We all gathered under the jacaranda tree. Dad was so grateful that we'd taken his place fighting the fire, so proud of us and his workers, and totally relieved that the danger was over. Us three younger Andersons, red eyed, covered in soot, smoke and sweat, looked like a comical trio of chimney sweeps as we sat round the paddling pool cooling our feet. Even Sirri had a story to tell about the fire, from where she'd been standing outside the house with Mango, looking anxiously up the hill.

Within a few hours, we'd all scrubbed up and were zig-zagging up the dusty escarpment to Nandi Hills in two cars. The candlelight carol service was inside the little Nandi church, and Mum and Dad glanced happily at each other, contented and proud to have their family filling the entire pew, with the added bonus of their little granddaughter. It really was some kind of miracle. Mum and Dad had lived in Nandi long before the church was built. Over the years Dad had helped with the electric wiring, read several lessons, and we'd attended various weddings and christenings in the friendly church, and this Christmas Eve, in the candlelight, we celebrated family. God was indeed good.

Bruce, Liz, Wendy and Karen drove down from their farm in Mau Narok. For many years they had been our only relatives in Kenya, and we'd always joined up at Christmas, but this was to be the last Christmas together. Bruce's father, Andrew Nicol, had spent his entire life working his farm in Mau Narok, and Bruce happily followed in his footsteps. However, a new Government Settlement Scheme forced Bruce, along with many other white farmers in the district, to sell their land. Once this land was taken over, it was to be divided into thousands of small plots or shambas for the Africans to farm, and hopefully develop successful co-ops. There were no options, no choices, and no negotiations. Now Bruce and Liz had only a month left in Kenya, before having to move off elsewhere to make a new life for themselves and their children. Bruce favoured Rhodesia, and Liz England.

Christmas Day was perfect, full of the easy chatter that flows between those who are used to one other. Sirri was so happy playing with her first present, that she never got round to opening any others. Mum had always liked the men to wear ties for Christmas dinner, so the boys wore ties, albeit with tee shirts! We girls wore long colourful cheesecloth or muslin skirts, with beads and flowers in our hair. Sitting at the crowded table, amongst the laughter and the chatter, my thoughts wandered to Lee, so far away, in a different world. Mum caught my eye, "You're missing Lee aren't you?" so we raised our glasses, "to absent ones".

As we'd always done on Christmas nights, we chatted and played games. The conversation turned to the supernatural, universal energy, and the power of the mind. We decided we'd try something for ourselves. Bruce was quite a big man, six foot, sturdy and strong. He sat on an ordinary dining chair in the middle of the lounge. Four of us, Linda, Liz, Robin and me, were the lifters. With only an index finger each under the chair seat, and on the count of "one, two, lift", we were going to lift Bruce on his chair. It was extraordinary. On the word "lift", Bruce, on his chair, rose up with ease, right up above our shoulders! I still recall Dad's face, eyes wide in a look of sheer astonishment.

On Boxing Day Dad stayed in bed. This was very unusual because he had never been one to let illness stop him. He said he was probably a little worn out with all the recent excitement. The rest of us enjoyed the company and a leisurely day on the veranda. All too soon it was time for everyone to say goodbye and return to work. Robin and the Nicols left, and then Mum drove up to Nairobi with Hugh and Linda. Hugh had a flight to catch to Malawi, but Linda was going to stay on with us for a couple of weeks. Back at Maraba, Sirri and I looked after Dad, who was not well at all. Sirri continually carried glasses of water through to Grandpa, and sat quietly by his side. Kipsang, our colourful headman, came to the house to discuss matters of the farm with Dad and me, and I was called out that first evening to apply a tourniquet to a calf bitten by a snake. Unable to save it, we uselessly watched the reflection of the setting sun in the calf's eye become misty and cloud over. Dad got up, and staggering to the shed with me supporting him, so he could show me how to work the generator for our electricity. He was having difficulty breathing and had a terrible cough and was very week. I phoned the local Doctor, who told me to bring Dad into his surgery in the morning. The doctor's room was twenty miles away, and when Dad said he'd rather rest, I agreed with him. I didn't want to drag him off, over the bumpy roads, through the awful dust to the shabby surgery room at Muhoroni.

However, on her arrival home, Mum was shocked at Dad's condition as she'd expected him to be up and about again. We did drive Dad over to the doctor's, and then straight on into Kisumu Hospital, about an hour away. On Friday, we drove back into Kisumu to visit Dad. Unfortunately, his ward was right beside the outpatients and maternity clinic, and a door squeaked terribly every time anyone used the toilet (which was often). Dad asked us to bring in some oil to fix the squeak. Then as we were leaving, he told me to fire the 22 twice each evening to let anyone with malicious intent know that even though we were women on our own, we were armed. 'Just a security measure', he'd said, as he was not home to protect us himself. There had been unrest in the Mteti Valley due to the edgy rebellious nature of the young tribesmen, and there had been several recent aggressive gang attacks on nearby farms. Dad had been given a permit for a 22 gun and some chemical mace. These were kept locked in a safe in the walls of the house, only to be used in extreme emergency.

The Catholic nurses told us that Dad had double pneumonia and pleurisy, but we still didn't realise how bad he really was. Late afternoon, as we left the hospital, Dad looked up at me and said, "Come back soon".

I never did.

How simple it would have been to do that, to follow my heart and hurry back. But with a flu bug myself, we thought it would be better to keep the germs away from Dad the next day and catch up on chores around the farm, returning to Kisumu to see Dad on Sunday morning. I didn't fire the gun, but stood instead beneath the jacaranda watching the sunset fade, suddenly scared that Dad was slipping away. Early Sunday morning we were up and getting ready to leave when the phone rang. It was the nuns from the hospital. Dad had just passed away.

The memories are jumbled, the emotions even worse, but I still recall Mango's kind, quiet acceptance. He insisted on coming into Kisumu with us and looked after Sirri when we first went in to the hospital. Later he knelt by the bed saying a wee prayer for Dad, before escorting Mum to the carpenter's to organize a coffin. Crossing to Dad's bedside, I needed to say goodbye, but Dad already looked different. I bent to give him one last hug, but felt only a deep icy-cold. He was so very, very cold. He'd already gone too far.

Numbness accompanied our shocked hearts home, but then we had to begin the nightmare task of letting people know Daddy had died. The phone lines were terrible, always crackling and often cutting out, and pleasantries were not an option. It was impossible to get through to Hugh, and when Mum rang Robin, he was not home. She had to ask Johnny Bannister to find Robin and tell him his Dad had died. Poor Johnny frantically searched for hours. Robin was likely to be anywhere after a Saturday night out in Nairobi. Eventually he was located and immediately hurtled his little rally car north again. Meanwhile Uncle Jim in South Africa, told us he'd get a telegram off to Hugh to break the sad news to him. Old friends, Ken and Pauline Archer, kindly offered to organize the funeral in Nandi Hills for us, and offered to provide refreshments at their house afterwards.

A loud, keen, high pitched wailing sliced the silence. Outside on the porch, Kipsang, with his gnarled feet and dangling ears, wept and wailed in unrestrained grief. Huge tears rolled off his bony cheeks splashing down into a wet puddle on the stone floor. If only we could be so uninhibited in expressing our grief. Instead we each retreated into our own space, and I found myself with little Sirri and Macora, in the shade of a thorn tree, gazing at the distant hazy hills, aware only of the birds' clear calls, and the droning buzz of insects. The sun was warm, and the afternoon gentle on my soul. We wandered down to the quiet, empty coffee sheds. An old woman, with paper-thin skin, was passing by, carrying a huge load of sticks on her back. She stopped to hold my hands and 'tut' and shake her head. Then eventually she started talking, and told me that all of life's experiences are beads, which we thread onto the necklace of our lives. "Bwana Kiko was a special bead," she said, "And we all have more beautiful necklaces because of him". What kinder place was there in which to lose a love one?

Returning home, we met Otunda on the path. Not smiling now, and with tears in his eyes, he asked, "Why does God always take the best ones?"

Robin arrived, then Liz and Bruce. As was the way in Kenya then, after the evening news there was a funeral announcement on the radio. "The death has occurred of Jim Anderson. The Funeral will take place tomorrow afternoon at 3pm at St Peter's Church, Nandi Hills". Norman, an old friend, kindly drove Dad in his pick-up, on his final journey up the Nandi Escarpment. Robin took the farm truck, bursting to the brim, with our African workers, dressed in their glad rags, to say farewell to their friend Bwana Kiko. We all collected outside the church in the afternoon sunshine for Dad's funeral. Friends had come from everywhere to pay their last respects, old and young, black and white. It was beautiful. Keifer, our old carpenter and foreman at Schiehallion, who could only have heard the news by 'bush telephone' walked the twenty miles to say goodbye. Young friends of ours had shared cars and driven for hours to be there. In spite of the country being gripped by drought, people had raided friends' gardens and the grave was surrounded by an assortment of colourful flowers. As they buried Dad, I looked out into the distance, past the Nandi Hills and down across the Songhor Valley, over tiny tin roofs twinkling in the sun, to the faraway silver streak of Lake Victoria. I knew then that it was right that Dad should die and be buried here, here in the land he loved.

Robin arranged for all the workers to have soft drinks and buns at the *duka*, while we had a cup of tea and talked to old friends at the Archer's. Before driving home, we visited Dad's grave again. It was now a large mound covered in lovely bright flowers. Now that we were alone, Mum's pain was all too clear. Poor dear Mum, she carried on so bravely, even though her heart was breaking.

As we started our journey home down the escarpment, large raindrops splattered on the windscreen, announcing a fierce storm. The drought had broken. Thunder roared and crashed above us, lightening split the dark grey sky, and rain pelted down on us as we crawled along the winding slippery road. As dramatically as it had begun, the storm ended. The clouds turned to glorious golden oranges and reds, as nature pulled out all the stops to say goodbye to Dad.

A day or two later we heard that a group of our young friends, travelling back to Nairobi from the funeral, had had an accident in the valley. They'd driven through a cloud of swarming bees. The car windows had been open, and the bees caused mayhem resulting in the car going off the road. The police, who attended the accident, refused to believe their story and locked our friends in the local jail for the night. A nasty repayment for all their efforts to get down to Nandi for the funeral. Days later the post office operator in Malawi phoned Hugh to read out the telegram. Either he was unable to read English well or he had a particularly bad accent, but Hugh was unable to make out exactly what the telegram said and fearing the worst, but still uncertain, had to drive miles to the post office to get the actual typed telegram before the message became clear. Poor Hugh, what a horrible lonely way to learn your Dad has died. All through the next few days I kept secretly hoping Hugh would walk through the door so he could be with us all and not on his own, but he had not even heard the news.

Death takes the dear departed and leaves the living to go on. Robin and Mum began the task of sorting through the farm and personal paperwork. They were staggered to see that Dad had absolutely everything up to date and in perfect order, as though he had known something. Office work had never been Dad's forte, and he generally avoided it like the plague, so it was strange to find loose ends tied up and everything dealt with. The priority now was to help Mum pack up all their things and move out of Maraba, so that a new farm manager could move in. Mum felt her only realistic option was to return to England to live. Previously, a house had always been provided as part of Dad's salary as farm manager. Now, not only had she lost her husband, she had lost her home, and income. Thankfully there was a little left from Schiehallion's sale, although the bulk had gone to finalise bank repayments. Norman and Jeanine Brookes kindly invited us to stay with them at Koru, giving us a hot meal, bath, bed, and good company every evening. Each morning we drove back to Maraba to continue packing up. Mango was a great help, sorting out boxes and tea chests of books, kitchen and household items to give to the EAWL charity. Mum gave all Dad's clothes, hat and shoes to the people of the farm, but asked them please not to wear any of it while she was still there. To a man, this was respected and carried out. We distributed blankets, bowls, kitchen utensils, and other bits and pieces to the women. Sirri gave toys, felt pens, and books to all the little African children, who giggled in excitement. She chose a soccer ball and skipping rope for Otunda's two elder children, handing Tubby, my dear old Teddy, still in his kilt and faded yellow cable knit jumper, to little Margaret. I remembered how I used to whisper secrets to Tubby when I was lonely at boarding school, and now Margaret would have him for a friend. As for Margaret the chicken, Otunda and I agreed that he'd look after her for us until we came back again. We both knew it would never happen. Macora was staying on at Maraba as the new manager wanted a dog and was happy to inherit her. Mango was also going to stay on working at the Maraba house, and said he would be happy to keep an eye on Macora.

We'd been packing up for three days, and now it was time to leave, forever. Our hearts were heavy. It was gut wrenching. The time had come to say goodbye to everyone. How could we leave all this behind? Wanting to give Macora one last pat, Sirri and I looked everywhere for her, whistling and calling her name. It was unusual for her not to respond to our calls. At last we found her, huddled underneath my bed, and as she came out, our wee dog literally had tears sliding down her face. It broke our hearts. Somehow she knew that this was the last day and she'd never see us again.

Already Maraba had a sense about it that something special was over. We shook hands with dear old Mango, Kipsang, Otunda and all the other *watu* on the farm, and drove sadly down the hill, past the coffee sheds and the dip, for the last time.

***

We spent a few days with Liz and Bruce, who were staying in Aunt Pix's cottage on the slopes of Menengai Crater. It was a pleasant brief respite, and we enjoyed the company along with the lovely views over Lake Nakuru. We walked up to the edge of the huge eight mile wide Menengai Crater. Sirri, Karen and Wendy played happily together, and included in their games and pretend tea parties, were 'the brudders', now joined by Grandpa.

A kind friend of Liz and Bruce, invited us for a flight in his little four-seater plane early one morning. With Dad in our hearts, nothing could have felt more perfect, as Sirri, Linda, and I, took off, climbing up over Nakuru into the still clear air. We soared above a pure blue Kenya morning. A silvery blue lake shimmered beneath us reflecting the sky above. Distant mountain ranges unfolded in pastel blues and indigo hues, and the misty plains stretched out to meet the cliffs and rocky ridges of the Rift Valley. What a beautiful cradle for mankind. We looped back cruising over the powder blue lake trimmed with pale pink fringes of flamingo. Descending, we glided above clouds of circling flamingo. Swirling shades of pink rose and fell silently beneath us, surging and drifting as shoals of fish. Like a beautiful ballet, the flamingo flocks danced an exotic fandango as they merged and flowed into the blue morning.

Our next stop was the Bannister's pineapple and cattle ranch near Thika, where Robin worked. He squeezed us three into his wee house. We lived on delicious pineapples and pawpaw for breakfast and lunches, and enjoyed our evening meals with Janie and Johnny. Sirri had a wonderful time playing with Sally and Andrew and their pet monkey.

We booked our flights home on the same day. Linda, now called 'Mama Chick' since she had told us the good news that she was expecting a baby, was flying back to join Hugh in Malawi. Sirri and I were returning to England. Meanwhile Mum was going to stay on with Robin in Kenya for a couple of weeks. Once her affairs were completed, she wanted to go down to South Africa to spend time with her parents, and brother, Jim. Then she felt England would be the best place for her to try and settle down and make a living for herself.

On the morning of our departure, Robin was driving us along the Thika Road to catch our plane. Sirri and I hurtled along in the little blue rally car, leaving as we began, oh so long ago – a lifetime ago. Suddenly we pulled over. Something was wrong with the car. Robin disappeared under the bonnet, but was unable to get the car going. Fortunately Mum and Linda were following and pulled over. We quickly hugged Robin goodbye on the side of the road and squashed into Mum's car with our cases.

As the plane lifted up over Nairobi, it circled round, doubling back. Through my tears, I recognised Thika town-ship below, and the rugby pitch. There, right in the middle of the pitch, was a tiny blue car, and I knew Robin would be waving like there was no tomorrow.

***

Mum wrote to us in England telling us she was hoping to stop-over in Kenya on her way back from South Africa and would join us at the end of the month. She also wrote,

"*Poor Aunt Pix. A week after she heard that Dad had died, she received a letter from him. Through her tears she read his words; 'My cup runneth over – to have all my family here together is very special, and it warms my heart to see our offspring have grown up into such decent, kind people'*. At the bottom of her letter Mum added; "*P.S. I remember Macora, tears running down her face – never known a dog cry like that. That is my memory of her, and of our evening walks through the coffee as she scampered ahead foraging, then she'd sit waiting for me to catch up.*"

Meanwhile Lee's insurance company had discovered he had another job, and when he was told to choose one or the other, he selected to stay on at the building site, where the wages were regular.

We met Mum at the airport. Cooking supper that first night, I asked her for news of Mango and Otunda. Her face froze as she looked at me. After an eternal pause, her face ashen, she whispered, "Otunda is dead. He was murdered outside his hut, hacked to death with pangas by a gang from another tribe."

Otunda? This was too dreadful to accept. How is it that such a kind, gentle soul could come to such a horrific violent end? Heaven knows what happened to his three little children. Were they there when it happened? Who took care of them? Where are they now? Were they able to stay together?

Otunda belonged to the Thiriki tribe, one of the smaller tribes from the Kakamega area. The majority of Africans living at Maraba and surrounding farms in the Mteti Valley were Nandi. In the mid 1970s there had been quite a lot of trouble with the young Nandi *torsik*. These were young men who had been circumcised but had yet to prove their manhood. As maasai morani traditionally completed their initiation into manhood by killing a lion, the Nandi torsik did this by hunting down and slaying a leopard. There were few leopards left, and new laws had been enforced making it illegal to kill leopard. The young Nandi torsik were frustrated and angry, which resulted in trouble in the Mteti Valley with gangs raiding farms as well as attacking other Africans. In the previous year, two of Mum and Dad's neighbours had been beaten up, and the Huntleys, a lovely gentle family and our closest neighbours, were fortunately out when they were raided. Their house was smashed up inside, outbuildings were torched, and several workers were killed. This was why Dad had been worried about us when he was in hospital, and had told me to fire the gun each night as a warning that we were armed. Sometimes these gangs resorted to attacking members of other tribes, and we think, this is what happened to dear Otunda. Norman, Maraba's owner, drove down from Nairobi when he heard about this, but was unable to shed any light on what really happened.

Mum stayed with us in our tiny flat and found an office job. She and I shared the double bed beside Sirri's cot in our bedroom, and Lee had a camp stretcher in the lounge. The main difficulties were in the early morning as Lee and Mum both got ready for work, made coffees and breakfast in the miniscule kitchen that was also a bathroom, as well as the passage way to the loo! Those days must have been so difficult for Mum. Her heart was still so tender, yet she was determined to carve out a life for herself in a new country and amongst strangers, but she never complained or even let on how hard she was finding it all. She moved into a ridiculously small bedsit just round the corner, which we christened 'the cupboard'. One afternoon, she told me that as a young woman, she'd always loved the English spring, the daffodils and blossom on the trees, but now she looked around blankly and felt nothing. She was numb. Nothing excited her, and nothing interested her. It was as though all her senses had been anaesthetized and she was just going through the motions. Poor Mum. I wanted so much to help her, but in all reality, little Sirri's smiles or arms around her neck were the only things that mildly touched her. I was also finding it harder to come to terms with Dad's sudden departure. It had all been easier to accept out in Kenya amongst friends and nature. Somehow everything seemed colder and bleaker now. It was not an easy time for any of us, but I'll always have the utmost respect for Mum and the way she held on and gradually pulled her life together again.

After a while Mum moved down to Haywards Heath in Sussex, where she got a job working as Assistant Manager in a book shop owned by a Mr Patel, also from Kenya. With her lifelong love of books, Mum started to find her job interesting and slowly, slowly began to heal. Meanwhile Lee, Sirri and I returned to New Zealand.

13. 360 Degrees

Hugh and Linda's little daughter, Clair, was born in Malawi at Mzuzu. Later, after the little family had returned to England, she was joined by little sister, Jax. With the family now based in England, Hugh continued the overseas working assignments on his own. In a letter he sent me, in October 1976, he described his working conditions in Saudi;

"... officially the country has no pollution, but because of the burning off of the natural gas, the desert is not the clean sterile place one imagines, but is in fact horribly filthy. When we work around the GOSPs we have to wash our hair every day and the muck that comes out of it is incredible. A GOSP is a Gas Oil Separation Plant and separates oil from the gas. 20 or 30 oil wells are linked to one GOSP. At the moment the gas is burned off by 'flares', which are huge balls of fire giving off great quantities of dense black smoke. If you can get hold of a copy of September's Readers Digest, the feature article '50 Million Years to the Gallon' deals with oil. Most of the work in Saudi now is connected with the Natural Gas Liquifiction Program. They have decided that instead of burning off the gas, they can purify it, liquefy it, and sell it. Some of the estimates out here reckon that the amount of gas burned off in the desert every day is the same as used in Britain during one month of winter. At one stage I was driving past the Uthmaniya GOSP2 twice a day and for the past three weeks I have been working at Jubail, which is just north of the big terminal at Ras Tunova. The desert here in Saudi's Eastern Province is very flat and the horizon is about as far away as when you are in a small boat in the middle of the ocean.

Next I am working in the Yemen Arab Republic, in Sanaa, although I am not yet sure what my job is, but I am hoping to be home for Christmas with Linda and our wee baby, and it will be good to see Mum again".

Another letter written on 25th December 1976

"I am sitting in Sanaa writing this on Christmas morning, and now don't expect to be home before February, provided we don't encounter any major problems. This is the first Christmas without Linda, and what makes it worse is that it is Clair's first real Christmas and I am sure as hell missing them both. We have a radio cassette player provided by the company because we need the radio for time signals for our astronomical observations, and we have a few locally

recorded tapes, including Abba, Grieg, Bert Kampfert, and Olivia Newton John, so we do have a little music to brighten our Christmas, along with what the BBC chooses for us. With the radio came a demonstration cassette 'Ob-la-di, ob-la-da' which has become our theme tune and I am sure will remind me of Yemen for the rest of my life!

Great to hear about your scuba gear, and remember don't dive alone! I am sure you'll obey all the dive rules, because although diving is a wonderful experience, underwater is not our natural environment. This was proved to me at least half a dozen times during our 15 months in Cayman, when people went out and didn't come back. So take great care of yourselves and each other.

Well folks, barakah na bahati mingi for 1977 ..."

Many years later, on Hugh's retirement, an article was published in Leica's 'Geometrics World', summarising his working career;

A 360° View by Ruth Badley

'When it has to be right.' The commitment Leica Geosystems makes to the professionals that measure the world could have been coined by its Support Specialist Hugh Anderson, who has retired after 23 years' service.

His technical expertise and contribution to the development of mapping software, photogrammetry techniques and surveying products over two decades is well known amongst the global surveying and geomatics community.

The presentations at his retirement dinner included an affectionate caricature showing a carefree, kilt wearer, at the wheel of an MG Midget. The hood is down, sunglasses are in position and a Leica cap is positioned at a jaunty angle. The other passenger is a Leica Total Station and the driver appears to be motoring through the Rift Valley, whilst a family of giraffes in the distance lope across the savannah. Arching above this idyllic scene is an oversized camera lens.

To encapsulate an entire career in a single illustration is always a challenge but how much more so when the subject has travelled through several continents, lived and worked alongside a multitude of different cultures, and can capture his experiences, in stunning panoramic and 360° panoramic photography?

Hugh joined Wild Heerbrugg at the UK base, Chatham in July 1989, shortly after Wild had acquired Kern. Prior to this Hugh had spent three years with D&H Surveys as a land surveyor where he used his practical experience and academic knowledge to write surveying software applications.

Soon after Hugh's appointment, and as a result of a merger with three microscopy companies, the newly named Wild Leitz moved to new UK headquarters at Milton Keynes.

With expertise in AutoCad and Leica's Geocom, he was well placed to provide the latest solutions, technical support and training to customers involved in major national and international surveying and engineering projects. When Leica Geosystems established a partnership with LISCAD surveying and engineering software in 1990 Hugh was closely associated with establishing the application in the UK and also supported project teams in Tripoli, Dubai, Nigeria and Sudan to use it.

In recognition for his service, a retirement gift from LISCAD includes return flights to Melbourne to visit LISCAD HQ, a long held travel ambition.

"What I am interested in has engineered what I do. I find computers and computer technology fascinating and was working at the right time in land surveying and engineering to immerse myself in this field and to utilise the programming skills I have. I was recruited to Leica because of that technical ability and have enjoyed the hard work that comes with new challenges," said Hugh.

Hugh has sat on an advisory panel for the development of new instruments at Leica Geosystems, Switzerland, and has also ensured presentations to the UK industry, at various roadshow events deliver the wow factor to audiences every year.

"When it comes to presentations, if it is not perfect, the imperfections are what you notice. I like it to be right, and 'when it has to be right' you have to live up to that claim – even if that makes me a bit annoying in rehearsal!"

<u>Culture shock</u> Born in Kenya, 35 miles north of the Equator, Hugh's arrival in London in 1965 to study land surveying at North East London Polytechnic was a definite culture shock. His father hailed from Glasgow but prior to 1965 Hugh had only visited the UK briefly on a family holiday.

The eldest of three children had grown up on an African farmstead where the nearest neighbour was twenty miles away from their tea and coffee plantation. Coming from a boarding school education in Nairobi to digs in London, the young adventurer did not intend to stay in the UK once he obtained his qualification and some experience.

Hugh recalls his first impressions. "It was like going from life in full colour to seeing everything in shades of grey. I was a student living in Walthamstow and working as a surveyor with J A Storey & Partners through the summer. The money I earned was paying my way through education. The plan was to get some training and go back to Africa."

When he returned in 1970, the effects of Independence on the local economy had set in. The division of land meant the family had to switch from growing tea and coffee to sugar cane and were cultivating the crop in a different area. There were no jobs to be had so the best bet was to return to the UK where J A Storey & Partners could offer the newly qualified surveyor an opportunity.

<u>Coral, communities and traditions</u> Within a month he was "back in the world of colour," and privy to a controversial scenario playing out in the San Blas islands, off the coast of Panama. With Alaskan oil just coming on stream, a hydrographic survey was undertaken as part of a project to accommodate super tankers and a terminal.

"Whilst it was very exciting to navigate a tiny boat through the canal, if the project had gone ahead, it would have destroyed the coral reef and the ancient communities that live on those beautiful islands. "I was delighted when the information became public knowledge and alternative schemes were adopted."

Just before leaving for Panama, Hugh had met Linda and they married in 1971. His Scottish heritage is a source of pride so Hugh got married in a kilt and the tartan is called into service for other family celebrations. "It harks back to the time when I was a student. It was family joke that I only wore jeans – I didn't actually have the money to buy trousers - so I am carrying on the tradition, but I like to wear the kilt when the occasion demands it."

Before the year was out Hugh had taken his new bride to the Caribbean where he ran the office working as a land surveyor for J A Storey & Partners in the Cayman Islands.

<u>Pioneering techniques</u> Hugh and Linda enjoyed a married posting to Malawi, sailing back to the UK in 1973 with three month-old Clair. A second daughter, Jacqueline was born in 1978 and the family remained in the UK for the majority of Hugh's subsequent overseas assignments.

"I had an unnerving encounter with a rhino in Kenya, and a risky time in Saudi Arabia when I thought I might get arrested for remaining in the country when my flight was overbooked. Luckily, a Saudi Prince wanted to fly to Bahrain that day so I got on his plane, although I was the only tourist class passenger on that flight.

"Yemen was a place of great contrasts. I was shot at there, but at the same time the local people we encountered were extremely hospitable. We camped in one village where the local sheik had arranged lunch to arrive for us as a welcome."

Cameras have been a source of fascination from a young age and using photography as a means of measurement was a natural progression. Mapping from aerial photographs for projects in the Cayman Islands, Kenya, Yemen, Tanzania, Nigeria, Oman, Abu Dhabi and Saudi Arabia was carried out before the development of sophisticated computer technology and software that could stitch the images together.

With hi-tech solutions still some years off, Hugh's pioneering approach to mapping the hidden corners of Annesley Hall, Nottingham resulted in a breakthrough development in 1974. By using a camera fitted with a fish eye lens he was able to plot the rooms using photographic intersection. A UK patent was granted for his 'Optic for Instantaneously Photographing an Horizon of 360°' but he lacked the funds to develop it – though others, including Kodak, eventually did.

Later, working for BKS Surveys, Hugh and a colleague developed and used the 'light line' method to survey railway tunnels, and close range stereo photogrammetric to record processing plant, well ahead of the academics who published their research papers on the topic at a later date.

Retirement has already presented a new opportunity for Hugh to utilise his skills to record and create panoramas. Working with a website developer he has produced virtual tours allowing visitors to 'look around' hospitality venues in Cheltenham and Twickenham managed by Keith Prowse and this is a service he hopes to expand. For more information visit www.360hugh.co.uk

"When I first got interested in using photography in different ways I couldn't find the information I wanted. I had to develop my own ways of working as there were no books or forums to share ideas. I think it is important to share what I learned because I know how helpful that information can be to others."

<u>Cultural exploration through Earth Sciences</u> Hugh's involvement with the British Schools Expedition Society as a scientific leader took him back to Tanzania in 2004 for a five week trek across the Gregory Rift and Crater Highlands. Data collected from the gravity survey using Leica GPS and TPS on the density and composition of the Ol Doinyo volcano was subsequently made available to universities.

"Experiences like this are life changing for young people. I know from my own career how important it is to see the world and different cultures at first hand, before life traps you with responsibilities. We all belong to Planet Earth - I'm nomadic myself. The diversity of cultures is interesting and more complex than we realise and organisations like BSES allow young people to experience a different culture in a safe and informed way."

And so to complete the 360° view, the MG Midget mentioned at the beginning, hints at a continuing interest in the fun side of motoring and a plan to be at the wheel for the annual Kop Hill Climb in Buckinghamshire. Each year veteran, vintage and classic car owners gather to take part in a charitable sporting event. Hugh has been persuaded to encourage owners and manufacturers of alternatively powered vehicles, such as those fueled by steam, electricity or pedal power, to take part. Retirement is supposed to be the time to slow down, after all.

Detailed information on creating panoramas and examples of many of Hugh Anderson's photographic projects and techniques can be found by visiting www.hugha.co.uk

<u>Projects undertaken by Hugh in various parts of the world</u>;
Large scale mapping of military, road routes, and other sites in the UK
Oil Tanker Terminal in the San Blass Islands on the north coast of Panama (which was fortunately abandoned due to conservation issues)
Cadastral and other surveying and mapping in the Cayman Islands
The Hadeja Irrigation Scheme in north east Nigeria (the southern Sahara)
Enugu to Umahia highway in south east Nigeria

Mapping for six different routes in the mountains of North Yemen, most of which was carried out on foot, with camels and donkeys carrying the equipment, tent and food.
Ground control for major infrastructure developments in Sultanate of Oman
Mapping for the Al Kharj Airforce Base and several other assignments in Saudi Arabia
Road project in Malawi to bring logs from the Viphya to the shores of Lake Malawi where a pulp mill was to be built by the Chinese, but this was aborted due to the political unrest that started in Mozambique whilst in Malawi
Mapping the location of investigation bore holes Mareb, Yemen
Abu Dhabi - Oil field pipeline surveys in Bu Hasa and in the Rub Al Khali
Mapping the desert for a new town at Ruwais in Abu Dhabi Emirate
Mapping of utilities in Al Ain in Abu Dhabi Emirate
Mapping Annesley Hall and Estate in Nottinghamshire
Survey of canal tunnel at Stoke Bruerne
Software training in Croatia, Dubai, Libya, Nigeria and the Sudan

In his spare time Hugh completed a Mathematics degree with Open University and continued to increase his own skills and knowledge as precision instruments and computer technology rapidly advanced. In 1989 Hugh had been asked to join Leica Geosystems as a Support Specialist to help with the establishment of LISCAD products. With expertise in AutoCAD and Leica's GeoCOM, he was responsible for providing modern solutions, technical support, and training to customers involved in major national and international surveying and engineering projects.

Hugh was involved with the development of new Instruments with Leica Geosystems. He patented "Optic for instantaneously photographing an horizon of 360°" http://hugha.co.uk/Acrobat%20PDF%20Files/Panoramic%20Optic.pdf

With David Stevens, he developed "Method and apparatus for photographic tunnel sectioning" http://hugha.co.uk/Acrobat%20PDF%20Files/Light%20Line.pdf

While he was with BKS, Hugh had pioneered Terrestrial Photogrammetry for building façades in 1974/75 and then developed it for measuring "plant" with Robin Douglass and David Stevens.

***

The infamous East African Safari Rally was held every year over Easter, when the drivers hurtled their cars over 3,000 miles of rough African terrain in one weekend. Originally the field consisted of local drivers with a few overseas rally drivers entered for the challenge of experiencing 'the world's toughest rally'. Gradually more and more works teams entered, with large companies like Peugeot, Ford, Subaru, and Datsun, manufacturing specially prepared rally cars, and it became more like a sleek big business operation. These companies brought with them more international drivers, support teams, a seemingly limitless supply of mechanics and technicians, every conceivable spare part, radio contact, and eventually their own helicopters to service and repair competing cars out in the field. No expense was spared. This of course made it harder and harder for the local drivers to compete, but it was not enough to stop them.

Robin entered his first East African Safari in 1972 with his old school friend, Andrew, in car number 72. However, they had been time barred and were returning to Nairobi on the long Mombasa Road. It was late at night and Andrew was at the wheel near Voi, when, at high speeds, they drove smack into the back of a lorry that was left parked on the side of a deserted road without lights. Fortunately, although Andrew and Robin were hospitalised, and it took them several months to recover, both young men were soon back living life to the full.

I had saved several letters that Robin had written to me when we were in New Zealand. Almost the entire airmail forms were filled with rallying accounts!

January 1976: *"... The rallying is still going well and I came 15th out of the 16 finishers last time, and we have another rally this weekend. In 1975 we drove in seven rallies and came 5th, 6th, 7th, 10th, 15th, and 18th overall, winning our class four times, were 2nd once and 3rd once. All in all very chuffing! However we have decided not to enter the Safari this year as we reckon it is just not worth it with all the money and preparation required for just one weekend (maybe even just one hour!). So we are going to buy another car for the 1976 local rally championships, which are far more fun, not nearly so hard on the pocket, and if you can't make it for one rally, there is always another one only a month away. Mind you I'll have to sell both my cars to buy half shares in the Datsun 120Y (purely a rally car), and to buy Brian out of the 1200 Datsun we have been rallying (this will become my personal transport). My Lancer is back on the road and I intend to do it up, re-paint it, and sell it with the blue Datsun as soon as possible. The world of Rob's high finance!"*

April 1976: *"I did actually go in the Safari after all this year. Johnny B and I were in a Lancer 1200, Number 45. There were only 66 entries this year. We went quite well for the first 300 kms and were 28th on the road until we got held up by the now infamous swollen river. We were the first car to arrive after it flooded and had to wait about 72 hours for the 10 foot waters to subside. Eventually we and a few others made it across, only to be time barred shortly afterwards. There was a huge furor about it as the 27 cars that got through before the floods were all works cars, and all those following were private entries and all were time barred because of the river. We are staying out of the hulla-baloo as technically the organizers were correct, but something could have been altered to allow those held up by the flood waters to continue the rally."*

Robin continued to push his 'nine lives' to the limit. There were several more minor prangs and near misses, but in October 1976 Robin was involved in a critical accident in the township of Thika. Driving along a main road at nine o'clock one morning, he was passing the Kenya Canneries turn off, when a lorry suddenly shot out of the side road, ploughing into Robin's car. School children heading into the school gates all saw the horrific accident. Robin was pulled from underneath the wreckage and had lost so much blood that they didn't think he'd survive. Someone raced him to hospital in Nairobi in the back of a pick-up truck, unsure if he'd make the 30 minute journey. A friend, Roy Wallace, quickly phoned Thika and Nairobi rugby club captains, who in turn contacted all the members of their teams, who, with their wives, rushed to hospitals to donate pints of blood in the hope that it would help to save Robin. Thanks to the incredible efforts of so many unknown people, Robin did pull through. In spite of serious internal damage, breaks and injuries to his face and legs, he was able to limp out of hospital on crutches four months later, looking thin and emaciated. Many more months of medication, physiotherapy, and the re-structuring of his leg, followed, caringly aided by Mum who had flown out to be with her son. At the time the accident occurred, she had been with her parents, Arthur and Sue, who were on holiday in England. Together they heard the news of Robin's terrible accident and that he'd already been in intensive care for three days. Each night they waited in their hotel in Brighton for a telephone call from Johnnie and Janie Bannister, updating Robin's tenuous situation.

But this was still not enough to keep Robin down, and once he'd recovered, he and his best friend Brian Haworth entered several local rallies together. Robin was especially proud of their efforts in the extremely wet ASA Rally, in June 1978, when he, as co-driver to Brian, spent much of the time pushing them out of the mud, but they came 5th overall and won their class.

March 1982: *"Your little bro is again going in the Safari, so keep your eyes skinned to any news of the rally on TV. Look out for Car No.10, a works Datsun Bluebird Turbo, driven by Johnny Hellier, with me sitting in the hot seat as co-driver / navigator. It all came about pretty quickly and at first I thought I was doing the wrong thing as I had to come up with $3,000 and I knew we couldn't afford it. Luckily I managed to get a business in Kericho to sponsor $1,500. Warrens sponsored $500, and I was given several smaller amounts, so now I am really chuffed and dying to go! I am trying to get fitter and have become a 7,000 feet up and down hills, high altitude jogger! "Eliminate all joggers!" We have just done a recce on a southern loop and our car doesn't like heat or low altitude much. The first leg takes us down to the coast, so if we get round the first leg, we stand a fair chance. The rains are very late, and for the first time in my life I want a DRY Safari, as the Turbo is best in fast, dry, flat out conditions. Johnny is pretty good. He won four rallies this year, has done 9 Safaris and finished 7, usually in the top ten. So little Mr Magoo hopes he is up to it all! Should be a* *fantastic experience and just hope we finish, which would be a fantastic bonus for my last Safari."*

July 1982: *"This year's Safari was a complete FU. As you know we were in a Japanese works car, no.10. We began well and were 10th overall and 10th on the road by the first control point at Mtito Andei. Then the car started blowing turbo chargers! We lost 45 minutes changing the first and dropped to 43rd. Into the Taita Hills and down to a mud hole where we were held up with everyone else, but as we'd done a recce through there a few days earlier, we knew the way through the mud, so hurtled on towards Mombasa, arriving 13th overall. Dirt roads down the south coast and we were 9th on the road. With Sheka Mehta and Mike Kirkland 20 kms ahead, both with broken axels, we should be 7th in ten minutes. Not to be – the second turbo blows up! This time a spare arrives within minutes with Brian Haworth, our support team, who had taken the first blown turbo to the Japs. Unbeknown to him, they had taken it out the back, cleaned it up, and given it back as "new turbo". Once Brian began to fit this by the side of the road, he realised it was the same bloody one. After another hour we get a message from chief Jap, "No more turbo, have one Nairobi yah yah, proceed Nairobi. If engine blow up Japanese understand, yah yah". So off we go like a Morris Minor to Nairobi, with clouds and clouds of smoke pouring out behind. We made it with one hour and twenty minutes to spare, so Japs change turbo (one hour ten minutes), but trying to get from railway bridge to the ramp (2 kms!!) we break down four times (nothing had been tightened properly), and are time barred by 12 minutes. So end of the rally. At least it didn't cost me much this time as I'd managed to find sponsorship. Obviously the main sponsor, a business in Kericho, would have liked to see us win, do well, or at least pass through Kericho. When I said sorry to him, he said he didn't mind because a cousin Patel, Shah or Singh had seen the No. 10 car in Nairobi and reported it back to a business competitor, who wanted to know how the hell the man from Kericho had his company name on No.10, a works car! So the end of the first leg of Marlboro Safari Rally 1982! Alas the end of car 10, and end of my Safari career.*

Robin still suffered sporadically from bilharzia, re-occurring bouts of malaria, as well as the after effects of his accidents, but he played down any ill health, refusing to be laid low for long. He missed the family a lot and was going through a difficult time with his relationships. Although Robin was never short of nice girlfriends, he had become especially fond of the wife of one of his best friends, but after much soul searching decided it would be best to steer clear of these dear friends. Fortunately he was to find love in the form of lovely Australian blonde, Kaye. Robin and his 'Aussie Spanner Girl' met at Thika, where Kaye was teaching. The attraction was instant, and Robin whisked Kaye away for a romantic interlude camping alone on the shores of 'The Jade Sea' - Lake Turkana. In this isolated place they only wore clothes occasionally to keep the sun off or the mosquitoes at bay! Kaye and Robin married in Nairobi in 1979. They had a little daughter, Tammy, and eighteen months later a son, Matthew.

Robin's rally driving experience came into its own when they had an emergency with their new baby Matthew. At the time Robin and Kaye were living in Tinderet, where Robin was managing a remote farm about 350 kms from Nairobi. A letter Robin sent from Kenya on 14th January 1981 conveys their nightmare;

"We very nearly lost our little Matt. He had septicemia and bronchial pneumonia, both due to a flu bug we'd all caught off a friend's young boy. Tammy had a bad dose but struggled through. She is still not 100% but is on the mend. Kaye has suffered too, getting the flu when she hadn't recovered from Matt's birth, hemorrhaging, and her D&C. It all began on Sunday 4th with Matt going 6 hours between feeds, as opposed to his usual 3 hourly feeds. On Monday he was becoming more lethargic, losing his colour, and sicking up his feed, so Kaye took him to the doctor in Kericho. The doctor didn't seem unduly concerned, gave Kaye some medication for both Tammy and Matt, and told her to come back in 48 hours if there was no improvement. The next day Kaye was very worried, and as we had no phones we drove down to Cath Wilson's. Cath, a nurse, was not there but we phoned the doctor, who now thought it might be meningitis or ....pelisses? both of which effect the brain. So we rushed to Kericho to get him checked over, were given a letter to a Nairobi doctor, and hurriedly set off for Gertrude's Garden Children's Hospital in Nairobi. We wasted half an hour in Nakuru trying to feed Matt, but he wouldn't take anything and now he's gone 7 hours without anything. He is also occasionally forgetting to breathe. Kaye does everything to keep shocking him into taking another breath, while I keep my foot to the floor. Getting into the outskirts of Nairobi, Matt stops breathing completely and Kaye frantically shakes him, and I drive the rest of the way like a bat out of hell. If we have a prang, its four of us dead for one, but we went for it. We got to the hospital after 10pm and he was immediately given oxygen and put into an incubator with a drip, oxygen, and a tube to drain his lungs. The poor little fella was not breathing because it was too painful and also there was no room in his lungs for air as they were so full of gunge. Kaye and I take turns all night, flicking his feet when he stops breathing, and the doctors take all sorts of tests, including lumber puncture, to find out what is wrong. Poor little mite was so white and cold, but a gradual improvement eventually meant that by dawn I 'know' he's going to be all right. By midday he is much better and I hurtle back to Tinderet to organize things on the farm, (no one even knows where I am), and to pack us some clothes etc before returning to Nairobi. Now our little man is out of the incubator and getting better all the time and comes out of hospital on the Monday. They all just need to rest to gather strength. Septicemia in one so young is not common and has 90% fatality rate. God got prayed to like I don't know what, but he performed

a miracle, and he has given our little Matt back to us – for that I cannot explain how grateful we all are.

More good news is that our application to reside in Australia has been accepted, and all the arrangements should be finalised this week. Malcolm, my boss, has been away on leave since 5th December and is due back on Sunday. It will just be great to hand over to him, sort things out, and then head off for a well-earned holiday on 8th Feb. Can't tell you how the Aussie trip is coming at the best possible time – so watch out kids – a hellova lot to celebrate when we get there!"

14. Down Under

After a couple of years in New Zealand, Lee, Sirri & I moved 'across the ditch' to Australia. Our second daughter, Savana, was born in Sydney, bringing her own special sweetness, love, and laughter to our lives. We lived in units on the North Shore, adjacent to Lane Cove Park, and near Lee's sister Char, Tony and their girls, and his brother Pat and Carol and the boys. We spent a lot of time together enjoying a typical Aussie life style, with BBQs and picnics, games of tennis, and days at the beach, swimming and playing cricket or soccer.

Mum timed a visit out from England to coincide with Robin and Kaye's Australian holiday. Robin and Kaye were thinking of leaving Kenya and wanted to have a look at Australia, with a view to settling here. Kaye was happy to return home to Australia permanently and looked forward to being closer to her family. Robin liked what he saw of 'the big country' and was keen to come 'down under'. After years of putting up with the endless bribery and corruption, and general downturn of things in Kenya he was ready to make the move. He was also adamant that he did not want his children to have to go to boarding school, which was a given if they remained in Kenya. Meanwhile, I was just thrilled to have my brother and his family living in the same country.

However, it proved difficult for Robin to get a job managing farms as he had done in Kenya. He was knocked back time and time again because of his lack of experience in Australian conditions. The only farming positions available to him were lowly farm assistants jobs. Kaye's Dad, Clyde, offered to help Robin get a job with him at Ford Motors in Melbourne, but Robin was resolute he preferred to work on the land and needed to be independent. Finally he took a job near North Star in northern NSW, and from here they could only go up! The family lived in a dilapidated old farm house, surrounded by a two foot high ridge of cans and bottles, formed by years of lazy employees simply tossing all their empties out the nearest windows and doors. On this particular wheat farm, Robin was required to drive a huge tractor up and down the vast fields for twelve hours a day. The only time the tractor stopped was to refuel or at shift change over. Robin would climb aboard with enough food and water to last the whole day. He alternated between the drone of the tractor, or the only available radio station, which played non-stop country and western. To stay awake, Robin decided to look out for emu eggs, which it was reported, were easily seen in the ploughed fields. He saw plenty of green pumpkins scattered over the field, but never any emu eggs, which he imagined would look similar to large off-white ostrich eggs. Confessing his lack of success to work mates, they all doubled over laughing, while Robin felt as green as the pumpkins he'd been driving over! Emu eggs are like huge dark green avocados, and there were no pumpkins at that time of year!

During a visit to Robin and Kaye, we all piled into the pickup for an evening drive. Robin was driving us along the fence line of a large flat field, when we chanced upon a pack of perhaps a dozen kangaroo bounding along the other side of the fence next to us. We were all buzzing with excitement and totally absorbed by these large marsupials bouncing along so close and at the same speed as us. Then, as one, the pack rose, producing an extra high leap and soaring up and over a wire fence as we collectively chorused "wow!" in enthusiastic appreciation. Suddenly we came to a shuddering halt, and those of us in the back were thrown off our feet. We had hit a fence. So caught up in the splendour of the kangaroos' leap, our driver hadn't noticed the same fence that the animals had floated over so effortlessly, ran across our own path!

Months later, numbed by the endless hours driving the tractor up and down fields for 12 hours a day, Robin took another job further inland. This was not much better but provided a new set of conditions to adjust to. The terrain here was equally flat and expansive, the temperature hotter, and the conditions ideal for growing cotton. The daytime heat was too extreme for the small crop dusting planes to fly low over the cotton fields, necessitating the pilots do this job at night. After dark, Robin and a co-worker would park their trucks at diagonally opposite ends of a vast cotton field, leaving the vehicle lights on to guide the planes as they sprayed the crop over several hours. Finally, when the pilots had completed their spraying, they'd buzz the house and the workers would head out to bring the trucks home to base before going to bed.

An hour after sunrise, the kitchen was as hot as an oven, and Kaye quickly became proficient at producing all the family meals in the microwave. Endless flat fields stretched out to the horizon without a crease, and relaxing with a cold beer on the veranda, we'd laugh as we caught each other out gazing at a lone distant windmill, the only thing in sight to rest your eyes on!

With Tammy due to start school soon, Kaye and Robin became increasingly anxious to settle down somewhere more pleasant, and after visiting Tamworth, they decided it would be an ideal town for jobs and school. The Andersons bought the worst house in a good street and industriously renovated the place, room by room, while they continued to work. Kaye, being a good, qualified teacher was in demand, and Robin started up his own taxi-truck courier business. 'Anderson Carriers' filled a niche in Tamworth, quickly delivering equipment and larger bulky packages to local businesses. The two children, Tammy and Matthew, thrived in their schools and in all areas of sport. Robin took on several coaching positions, encouraging youngster's participation, enjoyment, and commitment out on the sports field, and many young tennis, hockey and soccer players were coached to new heights.

Matthew became fond of playing typical schoolboy pranks with his mates, and reports started to come in from school about his escapades. Eventually a meeting in the Headmaster's office was required, after which Robin and Matthew had a discussion about the young fellow's behaviour. The situation stabilized for a week or two, until Matthew came home late one Friday. When asked why he was late, he explained he'd had to stay back in detention. His frustrated father sighed in exasperation, saying, "What now Matthew? I thought we'd left all that nonsense behind." To which Matthew replied, "Dad, it was only because I set the school clock five minutes faster so everyone could go home earlier!"

The house, garden, and new pool began to look very attractive, and the Andersons became an integral part of the Tamworth community. With the hard yards behind them, and looking forward to a break, Robin and Kaye were determined to take their children back to England and Kenya for a holiday. They wanted Tammy and Matthew to re-visit these places while they were old enough to take it all in, and still young enough to travel as a family. The Anderson's epic safari began with a wonderful long weekend with us in New Zealand. They took Savana with them for the next leg of their trip to the States and Disneyland, before continuing to England for Christmas with Mum, Hugh and Linda, Clair and Jax. After the festivities, and a visit to mysterious Avebury stones, our family's favourite place in England, the Andersons left for more good times in Scotland and Kenya with old friends. Ten year old Savana stayed on with Mum (Granny Peg) for an English winter holiday.

After their holiday, and back in Australia, Robin sat down to write a book. Sadly, unbeknown to anyone at the time, Robin only had little more than a year left, and only a few draft chapters were written by hand. Unfortunately these initial pages were more concerned with the history and politics of early Kenya rather than Robin's own personal experiences. However we have an excerpt from some pages written in early 1993. Robin mentions that he is writing on his desk made from Meru Oak, an African hard wood. He'd made the desk from planks of timber transported from Kenya by ship when they'd moved to Australia.

... By the time I finish writing this, or maybe by the time you read it, there will be no more Meru Oak left growing in the world. It is a depressing and very sobering thought, but one that is quite topical at a time when the civilised world is becoming conscious (outwardly anyway!) of looking after the environment. Thankfully, we, as a species of this wonderful planet, are at least aware of the destruction we have caused, and indeed still cause. Let us all hope that we are not already too late to stop the process.

My thirteen year old daughter, Tammy has just asked me what I'm up to. She pinched what I had written thus far, and I watched her face with interest. Utter disgust and 'why?' was written all over her dear wee face. Then we chatted and I told her a few of the family stories and she began to see the point of recording them. "Yeah, go ahead Dad! - if you ever finish it – no you'll never make it" Maybe she is right. I have felt the same way for at least six years, but I must make the effort. The Anderson family have always placed effort ahead of pure results, so here goes, and I do hope that there is at least a smile for somebody (is that you?), or a realisation for another (you, this time?), but not a yawn or a shake of the head, I hope. And if the latter is you reading this, you just be very careful – I may be watching you!

***

While Robin and Kaye had been trying to settle down, Lee and I were getting restless. We'd been working in Sydney, but outside our window, Australia was begging to be explored. Ensconced in routine, we felt the need for another adventure. Lee was on the cusp of changing jobs, and after some deliberation, we let the job go, stored our belongings in our friend Vanda's garage, and bought a used diesel short wheel base Toyota Land Cruiser. We loaded our tent and basic camping gear into the truck and, as a family, set out to explore Australia, complete with Brazil, the budgie in his cage. Savana was then three, and Sirri twelve.

German friends who had previously travelled right round Australia mentioned that there was an awful lot of nothing between distant towns, and while they drove through the heat and dust, over the endless straight roads, they'd be hanging out to reach the next town. On arrival, they wondered why they'd been looking forward to it! However, we soon discovered there was so much to see and explore just by getting off the beaten track, and we spent the next six months camping in incredibly beautiful places in New South Wales, Victoria, and southern Queensland. More often than not we had the world to ourselves and camped in idyllic settings by rivers and lakes where brilliant parrots flashed across the sky, and kangaroos grazed outside our tent at dawn and dusk. Brazil was given a new lease of life and thrived in his cage suspended in nearby trees, chirping endlessly to the wild birds. We spent our days swimming in clear lakes and rivers, under waterfalls, or in shady pools, or we'd go for long bush walks through the forests and clamber up massive rock formations to see what it looked like from the top. Each day was a new and unexpected adventure, and it was a gift to have so much free time to spend with our children in this remarkable environment. We shared much, and all look back fondly at the happy times we spent on our amazing safari in Australia. Camping in the beautiful New England Ranges we'd sometimes wile away an hour or two chatting with the rangers. We commented that we'd heard whip birds all around but had never sighted any. It was the same with the trial bikes that we heard roaring in the hills from time to time. Apparently the motor bike sounds and the 'whip' noises were made by lyre birds, wonderful mimics that can imitate to perfection any sound that takes their fancy. They certainly had us fooled! The ranger told us about an old Vietnam War vet who'd wandered into the mountains. He lived a solitary existence in a shack in the forest, playing his violin endlessly. Years later, strains of Beethoven and Bach could still be heard drifting through the hills. It was the lyre birds enjoying a classical revival moment!

Christmas was drawing near and we felt that Sirri would appreciate the company of other young people for a change. The ranger suggested we camp at Trial Bay Goal on the coast, and after a couple of phone calls, he informed us we were very lucky because there had been a cancellation at this popular site. We packed up and headed off to South West Rocks immediately. If we thought we'd been in heaven, we'd now arrived in paradise!

There lay a beautiful sandy bay, kissed by translucent turquoise waters, and sheltered by a rocky headland on which stood the ruins of the old goal. The goal and breakwater had been built by convicts in the late nineteenth century to establish a safe harbour for the ships that plied the coast between Brisbane and Sydney. Tents and caravans now surrounded the goal and campers enjoyed the million dollar view spread out below them. We pitched our tent underneath the palm tree, and were quickly made to feel welcome by our tented neighbours, who lent us surf boards, dropped freshly caught fish off, and told us where to acquire a tiny Christmas tree for our tent!

Sirri quickly made young friends and was off swimming and sailing all day. We joined other happy campers for a lovely atmospheric candlelit carol service amongst the ruins, and on Christmas Eve we were invited over to the neighbours. We joined the several families at a long table in a large communal tent. Although they offered us a beer, they explained that one of the uncles was an alcoholic, who'd caused a lot of strife because of his addiction. In order to help him, the entire family had decided not to touch a drop either, and now several years later they were all teetotal. There was much laughter and merriment and we had a wonderful night with these warm and happy people. In fact, in years to come, we would all look back on this Christmas as a favourite. We had expected so little that year, but the simplicity, camaraderie and kindness far surpassed the usual hectic Christmas rush of shopping, presents and feasting.

In the New Year we were joined by Lee's brother Pat, his wife Carol, their three boys and the dog. They had their own Land Cruiser and we all enjoyed the weeks that followed. Our their first day together was spent driving our 4WDs over the sand dunes to a gorgeous deserted beach where we swam, body-surfed, and slid down the sand dunes. After dark and a BBQ, Lee and I were skinny dipping when we suddenly discovered the delightful beauty of phosphorescence, where every movement creates tiny marine creatures to emit thousands of twinkling, sparkling lights. We rushed up the beach to get the others and soon we were all frolicking in the sea enjoying the incredible phenomenon. Our skin glistened, as laughing and shouting we splashed and danced around in the shallows, generating an amazing, ever-changing galaxy of glitters, gleams, and sparkles.

Young Savana had thrived in her freestyle, open-air kindergarten, and often amused us with her young wisdom and odd insights. Somewhere along the line she befriended an older lady and chattered away nineteen to the dozen. When it was time for us to leave, she was heard to say, "Come and see us sometime. You know how to get to our place don't you? You just follow the sun." Later, visiting Robin and Kaye after several months on the open road, she gazed out the kitchen window in quiet concentration, eventually asking, "Why there are two moons Mum?" Sure enough, outside the window, there were two circles of light in view, but they were just streetlights, which were novel to her after living out in the bush for so long! Sometimes she got her wires crossed, and as we drove behind a loaded logging truck, she exclaimed, "Oh look, that's nice, they are going to plant some trees!"

All too soon we had to cut short our adventures on the road, and return to the real world, work and school. Sirri began her secondary education at a large co-ed college north of Sydney, Lee found a job loading trucks, and Savana and I searched for somewhere permanent to live within the radius of Sirri's school. We had a series of three-month rentals, but finally found a log house on 25 acres of land where we were able to settle for a year or so, until, once again, the owners wanted to sell.

We loved living here amongst the gum trees, with lovely walks, swims in the quarry, and lots of barbeques with friends and family. We even experienced a bush fire that raged through the trees, coming as close to the house as the washing line. The next day the devastation was chilling. An eerie silence enveloped a monochrome world of thick grey ash and stark black charred trunks. The birds and little creatures had gone, and everything was still and quiet. Incredibly, only days later we noticed signs of regrowth, and within a week, a profusion of green had sprung up at ground level showing the rapid speed of Australian regeneration.

While living here, we were randomly selected for a survey and an attractive black girl came to give me the questionnaire. The two of us, she black and me white, sat down for coffee and a chat. She spoke with a hint of a London accent, and I asked her where she was from.

The black girl replied, "I'm from England. Where are you from?"

"I'm from Africa!" I replied. Like the two queens on a chessboard, we looked across at each other, grinned and burst into giggles at the comical irony of the moment.

Raucous caws awoke us early one morning. Large black cockatoos were gathering in the surrounding trees. We had never seen these birds here before, but now more and more were descending. They remained perched in the branches, cawing and waiting. We watched and waited. Surreal sensations stirred as the collecting black cockatoos continued to arrive, reminding us of the sinister Hitchcock film 'The Birds'. What was the meaning of this? Were we perhaps on their migratory path? An hour or so later the cries changed. The birds stretched their wings, and took off en masse flying into the distance like a huge black cloud, taking the questions and answers with them.

A more enlightening bird incident occurred another day, when about to hang out the washing, we noticed a kookaburra land on the washing line, and a smaller one alighted by its side. Savana and I watched quietly for a while, and then as the larger bird took off, without missing a beat, the little one instantly followed and actually gripped the tail feathers of its mother in its little beak as they set off for a flying lesson.

The lovely log house amongst the eucalyptus trees was suddenly sold and we received a month's notice. The new owners couldn't wait to move in, leaving boxes and crates piled up in our garage, and before they'd even got the feel of the place, they brought in a bulldozer to remove trees and grade a wide straight road to the swimming hole at the quarry.

15. Don't forget to remember me

Unable to find a suitable house to rent outside suburbia, we were persuaded to return to New Zealand, this time to Auckland. Our timing was out again, as we arrived in 1987, a year stock markets crashed and house prices soared.

During our nine year absence, New Zealand had progressed immeasurably. It had become of age, and was now a citizen of the world. Cities were pumping, and everywhere standards had improved as tourism gained momentum, and Kiwis broadened their horizons overseas. However, a thick 'PC' veil hovered over the country like a damp cloud. The racial harmony I had noticed in the early 70s had all but disappeared, and Maori activists were demanding compensation for the way their tribes were treated in 1840. While globalisation gathered momentum and the rest of the world attempted to integrate, New Zealand seemed to be heading backwards towards segregation. Well maybe that's a bit harsh, but it certainly seemed to want to create some sort of parallel state.

Lee's elder sister Irene and husband Brian kindly put up with us in their home while we searched frantically for somewhere to live. Fortunately we both found jobs straight away, the girls settled into schools, and we found a temporary rental while owners went overseas. Concerned that the current high rents would quickly devour our savings, the only option was to buy a dump and do it up ourselves. We eventually managed to find a house for sale that was almost within our price range. The house appeared solid although it was in a shocking state. It was so disgusting that everything that could be ripped out, was! We stripped everything down and began the long slow process of doing it all up again. Brian was a fantastic support, toiling away with us every night until midnight. He'd often hand me a little package as he arrived, saying "Present for you", and inside would be sealant or a scraper, or something he knew would be needed soon. Lee and I both had jobs in the city, so Sirri collected Savana from school and looked after her until we arrived home. We'd crawl home through the peak hour traffic, eat a basic meal with the girls, don overalls, and get stuck in. About midnight, we'd wash and fall onto our mattress. Six hours later, we'd be up and showered, and with Lee in a suit and me in smart city outfits and high heels, we'd head off to work. No one could possibly imagine the double life we were leading! Alas, not six months into this, and a week before Christmas, I was made redundant.

Companies were 'down-sizing' like the plague, and generally the last employees to arrive were the first to go. In January the same thing happened to Lee. It was not a good look, with no jobs, and a mortgage to pay with current interest rates of 22%. Our dear friend Cobber Brian, 'The Godfather', who was working as chief cook on the ships, came to our aid, lending us a couple of month's mortgage and keeping us cheerful with his stories and wacky sense of humour while he was in port. We managed to find new jobs and somehow struggled through it all.

My friend Hon and I had continued to write to each other through the years, and while we were in Australia, Hon wrote lengthy letters about a great guy she'd met. Bobby Campbell was a Scottish sports journalist working for the Express in London. Hon and Bobby had a wonderful whirlwind romance and married in a registry office with family and friends. Hon, who had always been fantastic with children, longed for her own babies, but was unable to conceive. Hon and Bobby went through all the IUV programs, associated indignities, and heartache, to no avail. Eventually, tired of all the shenanigans they gave up and settled back into a normal London life. Like most Scots and journos the world over, Bobby was partial to a whisky or few, but fate played its part when Bobby went for a routine health check. His doctor advised him, "You know Bobby, there are veins showing on your testicles, similar to varicose veins. If you give up drinking completely you will find they disappear, and I wouldn't be surprised if it doesn't make you more fertile as a result". Bobby instantly gave up the drink, and it wasn't long before Hon rang him at work. "Sit down Bobby, I've got something to tell you. I'm pregnant, and we're having triplets!" The triplets duly arrived, three healthy boys, Roderick, Fergus, and Diarmid. One baby had a mop of dark hair and others were little red heads. The joy the boys gave Hon and Bobby was infectious, even in letters to the other side of the world.

Hon, Bobby and their boys lived in London for a couple of years before moving to Scotland where they bought a house and settled in Edinburgh. At much the same time we'd travelled around Australia and moved to New Zealand. Consequently Hon and I didn't know each other's new addresses and lost touch with one another. It felt strange not being in contact with Hon as, even separated by oceans, we'd always remained close by writing to each other. Out the blue, I suddenly remembered Hon's mother's address in the Lake District. I wrote a newsy letter to Hon's Mum, asking her to forward it to Hon. A couple of weeks passed and I was thrilled to find a letter from Hon's Mum in the mail box. Alas, it was a bearer of impossibly sad news. Hon's Mum explained that dear Hon had died about six months before. Diagnosed with breast cancer, Hon had died within twelve months, in spite of chemotherapy treatment. It was devastating news. I couldn't believe my beautiful friend, always so vibrant and full of life, had died so young. I felt awful that unaware of Hon's sickness, I had been unable to help her through her ordeals. For Hon, the agony of knowing she would have to leave her wee children motherless would have been unbearable. The little triplets were only five when she died. She would have been a fantastic mother. She was a fantastic friend – the very best.

Many years later I was fortunate to meet Bobby in Edinburgh. The entrance hall in their house was covered in large black and white photos of the triplets growing up with Hon and Bobby, echoes of happier times as the little family laughed and played together. Bobby and I instantly clicked, and spent a wonderful night chatting about Hon and the things we'd done. Bobby filled me in on the missing years as we shed tears and laughed at the way it used to be. The three boys, now ten, were delightful wee Scottish lads, enthusiastic soccer players, and very musical, each learning their own instrument.

Bobby described a poignant moment during their last Christmas together, only a few weeks before Hon died. She was lying on the couch listening to Bobby and the three boys who were standing by the fireplace giving a musical concert. Feeling as though he was towering over the boys, Bobby knelt down so he'd be on the same level as the wee lads. Still playing, and without missing a beat, the boys thought this must be the thing to do, and as one, knelt down too! Hon and Bobby's laughter rippled through the sweetness of the tune.

Bobby also told me this. After Hon's funeral, a gift of money was paid into his bank account. The same payment continued to be made month after month, year after year. Nobody ever mentioned or acknowledged this when Bobby asked around, and he was never able to get the bank to reveal who was making these deposits, and was never able to thank this kind soul.

When I returned to New Zealand I received a couple of letters from the boys. Alas more was to befall the Campbell family. Bobby threw a party for the triplets on their thirteenth birthday, and after a noisy happy party, the young guests left and Bobby and the boys cleaned up and went to bed. One of the boys went to wake Bobby up in the morning for work and school. Bobby couldn't be roused. He had passed away in his sleep during the night. These young lads, who'd had such special parents, were now suddenly orphans.

Fate deals some strange hands. Fortunately Hon's brother, Brendan, who was working as a male psychiatric nurse in Edinburgh, was able to come to the rescue and moved in with the boys, and continued to look after them as they grew up.

***

Excitement arrived with the 1990 Commonwealth Games in Auckland. Lee and I had often said that if we were ever in, or near a country hosting the Olympic or Commonwealth Games, we would make a point of being there. Now living in Auckland, we were thrilled that the Commonwealth Games was to be held right on our doorstep.

Having grown up in the Nandi Hills, I had always taken a keen interest in Nandi's incredible long distance runners. The majority of Nandi athletes lived and trained between 6,000 and 7,000 feet above sea level. At high altitude the air is thinner as there is less oxygen in the air. The heart beats faster, and as it works harder, it produces more red blood cells with haemoglobin. The more haemoglobin the blood contains, the more oxygen can be transported throughout the body. The native children grow up in the high altitude of the Nandi Hills where running is as natural as breathing. They race each other to school over rough terrain every day, and it is a common sight to see the tall, lithe bodies of the Nandi loping along a hillside and away into the distance. In the early days, a few fortunate runners who had been selected because of their potential were able to live and train at St Patricks School in Iten, where a catholic priest provided food, shelter and schooling, while he coached the young men, training them as long distance athletes.

My memories took me back to a day when we lived in Eldoret, and Mum and Dad took us to our first track and field meeting at Iten. A straight dirt road lined with gum trees led towards the athletics field and chattering colourful crowd. Excitement filled the dusty air, as we anticipated the day ahead, and the chance to watch one Kipchoge Keino, rumoured to be a very fast runner.

Over the years Kip Keino's running went from strength to strength. Always improving, first at local events and then internationally, Kip Keino emerged as a leading distance runner in the mid-1960s, breaking two world records in 1965. He broke his first world record, the 3,000 metres, by a staggering 6 seconds, having never raced this distance before. A few months later he broke the 5,000 metre world record in New Zealand.

In London in 1968, I watched on TV as the Kenyan runners took the world by storm. During the Mexico City Olympics, known as the 'high altitude Olympics', Kenya claimed an amazing three gold, four silver, and three bronze medals, setting the pace for the hundreds of future talented Kenyan athletes. It was thrilling watching the middle and long distance runners from home, from the Nandi Hills, compete so brilliantly, gaining the attention and respect of sports fans all over the world.

Kip Keino won a gold and silver medal at these Olympics, and stood tall on the podium, proud yet humble. Later I was to read how even more astonishing his efforts really were. Keino had run six distance races in eight days, while suffering severe abdominal pains. During the 10,000 metres, with two laps to go, Keino collapsed, but managed to stagger to his feet to finish the race, even though he had been officially disqualified. Doctors diagnosed an acute gall bladder infection and advised him to rest, telling him that it could be fatal to compete in his condition. He reluctantly conceded to doctors' warnings and remained behind at the Olympic Village on the day of the 15,000 metres. American, Jim Ryun, the 15,000 metre world record holder, unbeaten at this distance for three years, was tipped to take out the gold medal.

A restless Kip Keino suddenly decided he could not sit around watching the race, he had to be in it! Grabbing his kit, he caught a bus to the stadium, but a traffic jam brought everything to a complete standstill. Not to be defeated, Kip Keino leapt off the bus and ran the last three kilometres to the stadium, arriving just in time to line up for his race. With the help of his team mate, Ben Jipcho, who set a grueling pace, Kip Keino stretched out in front to take the race, beating Ryun by a an incredible 20 metres. He had won his first Olympic Gold Medal, and set a new Olympic Record. He also won a silver medal in the 5,000 metres and became a National hero.

Kip Keino continued to run distance races at international level and his performances are legendary. However, Kip, ever humble, is quick to point out that his children are what make him really proud.

Orphaned at an early age, Kipchoge Keino herded goats in the Nandi Hills, and at 19 he joined the police force. He participated in a variety of fitness programs and sports activities, taking his responsibilities seriously, and progressing to Police Physical Training Instructor. It was while he was with the police that he was given the opportunity to train and enter local track and field events. Kip retired in 1973 to devote his time to his Orphanage. In spite of his international success, he earned very little from his exceptional distance running career, but the $20,000 he had received in prize money was enough to buy his small farm near Eldoret. Kip and his young wife Phyllis, opened their home and their hearts to some abandoned children he had found while on duty as a policeman. The Keinos had seven children of their own, and as more destitute children arrived at their doorstep, they were welcomed into the ever-growing family. Over the years another farm was purchased and both Baraka Farm and Kazi Mingi (meaning much work) are self-sufficient. The farms provide the orphanage with fresh produce and an opportunity for the children to learn farming and life skills. Everyone in the home, no matter how small, participates in day to day chores, milking, growing maize and vegetables, washing or cooking. As Kip explained once during an interview, "My mother died when I was three. I don't want anyone else to grow up with that problem. I can't help everyone but I can do what is within my ability".

Phyllis and Kip had been caring for destitute children since they married in 1964, and they were pleased to move the orphanage from its original sight in 2003. The Lewa Children's Home is now adjacent to Baraka Farm and the Kip Keino Boarding School. The buildings have been upgraded and the school for three hundred children is modern and well equipped thanks to fundraisers and contributions from overseas. Phyllis and Kip consider a proper education essential and the school has a very good reputation. Many of Phyllis and Kip's children from the home have gone on to take up scholarships in overseas universities, join the police force, become doctors, or other useful members of society. Baraka Farm also hosts 'Farm Days' for local farmers to learn new innovative techniques to improve crop yields and at the same time protect the environment.

More recently, Kip Keino opened the international Kip Keino Training Centre, an IAAF High Performance Training Institute. At an altitude of 6,800 feet above sea level, the centre provides up to the minute facilities and training for serious athletes from all over the world. Many Kenyan athletes have taken the opportunity to run and study in other parts of the world, and others have used their earnings or prize money to contribute to their communities by establishing local institutions such as schools, hospitals, stadiums or training centres, or have set up local factories and businesses. The once small town of Eldoret is now thriving, with an international airport, university, four hospitals, a variety of schools and polytechnics, and abundant hotels for the constant flow of tourists who now visit the area because of its athletic reputation. China is currently interested in investing money into restoring the dilapidated Kipchoge Stadium to international standard.

Meanwhile, in New Zealand, the 1990 Commonwealth Games in Auckland drew closer, and we arranged to take our holidays during 'The Games', and booked seats at the stadium. The city's preparations were in full swing when we heard the disappointing news that the Kenya team would probably boycott the Games in protest of apartheid in South Africa. Then at the eleventh hour decisions were made and it was confirmed that the Kenya team would be competing in New Zealand after all!

Teams from the Commonwealth flew in, tourists gathered in anticipation, and we all looked forward to the coming weeks. Wanting to send the Kenya Team a card to welcome them to New Zealand, I phoned around trying to get an address. At the time I was working as a receptionist on a switchboard, and did this between incoming calls. Finally I was given the number of the Commonwealth Games Village, and phoning there, I explained I needed an address for the Kenya Team. Before I knew it I was connected to the Kenyan Commonwealth Games HQ, and found myself talking to Stanley Wachanga, the contingent's Executive Officer! As soon as Stanley realised I was from Kenya he started talking to me in Swahili. It was so long since I had last spoken Swahili, but it all came straight back and we had a wonderful lively chat on the phone. Caught up in the excitement of the moment, I was completely oblivious to the abandoned switchboard screeching in alarm, and bringing concerned staff scuttling out of their offices. We nattered away like old friends and Stanley suggested we come down that evening after work to meet the team. Wow! How lucky can you get? Lee and I duly arrived at the entrance to the Games Village and were checked out and given ID's while they sent for someone to escort us to the houses allocated to the Kenyan Team. It was fantastic to be welcomed by such friendly happy people and we spent a great evening talking and laughing with the athletes and officials, and were told to bring the girls with us next time.

We turned up with Sirri and Savana on the Saturday and all the Kenyans came out of their houses to sit in the sun and chat. Africans have a natural affinity with children, and Savana had the time of her young life with all the friendly attention she was getting, and it wasn't long before a small group took her off to the Commonwealth Village dining hall. Lee was absorbed in discussions with Peter, the boxing coach, and lads from the boxing team, while I was on cloud nine. After so long away from home, it felt great to be talking Swahili and spending time with the Kenyans, enjoying their warm, easy going ways. One of the young men wanted to marry Sirri! The usual jokes about a bride price and how many goats or cows we thought she was worth were banded about, and everyone enjoyed a lighthearted morning. That is, with the exception of the young, now sullen, coach who had wanted Sirri for his bride, who was less than pleased that no one had taken him seriously.

We had an open invitation to visit the Kenyans, but decided to keep a low profile once the heats began, so the athletes could focus on their events. We visited the team the next Saturday, and on the Sunday escorted a little group to the markets. During the week Lee and I took Irene and Brian to the track and field events at Mt Smart Stadium. We had a wonderful day soaking up the atmosphere, enjoying the competitions, and yelling for Kenya, and England, and New Zealand! One special race will be etched in our memories forever. John Ngugi was running for Kenya in the 5,000 metre final. He was going well when he had a nasty fall and the other runners surged past him. Ngugi got to his feet and sprinted off, but he was a long way behind. We watched in awe as he dug deep, and metre by metre he hauled his way up to join the group. Then, unbelievably, he proceeded to pass everyone. Now he was in front and giving his all down the home straight. We were on our feet, with our hearts in our mouths. The applause was deafening. What an incredible, superhuman performance! Suddenly Australia's Andrew Lloyd found some extra strength, powering forward to chase down Ngugi as they approached the finishing line. It seemed that Ngugi was unaware how close the danger was, as exhausted he forced himself home, but with a final burst of speed, Lloyd threw himself in front just before the line. The fierce determination, endurance, and strength we witnessed epitomizes the height of sport and human effort, and we were privileged to be there watching that phenomenal race.

The Marathon was scheduled to run early in the morning, and the route, along the waterfront, wound back on itself a few times, so by standing in one place spectators were able to view the runners pounding past several times. Kenya had three entrants, with Douglas Wakiihuri the main hope, and a serious rival in the form of Australia's Steve Moneghetti.

Douglas Wakiihuri's dream had always been to be an Olympic runner, but because the competition from hundreds of other young Kenyan track runners was so intense, he decided he'd have a better chance if he became a marathon runner. He took this seriously and was prepared to take any opportunities that came along and asked around for assistance with training. His good fortune came, when at 18, he was offered a chance to study under a renowned Japanese mentor. This was thanks to a Japanese journalist living in Kenya, who had asked the Japanese marathon expert, Kiyoshi Nakamura if he would agree to take the young Kenyan under his wing. Wakiihuri studied in Tokyo for the next four years, becoming fully conversant with the language and totally embracing the Japanese way of life, culture, and philosophy. His attitude when running the marathon being, "the number of kilometres you run is not important. What matters is how you run every kilometre".

Lee, Savana and I, dressed in red, green, and black, and with Rabbi, our mascot rabbit, wearing his knitted Kenya flag jumper, found a place away from the cafes and crowds to support the Kenyan runners. Madly waving and shouting, we put our hearts into cheering the runners on, to such an extent that listening to the marathon on the radio in Australia, Robin heard several comments about the enthusiastic support Kenya was getting. Meanwhile in England, Mum was sitting down to supper on a tray while she watched the marathon live in New Zealand. She knew only that we'd be out there somewhere to watch the marathon, and that we'd probably find a little spot away from the masses. Suddenly there we were in front of her! She was ecstatic as she watched us 'live' on TV, waving and yelling on the other side of the world. It must have been thrilling for her to share that moment with her family, even though we were so far apart.

The marathon runners continued to pound the concrete courageously, enduring the heat and the fast pace. Our respect for their tremendous efforts was immense. After they'd passed us on the last lap, we decided to hurry over to the finishing line to welcome them home. We were still a couple of hundred metres from the finish when the leaders returned, throwing in their finishing kicks with everything they could muster. Young, and fit, we raced along our path, but the marathon runners, in spite of the distance they'd travelled over the last two hours, still had far more power and speed than we did, and needless to say they easily beat us back. It was an incredible endurance event, duly won by Wakiihuri, followed closely by Moneghetti, only seven seconds behind, with Tanzanian, Naali coming in third.

On the Sunday I found myself sitting with a group of the younger Nandi distance runners, while they relaxed watching a replay of the marathon and chatting about tactics. How many athletes would give their eye teeth to be in a room with Kenyan runners discussing running, techniques, and strategies? Even though my Nandi was pretty rusty, it was insightful and I felt honoured to be a part of this magical moment.

We enjoyed a wonderful day out with Sammy Tirop and Nixon Kirprotich. They had completed their events, having won gold and silver medals in the 800 metres, against England's Sebastian Coe and Matthew Yates. We took Sammy and Nixon to meet Lee's Mum before driving north to Red Beach, a beautiful wide, long beach at Orewa. Both men thought New Zealand should have far more world class athletes considering the amazing natural facilities here, and they talked of

John Walker with such admiration. In fact all the Kenyans had the utmost respect for him. Sammy and Nixon took Lee for a jog along the beach with them while Savana and I lazed in the sun. On the return journey, passing lots of gum trees, Nixon commented how similar the scenery was to Eldoret, and chatted about his family. Then the conversation turned to the masses of hopeful runners in Kenya and the incredibly fierce competition to get selected. To the majority of Africans, to become an athlete was their only chance to change their lives, "But," said Sammy, "For every good runner, there are a hundred others ready to take your place. You can never relax because at every trial or race meeting there are those whose lives depend on being faster than you."

They explained how some of the younger members of their squad had only just made it to the trials for the Commonwealth Games at Kisumu. The hard track surface was murram, a mixture of clay and very small stones. An unknown competitor, Lena Chesire, running with bare feet and in her only dress, won her race at an impressive speed, but her feet were torn and bleeding. A spectator started a collection to raise funds to help her, and thanks to a very generous African crowd, enough money was collected for some running shoes for Lena, and a tracksuit too.

Sixteen year old Joseph Kibor, had already made his way into Kiwi's hearts after a sports commentator had broadcast his story on TV. Joseph had sold his family goat in order to buy a return bus ticket to the trials at Kisumu. Against all odds he ran an incredible race, almost collapsing afterwards as he had not eaten properly for days. He was running on a slice of bread. New Zealanders nicknamed him 'The Goat Boy' and the city of Wanganui 'adopted' him and raised money to purchase more goats for his family.

Throughout the Games it had been difficult for the public to buy tickets because all the seats had been allocated to bulk bookings, although the stadium was half empty on any given day. However the stadium was crammed full for the Closing Ceremony. We had been very fortunate obtaining tickets from friends of friends, and for our little family it really was a once in a lifetime experience. Mount Smart Stadium was jam-packed, the heat intense, and the atmosphere electric. Sirri, Savana, Lee and I enthusiastically cheered the Kenyan relay team home to victory and watched, with lumps in our throats, as they stood on the podium, while the Kenya flag was raised to the stirring notes of our national anthem. Later, after the general formalities and the Queen's speech, it was party time! The stadium erupted with music and dancing, as all the athletes spontaneously surged out onto the track to dance and join in the jubilant festivities, singing, 'This is the Moment'. The evening closed with Dame Kiri Te Kanawa singing a beautiful rendition of 'Now is The Hour'. What a fitting end to our unexpected and truly wonderful time with the Kenyans at the 1990 Commonwealth Games in New Zealand.

16. Further than the stars

March 12th 1994 was a normal Kiwi Saturday morning and I'd hopped on Savana's bike to ride up to the bakery for a loaf for lunch. It felt good to be cycling again, so I dropped the bread off at home, riding on around the block and through the playground. I approached a short steep bank up to the road and took a run at it. I failed. I had nothing in the tank, and getting off the bike to walk up the slope, my legs turned to jelly, my heart was pounding and I felt as though I was going to faint. What was this? I couldn't believe I was so out of condition. I was young, fit, and healthy. I staggered home and collapsed on the steps, totally exhausted. Suddenly I burst into tears and rushed through to the bedroom, followed closely by Lee wondering what on earth was wrong. I couldn't explain it, but continued to sob my heart out. Eventually I recovered, and the rest of the day continued much as usual, with the bonus of Sirri, and her wee boy Jay, arriving on a visit from Waihi. The phone rang early evening. It was Kaye in Australia, and I greeted her warmly, happy to hear her voice. She quickly said, "No, no, it's not like that – I have to tell you bad news – Robin died this morning..."

My little brother, dead? Robin was only 42 and we were unaware he had even been ill. Apparently he had woken with chest pains during the night. Kaye had rushed him up to Tamworth Hospital, where they ran tests and fitted him with an angina patch, before sending him home to rest. The next morning, ten year old Matthew went off to his Saturday sport, and Kaye and Tammy drove down town to get some groceries. The poor souls returned to find Robin collapsed on the floor. Kaye immediately tried CPR, but to no avail. Robin had already gone. Wee Tammy, only 13, couldn't take in the magnitude of this, desperately clutching at any hope, called out, "I know Mum, he's just joking. He's tricking us". It must have been dreadful for them. The next thing Kaye had to deal with was Matthew. After his hockey match, he and a group of friends had gone off on their bikes, which they normally did at weekends, but no one really knew exactly where the boys were. Kaye didn't want to tell anyone about Robin, in case the news got out before she'd had a chance to tell Matthew herself. Hence it was several hours before she was able to ring us in New Zealand, or Hugh and Linda in England. I only remember feeling very small and vulnerable, as I sat out under the stars, gazing up into eternity, realising that my dear little brother was now as unreachable as the stars.

Twenty Miles to say Goodbye

It was many months before I could look up at the night sky again, because it was just too hard to bear.

Over in England, Hugh was to break the sad news to Mum. He set off on the three hour journey to Mum's in Wiltshire. It had been Mum's birthday the day before, and she was having a few friends round on Saturday afternoon to celebrate, completely unaware of what had happened. A shattered and heartbroken Hugh arrived in Calne, and waited outside, alone with his thoughts, until he could see all the guests had left. It was now time to do what he must. Later he acknowledged that this was the worst thing he'd ever had to do in his life. He knocked on the door knowing that Mum would go from joy to heart rending despair in an instant. How could he tell her her son had died? Mum opened the door, to see Hugh, with tears rolling down his cheeks, holding his arms out to her in hopelessness. In a moment would come the words that would change her life forever, the heart-breaking words no mother, anywhere, ever wants to hear. Later Hugh helped Mum pack a few things and took her back to his family in Towcester.

Ah Robin, always so easy to be with, so hard to be without. I was to represent our family at Robin's funeral in Australia. After endless queues to obtain an entry permit, a quick flight, and a long drive through the night, I arrived at the Anderson's house in Tamworth. Kaye who had been waiting up, ran out to the car and we just hugged each other tightly. There were no words, we could only hold on to one another.

The church was packed with all the many people Robin had touched during the few years they had lived in Tamworth. There were children from the sports teams he coached, business people he'd met running his Taxi Truck Couriers, and many friends from near and far. Kaye's brother Phil joined her parents, Gwen and Clyde, who had flown from Melbourne to comfort their daughter and grandchildren. Someone kindly made a tape recording of Robin's funeral for Mum and Hugh in England. It was lovely to hear Robin's friends talking about him, but sad the rest of the family weren't with me to share the memories. A friend told me how much Robin loved the tune 'Flower of Scotland' and that whenever he sat down with his mates to watch a Scottish international rugby match, he'd turn to them with watery eyes, saying, "I defy anyone to listen to that tune without feeling something." Of course they teased him mercilessly, but I'm sure, for the rest of their lives, they'll remember Robin whenever they hear 'Flower of Scotland'. As will we.

The day after the funeral, I went for a long bike ride with Tammy and Matthew. They took me sightseeing all round Tamworth and we ended up at the BMX track, timing each other's laps, and having very fast, competitive races over the bumps and humps. It occurred to me that I wasn't unfit at all, and as we worked out the time difference between countries, including day light saving, the exact time of Robin's final heart attack was when I had felt weak and overwhelmed on that bike ride round the block in New Zealand.

I was grateful that Sirri was up in Auckland with us when we received the news about her Uncle Robin. Savana was staying with a friend's family, and they'd all gone to another suburb for the weekend. Brian and Sirri kindly went to bring her home so we could all grieve together. A few weeks earlier, Sirri had mentioned a dream she'd had. In this dream Uncle Robin had tucked her in and said good night. They were in an unknown house. Later, on the night Robin died, Sirri immediately recognised this house when she and Brian pulled up to collect Savana. Although she had never been here before, it was the house she'd dreamt of with Uncle Rob.

Several months later, mentioning these odd co-incidences to Mum, she revealed a couple of strange little incidents she had experienced herself. Only two nights before Robin's heart attack, she had been at the theatre with friends, and felt Dad's presence beside her. It was a strong sensation, but she thought this odd as he had never particularly liked accompanying her to the theatre, and so put it out of her mind. Tidying up the next morning, Mum was about to dust along the two shelves of family photos by her bed. She always kept her young family's photo frames on the top shelf, and those of loved ones who had passed on, were kept on the lower shelf. Mum noticed that Robin's photo was lying on the bottom shelf. Wondering vaguely how it got there, she picked it up, dusted it lovingly, whispering something like, "No. You don't belong down there" and placed him back on the top shelf.

Karibu – our welcome home

Early in our marriage, Lee and I had dreamed our own dreams and hoped to be able to own a freehold home in a nice natural environment. During our years in Australia, and now in New Zealand, whenever we'd travelled anywhere, we'd kept our eyes open for any potential 'dream' sites. We'd come close a few times, but something had always prevented it happening at the eleventh hour. Our Auckland house was a stepping stone to our dreams.

We stayed in Auckland for nine, often quite difficult years. I started getting up an hour earlier, and I spent this quiet time meditating and working on goals, and affirmations. A 'self- development' book I was reading, 'The Artist's Way', discussed left and right brain functions and suggested focusing on your dream, visualizing all your requirements in vivid detail, then writing it down using your least dominant hand. I duly did this, repeating it every day, believing it would come about. I still have the original piece of paper, with very untidy left hand scribble, which reads; *'wooden house - north facing for max sun - easy access - flat house site - native birds - walks - nice garden - stream with little bridge - wooden seats in lovely settings - forest environment - hammock - happy family atmosphere - quiet and private - good places for Jay to play - time to enjoy it all - inspirational and creative results.'*

I answered the phone at work one morning and Sirri was on the line. An advertisement for a couple of acres had just appeared in her local paper, and it sounded perfect. I phoned Lee and we both took the afternoon off and drove down to Waihi. Sirri had contacted the real estate and the land owners, and she, Jay, and baby Sancha were waiting for us at the site. We walked around the land. It was a paddock then, but a river bordered it on two sides, and it faced a lovely sloping native forest. It was perfect! Then the owner mentioned that another buyer was interested too, and our hearts sank. Lee suddenly upped the anti and offered the asking price, plus a bit extra to cover their survey costs. Our dream was coming true!

Originally the idea had been to continue working in Auckland, and come down to Waihi at weekends to plant trees and get a feel for weather patterns and house positions. However, we'd had enough of the rat wheel and sold our much improved Auckland house fairly quickly and moved down to Waihi, where we rented an old shaky miners cottage for a few months while we commenced building. Waihi is a gold and silver mining town with open-cast and underground mining actually operating within the town. The area has a rich mining history and hundreds of kilometres of old mine shafts and tunnels exist in multilevel warrens beneath the houses and streets. On the surface, dairy farms stretch out between the spectacular Karangahake Gorge and beautiful Waihi Beach.

As we would be building the house ourselves, we had chosen Fraemoh's, a kit set wood system, based on the old Scandinavian log cabin principle. We selected our own house design plan, and all the materials arrived in a semi and trailer. It was a terrifying moment. Knowing that we had put all our life savings into something we knew nothing about, we watched, hearts in mouths, as a huge truck and semi delivered massive loads of timber, windows and doors. Our first problem arrived instantly – the truck was too wide to get through the gate! A post had to be pulled out, and was duly replaced by our thoughtful new neighbour with his tractor immediately the truck had delivered its load and exited.

Council building plans required the foundations, electrical work, plumbing, and roof alignment be done by professionals, but the rest was up to us! Coincidentally Sirri and Martin were working on the next door dairy farm at the time, and their boss, John Campbell, a family man himself, generously allowed Martin to come and work on the house all day as long as the milking was done on time twice a day. So Martin did the early morning milk before joining us at the building site. Sirri turned up a little later with the children and a basket of welcome baking. Then she and I became skilled 'gofers' while the guys worked on the construction. The thick interlocking pine planks had been pre-cut, laminated, and numbered, while each wall was labelled alphabetically. Thus the inside and outside of say the lounge north wall was labelled "B" and numbered in ascending order from the floor to ceiling. Up ladders, banging planks into position, the guys would yell, 'Where the f...'s B13? Need it now!' Of course the delivery man had just hoisted everything off the truck and things weren't always in organized piles, so Sirri and I rushed around like scalded cats looking for the required pieces - before they were needed if possible! It was a fantastic team effort, and the children were great, with four year old Jay helping out wherever he could, and wee Sancha keeping us all cheery with her delightful easy-going company. Hopping off the antiquated school bus, Savana joined us for a cuppa before taking the children back to their house for baths and supper. Sirri and I roared off on the quad bike to round up the cows and do the evening milking. The lack of light forced us to take our aching bodies off to bed until the next day when we did it all again! The house walls went up very quickly, although other things took longer, but we reached 'lock up stage' in just over a month. We had to install a septic tank, and later a large tank was connected to the guttering to collect rain water off the roof, and an electric pump delivered running water to the house. It was great to have been able to experience building our own house, but it meant so much more that we had done it 'as a family', and we were privileged to have had the chance of working on something major together and our beautiful little wooden home retains its family spirit.

Once we'd settled in, we started on the grounds. An immediate priority was the rapidly invading brambles and honeysuckle, which initially we had to attack using pangas and scythes! We acquired four young steers, known as 'the Burger Boys' to keep the grass down. Everyone pitched in with the on-going tree planting, and we planted a couple of shelter belts, which necessitated quick growing gums, grevillea, and macrocarpa, and gradually we added a variety of more decorative trees, an orchard, and a lovely garden. We planted our own 'family tree', a jacaranda, even though we knew conditions weren't right for it here and that there were no other jacarandas to be seen in the area. Initially the little jacaranda sapling struggled to survive, and Savana even managed to give it a 'number one flat top' with the lawn mower! But it hung in and we covered it in frost cloth during its first winters. Now it has grown too tall to cover, and we wait and hope that it will flower next summer.

My thoughts turn to Dad, and in my mind's eye, I see him, pipe in hand, gazing across a field. I feel close to him, as I watch our scattered seeds rise up and grow in spirit.

Our home and shamba are called 'Karibu', Swahili for 'welcome, you are safe here'. A suitable name for our little haven, especially so as we have resident 'welcome swallows' who nest in the cliffs by the river all year round, but equally important, the name is due to serendipity. Years ago in Australia, Robin made engraved wooden house signs for everyone for Christmas. He carved Hugh and Linda a sign 'Casuarina' for their door in England, but when he came to us, there was no name as we were renting, so he solved the problem by carving 'Karibu' on our sign, and consequently wherever we have lived, it has always been Karibu!

Hearing of another Kenyan living in the district, I popped in to say 'jambo'. It transpired that Tony was the son of the Belchers mentioned in the Zanzibar Chapter. He left Kenya to study at Massey University and was now exporting organic blueberries and running a café. In Nairobi, we had been at schools only a mile apart, and although we had never met before we had much in common and Tony soon became a good family friend.

Sirri and her family stayed in the area while the children were growing up, and Savana and her little boy Quinton moved back to Waihi, so we have all been able to enjoy many years of incredible family times together. Like most families these days, we've faced some tough times along the way. Sadly one of us left our midst without a word to anyone, and that absence weighs heavy on us all. Questions aren't always answered, and we carry on, drawing on the love we share and the spirit from whence we came.

We have been blessed to have most of our overseas family come and stay at some time or another, but the only one unable to come was Mum. Living in England and unable to travel, she kept in touch with us by mail and phone. Always a great letter writer, she loved to correspond with her overseas family and friends in regular, long, slow conversations. Throughout our school years Mum had written to the three of us individually every week. In return she received a regulation weekly letter that all boarders were required to write to their parents. On Sundays at school it was just another thing we had to do, and the general idea was to fill your page up as quickly as you possibly could so you could go outside and play. Consequently Mum and Dad received three letters every week, all with rather large handwriting, more or less to the tune of;
Dear Mum and Dad,
I am well and happy at school.
I hope you are well and happy at home.
Love from Hugh, Heather, or Robin xxx

As we grew up, our letters improved somewhat, and we enjoyed the on-going correspondence with Mum as much as she did. The newsy letters traversing the oceans and continents kept us all in touch, and Mum's grandchildren, and great grandchildren, became familiar with the colourful character who was their Granny Peg.

Ever observant, Mum usually managed to find something of interest amongst the mundane, and she'd include odd little incidents in her letters;

A 'thing happened' recently, and she'd fill in the details. *On the train to the Andersons for Christmas, I was at the rear of a packed carriage, and noticed two rather colourful eccentric punks towards the front. The majority of passengers huddled into themselves ignoring the punks, but when we arrived at our destination, these two young men stood by the door giving a hand to those struggling with bags and parcels, and calling out cheery Christmas greetings to the indifferent passengers. The punks helped me down the carriage steps and carried my case for me, chatting as we went. Their friendly helpful manner really lifted my spirits, and was a welcome contrast to that of the bulk of somber souls supposedly heading off for a happy Christmas.'*

Or she'd write, *'having a coffee in a large food court, I noticed a group of disabled people at a nearby table. My eyes met those of a lad with downs syndrome, and I smiled. Later, when the group got up to go, this young lad walked over to my table, bent down, and kissed me on the cheek, before saying goodbye.'*

It is thanks to Mum's letters, her wonderfully descriptive journals, her great memory, and our long phone conversations, that these stories are so clear. From different sides of the world, we pleasantly whiled away the hours together, Mum with a cup of tea in an English afternoon, and me rugged up in New Zealand during the wee small hours. Appreciating the modern international telephone services, we talked of current events, films seen and books read, or we travelled back in time to long ago sunny days in Kenya. We were both well aware of how quickly things had changed, were changing, and we were truly appreciative of the fantastic experiences we'd had in Kenya, knowing that we'd been fortunate, indeed privileged, that things were as they were, then. Now we heard so much chilling news of violence, famine, and poverty, in what was once our beautiful homeland.

We discussed the dreadful situation at Lake Naivasha, once a large, beautiful, fresh water lake, spread across the floor of the Rift Valley. So often we'd picnicked or camped by the clear waters, fishing, water skiing, or bird watching in the incredibly beautiful natural surroundings. As a teenager I loved to lie on the prow of a boat, the sun warm on my back, as I gazed down into the transparent depths of the crystal clear water. Shafts of sunlight kissed the slender golden strands of weeds with promises that could never be kept, while unheeded, on the surface, the winds of change whispered warnings of disaster to come.

Now we learnt that huge commercial flower growing operations surrounded the lake. It was the ideal location for growers, with warm days, cool nights, endless water supply, cheap labour, and only an hour away from Nairobi Airport where massive volumes of fresh flowers were flown out every night to insatiable European markets. Vast acres of nurseries and plastic hot houses cluttered the shores and residue from fertilizer and other chemical products flowed into the once translucent waters. However, an even bigger problem had been created on a massive humanitarian scale, as thousands of desperate people flocked to the area in hope of work. Only a minority of workers were fortunate enough to have steady work, and about 65% of these were women, preferred for their delicate dexterity in handling the flowers, their obedience, and minimum wages expected. Crowds of hopefuls collected outside the various gates daily at dawn, begging to be picked and taken off in trucks for a day's temporary work, but thousands were rejected and turned away to return empty handed and hopeless to the slums and the vacant eyes of their starving families. Desperation led to poaching the once abundant wildlife and birdlife, and poachers fished the lakes at such a rate that the fish could no longer breed. Displaced societies squashed into the squalor of the newly created slums, where there is no electricity, running water, or sewerage, and it is reported that samples taken of the lake water show human waste is filtering into the lake in such alarming quantities, that it is as much of a problem as the chemical pollution from the flower industry. Meanwhile the realities of life in the unhygienic, squalid, poverty stricken slums have led to violence, corruption and lawlessness in a place where there are no answers, and there is no hope.

It is unbelievable that this once beautifully pristine environment had been destroyed so quickly, and harder still to imagine the resulting misery and poverty, in order to provide someone far away with the fleeting pleasure of some flowers on their table or in their hotel room. 'Say it with flowers' has become an ugly lie, at the expense of people desperately struggling to survive in an environment that has been annihilated by greed, and by need.

The frightening thing is, that this is just one place we know, insignificant in the entirety. Exploitation of the land and its people is happening everywhere. Destruction marches on, more relentless and cruel than any army, depleting the forests of the world, polluting the oceans and shores with thousands of oil rigs, coal mines that suck the earth dry and fill the air with toxic waste as industry demands more, quicker, faster. Diamond, gold, and silver mines exploit the locals, robbing them of their wealth, and leaving them in poverty in a land now scarred and barren.

It was not long after this discussion with Mum, that we had both been horrified by a documentary. It was called 'The Indian Ocean', and the young presenter went out to sea in dugout canoes with a group of island fisherman. The men dived to spear fish all day, returning in the evening with only three fish between them to feed their hungry families. The film crew then crossed the stretch of water to the south west coast of Mauritius, where they spoke to villagers, fighting for survival in a barren and much eroded environment. An old man told him that when his people were hungry and their bellies were empty, they 'took a real deep breath and filled their lungs with air'. Later the documentary moved to a city in the north east, and barred from entering the docks, the crew filmed through a tall wire netting fence. Huge cranes were hauling massive nets filled with tons of fresh tuna, loading them onto waiting ships. Apparently these processing ships were taking the fish to the UK, where it would be tinned and put on supermarket shelves. How shocking that we have come to this. That to provide variety in a faraway supermarket, and increase profit margins and bonuses, the local people must starve and die because their own waters have been commercially fished out.

Those who've lived in third world countries, or struggled through wars or difficult times, hate waste, tending to be frugal, using something in multiple ways, until it is worn out and no longer has a use. Uncertain where the next meal will come from, or how to keep the winter chills at bay, they are inclined to preserve what they can, and share more. If we all followed their examples, made do with what we have, bought less, gave away more, then perhaps, in some small way, we could stem this addictive consumerism, this dreadful tide of demand and supply. Certainly it's only a drop in the ocean, but as the Afghanis say, "drop by drop a river forms", and, we all know, we need to do something. Would it change anything, make any difference? Well, as the joke goes, if you think one small thing can't make a difference, try spending the night with a mosquito!

17. Kwaheri Mum

As old age staked its claim, Mum's tired body staggered on behind her bright mind. Like any elderly person, she'd gradually had to give up the things she loved to do. The first thing to go had been her travels. No longer able to visit her family in South Africa, Australia and New Zealand, she settled for local day trips, and walks, but eventually she was unable to step outside her door. Getting dressed, holding a book, knitting, or writing, were agony and became impossible. Remarkably, Mum managed to retain her dignity and independence, counting her blessings and staying positive and interesting for her welcome visitors. Hugh, Linda, Clair and Jax, who lived near Mum's village, provided a fantastic support system for her, and were always there to lend a hand, sorting through red tape, shopping, cleaning, repairing gadgets, and above all, visiting, often with their own young families and friends.

I put down the phone. I have been talking to Hugh and Linda, in England. It doesn't sound as though Mum will last this day. I sit here on this summer morning, birds sing, the river murmurs, and a light drizzle falls. During the fifteen years we have lived at Karibu, Mum had been unable to visit us. She would have loved it here, spending unimaginable hours relaxing in the garden, enjoying the birds, the trees, and the river rushing by. Life goes on, but not for Mum. At last her time has come, for she has been waiting to go for many years, tired of the endless struggles with her pain-wracked old body.

Everything that is born must die. Why is it then that I feel like this? Like, I don't want her to leave. Like, I won't cope without Mum, my oldest friend. How selfish and confused I feel. I have always been aware how blessed we are, that at 93, Mum was still sharp and related well to everyone. But now it all has to end, and I don't really know how to let go. Although I understand Mum is drifting away, I am suddenly gripped by an urge to talk to her – one last time – if I still can? I phone the hospital in England and speak to a ward nurse, who tells me gently that Mum is beyond conversations. This nurse is from West Africa. She is kind, and I know she knows about distance, as she offers to give my love to Mama.

Ah dear Mum, what an incredible safari it has been.

Epilogue

Back here at Karibu, the hot summer days wrap themselves around, warming the memories and drying the tears.

For quite some time, Lee and I had been thinking of extending our deck, and not long after Mum died, Rod and Sirri surprised us by turning up with a huge trailer load of wood, cement, and tools to do the job. Jay and his girlfriend, Amanda, along with Rod's teenage daughter, Haidee, followed in their car, and soon Savana and Nik, with young Quinton, and their new baby, Summer, arrived from Auckland. Lee began digging the holes for the foundations and the guys got stuck in immediately. Sirri and Savana catered for us all. For the next three days, while the guys toiled away in sweltering conditions, we provided them with endless drinks and cheery company, in between swims in the river and cuddles with little Summer. How Mum would have loved it all.

Someone suggested that the deck would be our tribute to Mum - Granny Peg - GGP, and since we were all together, the time was right to say *kwaheri,* goodbye. The completed deck looked lovely in the evening light, decorated with sunflowers, and candlelit lanterns strung around. Music played in the background, and while the family watched black and white images of Mum, I read the eulogy that Hugh and I had written together via email, and which Hugh would be delivering the next day at Mum's funeral in the church at Greens Norton in England. We captured the essence of Mum's 93 years of travels, adventures and family life, giving those who hadn't known her a glimpse of her unique personality, and the rest of us a fond reminder of a dear and special person. With tears in our eyes, and love in our hearts, we played 'Sailing', a favourite of Mum's. Then, on a more upbeat note, ten year old Quinton played us his own composition for Great Granny Peg – a sort of hip-hop groove created on Garage Band!

Twenty Miles to say Goodbye

ebooks & single or bulk paperbacks can be purchased on-line at Lulu.com, Amazon, Kindle, Barnes & Noble, ibooks, Oyster.

Printed in Great Britain
by Amazon